Higher Education Investment
in the Arab States of the Gulf:
Strategies for Excellence and Diversity

The Gulf Research Centre Book Series at Gerlach Press

The GCC in the Global Economy
Ed. by Richard Youngs
ISBN 9783940924018, 2012

Resources Blessed:
Diversification and the Gulf Development Model
Ed. by Giacomo Luciani
ISBN 9783940924025, 2012

GCC Financial Markets: The World's New Money Centers
Ed. by Eckart Woertz
ISBN 9783940924032, 2012

National Employment, Migration and Education in the GCC
Ed. by Steffen Hertog
ISBN 9783940924049, 2012

Asia-Gulf Economic Relations in the 21st Century:
The Local to Global Transformation
Ed. by Tim Niblock with Monica Malik
ISBN 9783940924100, 2013

A New Gulf Security Architecture:
Prospects and Challenges for an Asian Role
Ed. by Ranjit Gupta, Abubaker Bagader,
Talmiz Ahmad and N. Janardhan
ISBN 9783940924360, 2014

Gulf Charities and Islamic Philanthropy
in the 'Age of Terror' and Beyond
Ed. by Robert Lacey and Jonathan Benthall
ISBN 9783940924322, 2014

State-Society Relations in the Arab Gulf States
Ed. by Mazhar Al-Zoby and Birol Baskan
ISBN 9783940924384, 2014

Political Economy of Energy Reform:
The Clean Energy-Fossil Fuel Balance in the Gulf
Ed. by Giacomo Luciani and Rabia Ferroukhi
ISBN 9783940924407, 2014

The Silent Revolution: The Arab Spring and the Gulf States
Ed. by May Seikaly and Khawla Mattar
ISBN 9783940924346, 2014

Security Dynamics of East Asia in the Gulf Region
Ed. by Tim Niblock with Yang Guang
ISBN 9783940924483, 2014

Islamic Finance: Political Economy, Performance and Risk
Ed. by Mehmet Asutay and Abdullah Turkistani
ISBN 9783940924124, 3 vols set, 2015

Employment and Career Motivation in the Arab Gulf
States: The Rentier Mentality Revisited
Ed. by Annika Kropf and Mohamed Ramady
ISBN 9783940924605, 2015

The Changing Energy Landscape in the Gulf:
Strategic Implications
Ed. by Gawdat Bahgat
ISBN 9783940924643, 2015

Sustainable Development Challenges
in the Arab States of the Gulf
Ed. by David Bryde, Yusra Mouzughi and Turki Al Rasheed
ISBN 9783940924629, 2015

The United States and the Gulf:
Shifting Pressures, Strategies and Alignments
Ed. by Steven W. Hook and Tim Niblock
ISBN 9783940924667, 2015

Africa and the Gulf Region:
Blurred Boundaries and Shifting Ties
Ed. by Rogaia Mustafa Abusharaf and Dale F. Eickelman
ISBN 9783940924704, 2015

Rebuilding Yemen: Political, Economic and Social
Challenges
Ed. by Noel Brehony and Saud Al-Sarhan
ISBN 9783940924681, 2015

Science and Technology Development in the Gulf States:
Economic Diversification through Regional Collaboration
Ed. by Afreen Siddiqi and Laura Diaz Anadon
ISBN 9783959940023, 2016

Higher Education Investment in the Arab States of the Gulf:
Strategies for Excellence and Diversity
Ed. by Dale Eickelman and Rogaia Mustafa Abusharaf
ISBN 9783959940122, 2016

Iran's Relations with the Arab States of the Gulf:
Common Interests over Historic Rivalry
Ed. by Maaike Warnaar, Luciano Zaccara and Paul Aarts
ISBN 9783959940047, 2016

Egypt and the Gulf: A Renewed Regional Policy Alliance
Ed. by Robert Mason
ISBN 9783959940061, 2016

Intellectual Property Rights:
Development and Enforcement in the Arab States of the
Gulf
Ed. by David Price and Alhanoof AlDebasi
ISBN 9783959940108, 2016

The Arab States of the Gulf and BRICS:
New Strategic Partnerships in Geopolitcs and Economics
Ed. by Tim Niblock, Alejandra Galindo and Degang Sun
ISBN 9783959940085, 2016

The Arms Trade, Military Services and the Security Market
in the Gulf States: Trends and Implications
Ed. by David B. Des Roches and Dania Thafer
ISBN 9783959940160, 2016

Gulf Research Centre Cambridge
K n o w l e d g e   f o r   A l l

Higher Education Investment
in the Arab States of the Gulf:
Strategies for Excellence and Diversity

Edited by Dale F. Eickelman
and Rogaia Mustafa Abusharaf

First published 2017
by Gerlach Press
Berlin, Germany
www.gerlach-press.de

Cover Design: www.brandnewdesign.de, Hamburg
Printed and bound in Germany by Hubert & Co, Göttingen
www.hubertundco.de

British Library Cataloguing in Publication Data.
A catalogue record for this book is available from the British Library.

Bibliographic data available from Deutsche Nationalbibliothek
http://d-nb.info/1106344731

ISBN: 978-3-95994-012-2 (hardcover)
ISBN: 978-3-95994-013-9 (ebook)

Contents

Acknowledgements   vii

Preface: GCC Higher Education Comes of Age   1
Dale F. Eickelman

1 Building Universities that Lead: The Arabian Peninsula   8
Dale F. Eickelman

2 Western and Islamic Models of Higher Education in
Saudi Arabia and Iran   23
Keiko Sakurai

3 Higher Education and the Changing Aspirations of
Women in Saudi Arabia   42
Namie Tsujigami

4 Making a Branch Campus "Work": Georgetown University's
School of Foreign Service in Qatar   55
Daniel C. Stoll

5 Journalism and Scholarship: How One Learns in Qatar   72
Mary L. Dedinsky

6 Education as Public Diplomacy: The Soft Power
Potential of Qatar Higher Education   92
Alieu Manjang

7 The Health of Nations: The Evolution and Structure of Public Health
Higher Education in the GCC   106
Muhammad H. Zaman and *Katie Clifford*

8 Science and Engineering Education in the GCC:
Challenges and Transformations   123
Afreen Siddiqi, Laura Diaz Anadon, and *Venkatesh Narayanamurti*

9 Afterword: State-Society Dialogues in the GCC Knowledge Economy 135
Rogaia Mustafa Abusharaf

About the Contributors   141

Index   143

Acknowledgements

One of the major activities of the Gulf Research Centre (GRC) is to foster research through its annual meetings at the University of Cambridge, the sixth of which was held in 2015. All but one of the chapters in this volume were first presented in the workshop, and all papers have been significantly revised to take into account the discussions and critical feedback at the meeting. The GRC workshop provided the critical mass needed for the volume's contributors to compare their approaches and enable their own contributions to realize their full potential.

The GRC staff facilitated the workshop at all stages. The editors thank the chairman of the GRC, Dr. Abdelaziz Sager, and Dr. Christian Koch for creating these annual meetings as a vehicle for academic exchange, and for their role in providing a strong framework so that workshop directors could focus on their tasks. Elsa Courdier and Sanya Kapasi of the GRC staff managed the multiple tasks making the entire process from the creation of workshops to publication run smoothly.

Emily F. Albrecht prepared the index, and at the publication stage Kai-Henning Gerlach and Malcolm Campbell of Gerlach Press facilitated turning the manuscript into a book.

Preface

GCC Higher Education Comes of Age

Dale F. Eickelman

Let us move back in time to the early 1970s. The Sultanate of Oman established its first Ministry of Education needed textbooks fast. They came without cost via *dhow* from Qatar, and to this day Omanis of a certain generation, including a retired government minister, remember with gratitude these books, used until the early 1980s, when they were replaced with books commissioned by Oman itself. The Qatari donation was not the result of a formal state-to-state accord, but a gift based on personal ties between Omanis, some of whom had worked in Qatar in Oman's pre-1970 era and Qataris.

The Qatari book donation was an expression of the largely informal private initiatives behind the pre-1970 mosque-schools in Oman and elsewhere, and suggests the value placed on both religious and secular learning in the region. The official Oman Ministry of Education website lists some of the pre-1970 private initiatives and the few state ones for the same period.[1] Similar initiatives can be found throughout the region. For Kuwait, Bahrain, and Qatar, the facts, figures, and narrative provided by Sheikha al-Misnad's pioneering 1985 study[2] show the results of multiple tentative individual and state undertakings when the initiatives of a relatively small groups of people, Arab Gulf citizens, Arabs from elsewhere, and others set the foundation for schools that have vigorously grown in more recent years. The spread of educational institutions long ago surpassed the speed and capacities of the region's remaining dhows so crucial to Oman's first steps in the 1970s.

Higher Education Investment intends offers a framework through which recent developments in higher education can be understood in a fresh light. The first chapter, "Building Universities that Lead," places the developments of the last half century in a wider perspective, both with the expansion of state-sponsored education and the accelerated emergence of private higher education since the late twentieth century. With this expansion, a mix of local and international accreditation has also emerged, with some local accreditors offering more rigor and transparency than the "holy grail" (as seen by some) of international accreditation. Of course, the quest for contributing to the global "knowledge economy" is not confined to the GCC region, although some of its constituent states have more resources to invest in education at all levels. Yet the results in rising quality, as several contributors indicate, do not necessarily match the heavy investment. Declining oil revenues have severely crimped expenditures on higher education throughout the GCC, and some states have racheted back educational spending by as much as 30 percent. Nonetheless, recent growth has been formidable in numbers if not always in quality.

Of course, aspirations to create a knowledge economy is equally pervasive in other world regions—China, Southeast Asia, and India, as well as Europe and North America—but in the smaller compass of the GCC states, the juxtaposed mix of public and private universities, branch campuses and autonomous local ones, universities with a broad range of programs and others with a narrow compass of technical or business offerings is vast. So is the choice of languages of instruction, with English prevailing in many but not all fields of study and sometimes reversals between preferences for English or Arabic due to political and cultural influences, as well as "gender separation"—seen by some as a handicap because the academic performance of women in most regional universities is significantly better than that of men. The term "liberal arts" may not be readily understood any better among decision makers in the GCC states than in Europe or North America, but the idea of encouraging critical thinking, allowing citizens to contribute to the knowledge economy, remains a shared goal.

Keiko Sakurai's "Western and Islamic Models of Higher Education" (Chapter 2) offers a probing contrast between models of higher education in Iran and Saudi Arabia. All GCC countries profess adherence to Islamic religious values and almost all have faculties of religious studies within their state universities, but only Saudi Arabia, like Iran, has sought aggressively to "ensure Islamic norms while adopting the institutional characteristics of Western universities" (Sakurai, this volume). Both countries have been selective in adapting modern forms of higher education in order to ensure adherence to Islamic norms as locally understood. Iran allows gender-mixed classes although women must adhere to enforced dress codes. Likewise, Iran has entry quotas for women in many fields, although these have varied over time and universities have sometimes been allowed to re-introduce gender separation.

Saudi Arabia, in contrast, enforces strict gender separation at all levels of instruction except nursery schools and kindergarten. Many universities accept both men and women, but women must study in a separate part of the university and are excluded from many fields regarded as "counter to women's innate nature," such as mining, agriculture, and forestry at King Saud University. The sciences and engineering are seen as more value neutral and thus receive higher levels of investment than other fields, which also must avoid themes contrary to Islamic values, again as locally understood.

The King Abdullah University of Science and Technology (KAUST) breaks the pattern of other Saudi universities. Exempt from supervision by the Ministry of Education, it only provides postgraduate courses in science and engineering, with no required courses in religion or Arabic. The school attracts a large number of international faculty and students. Both countries also have highly developed Islamic universities that have developed in significantly different ways. The Iranian universities combine studies in the humanities and other academic fields with seminary training, facilitating an international outreach. Saudi Islamic universities, like the Islamic University of Medina, also serves to train preachers and missionaries, both under state control, but with curricula modeled on Western universities.

Namie Tsujigami's assessment (Chapter 3) of the implications on higher education for the changing aspirations of women in Saudi Arabia is remarkable in providing the view from below—that is, from the perspective of students—of what education means. In the aggregate, she writes that women's academic achievements, higher than those of men, has not resulted until recently in more employment opportunities. In recent years, however, the most highly educated women have successfully competed for the best wage-labor jobs, although women with lower educational attainment continues to lag behind.

Tsujigami makes an important point that many observers overlook. In pre-oil Saudi Arabia, tribal women played important economic and ritual roles. Only upper- and middle-class urban women were excluded from economic activity. Initial resistance to education for women in Saudi Arabia, and to access to higher education, began to erode by the late 1980s. Her close reading of statistics and ethnographies reminds us of how quickly attitudes toward education can change. Thus the events of the Arab Spring of 2011 accelerated educational reforms in Saudi Arabia and also the access of women to more important roles in society.

Another important development, seemingly a detail but with probably unintended consequences, has been the provision of dormitory accommodations for women. Their movement between campus residences and classrooms is carefully monitored, which means that women's reputations are protected from social and religious conservatives. Female students from distant parts of Saudi Arabia or living at a distance from the university were most likely to have dormitory accommodations.

For these students, education and residence away from kin and family offered opportunities to create non-kin ties to extend their social worlds, something that only married women could do before with advent of accessible higher education. Men can secure employment without higher education, but not women, and the stipends that the government pays for female students to live at the university makes studying at public universities "strategic and profitable" for the students and their families. The opportunity to build non-family social networks in the dormitories was also seen as an advantage, enhancing their access to jobs in an economy that increasingly depends on the participation of educated Saudi women.

Daniel Stoll's "Making a Branch Campus 'Work'" (Chapter 4) offers an insider's view on how to set up a quality branch campus. The profiles of new universities established over the last quarter century are varied, but at least half of them are "branch" campuses of one sort or another. In fortunately rare cases in the U.K. and the U.S., provosts and other key main campus administrators have injudiciously said in published interviews that their purpose in establishing branch campuses is to generate income for the home campus.

Stoll, intimately familiar with Georgetown's decision to establish a branch campus in Qatar, outlines the "win-win" reasons for the move. For both Qatar and the parent university, such a branch campus was an extension of "soft" power, to use Joseph Nye's term. It was a quick way of establishing a benchmark for ensuring quality research, teaching, and admissions standards. Discussions began in 2003 and the first class was admitted in August 2005. Financing, faculty governance, academic freedom, and faculty recruitment and retention are among central issues that had to be resolved. Georgetown's creative solution to creating a tenure-like system of promotion and peer review in a country where non-national faculty are not granted permanent residency merits special attention, as does the recruitment of local, region, and international students and the challenges of establishing student and faculty communities. Stoll may not have intended his chapter as a mini-handbook for how to build a branch campus, but it offers a good start for university administrators so inclined.

Mary Dedinsky, "Journalism and Scholarship: How One Learns in Qatar" (Chapter 5), compares the teaching of journalism in Qatar with her classroom experiences in the U.S. and her work as Managing Editor at the *Chicago Sun-Times*, and makes a strong argument for parallels in critical investigative journalism and scholarship. Both enterprises should be based on "a foundation of fact and reliable analysis," as she points out. The divergence is when the journalist must present "news" and develop information with "immediate public interest and value," or developing a story so that long-term issues, such as water and food security, can be made "newsworthy." Academic research sometimes ventures into the realm of the newsworthy, but good work is usually judged by the evaluations of senior like-minded peers, often creating highly specialized information and analysis.

Dedinsky's classroom and related "experiential" learning introduced Qatari student journalists, and herself, to the Qatari environment. Issues such as the waste management, the abusive treatment of housemaids, and perceived deficiencies in public education were delicate subjects. Officials were often reluctant to meet with the students, but many students used their extended social networks, or those of relatives, to secure interviews. Some of the most interesting stories used the students' local knowledge to obtain fresh perspectives on long-term trends. For example, one study noted that the earlier subject matter at regular informal gatherings of Qatari women (*majalis al-harim*) that used to focus on diet and children now concerned how to start a business. The lasting value of her chapter is to offer insight into how issues of academic and press freedom are introduced to wider audiences. They require learning not only by students, but by the intended audiences. Engaging in journalism by Qatar is not just top-down learning but a negotiation of boundaries of what can be said and where.

Alieu Manjang's "Education as Public Diplomacy" (Chapter 6) examines the "soft power" potential of Qatari higher education as lived experience. Manjang, a Gambian who is currently a doctoral student at the Gulf Studies Center at Qatar University, previously spent six years at Egypt's al-Azhar, followed by a master's degree at one of the Islamic studies programs at Qatar's Shaykh Hamad bin Khalifa University. Like Stoll, Manjang builds on Nye's notion of soft power. In Qatar, the offer of scholarships to foreign students is potentially one way of increasing a country's soft power potential. Using a survey administered to 113 international students, both female and male, at Qatar University, he indicated the strength and limits of education as soft power.

One finding was the limited contact with Qatari students outside of the classroom. His sample group included students residing with their families in Doha (and locally considered "international" students), those living in university dormitories, and a smaller number living alone away from the university. All groups reported minimal opportunities to socialize or study with their Qatari counterparts outside of the classroom. Qatari women often left the university immediately after class, and the men often had full- or part-time jobs away from the campus.

Another detriment to the soft power of education was that most international students—almost half from the Arab world and nearly a quarter from non-Arab African countries—disagreed with the idea that they would return to their home countries after graduation or they had not made up their minds. Manjang is acutely aware, however, that the social and cultural distance between Qatari nationals and international students is in flux and can be shaped in many different ways. His conclusion reads like policy recommendations, suggesting ways in which the Qatari university experience can be a base for building stronger ties among all its students, citizens and "international" alike.

Muhammad Zaman and Katie Clifford's title, "The Health of Nations" (Chapter 7), evokes Adam Smith's *Wealth of Nations*. They acknowledge that some of the region's hospitals are outstanding and some public health issues, such as water and sanitation, have been effectively addressed. The challenge is improving *public* health—providing adequate coverage for citizens and noncitizens alike, training a local workforce to staff the public health system, and meeting the challenges of endemic health issues, including diabetes and cancer, that have accompanied massive and rapid urbanization. In some GCC countries, 87 percent of the population is foreign, including both long-term expatriates and the generally lower-income migrant population of construction workers. Health care for citizens is generally free, but not the services offered to expatriates, the lower income ones of whom often lack access to adequate health care. Three-fourths of hospital clinicians and health care workers are foreign, many of whom lack Arabic and incentives to remain in the region.

Many observers will be surprised to learn that the Sultanate of Oman, more financially challenged than the neighboring GCC states, has the best record in developing a local health strategy, have begun long-term Omanization training in 1991. The Sultanate established not just hospitals and clinics but also a medical education infrastructure and distributed its graduates throughout the country, also providing them with continuing professional education.

Zaman and Clifford survey the development of medical and public health infrastructure throughout the region. They underscore the low levels of investment in medical research, suggesting ways in which regional and international partners can be better connected, and links made between the region's public universities, private universities, and the state. The country-by-country survey of public health initiatives indicates points for future development. The high dependence on non-local health staff, the emphasis on individual over public health, and the exclusion to date of public health from local research and development comes at a price. The GCC states are not alone in emphasizing high-end individual care over population health, but its health care institutions and infrastructure are young enough to offer hope for timely redirection that will benefit both health care and higher education in the region.

Afreen Siddiqi, Laura Anadon, and Venkatesh Narayanamurti, "Science and Engineering" (Chapter 8) also pursue the role of university-industry linkages, often emphasizing science and technology education over other fields. In addition to looking at the surprising recent jump in scientific publications for one GCC country, the authors note the near stagnation in others. The causes are multiple, and their extensive interviews with scientists, deans, university presidents, and others point to the chronic shortage of human capital. Some "stars" have been recruited, but the key challenge is long-term institutional growth, not short-term measures of patents, innovations, and publication in peer-reviewed journals often made possible by collaboration with scientists from outside the region. Key to healthy long-term development is the continued recruitment of trained researchers, and providing returning graduates with the means to continue their careers with adequate support systems.

If key people depend on short-term contracts and short-term visas, then the constant churn of personnel will restrict long-term development. Moreover, the lack of preparation of students for scientific research because of poor preparation in mathematics, science, and English at lower levels of education, a social problem that has political implications, deflects from the local development of science and engineering. The problems are not just technical. Policy decisions require rethinking issues of national identity, adequate leadership, and a renewed respect for careers in science and engineering.

Rogaia Abusharaf's "Afterword: State-Society Dialogues" (Chapter 9) returns to the broader questions of national identity. Her point of departure is the Qatar National Vision 2030, which she deconstructs to involve abstract struggle between "authenticity" and "modernity," evident in the development of higher education in the region. Higher education erodes boundaries between nations and often among existing fields of knowledge. Yet without exception, in the name of authenticity, the societies of the region raise barriers to citizenship and integration into local society.

The knowledge economy requires not just start-up institutions and realizing short-term objectives, but developing stable and enduring long-term capacities. Several chapters in this book suggest ways in which these problems have been or can be addressed— workaround systems of promotion and retention not based on "tenure without term," to use the American phrase, and offering economic incentives that have become hard for researchers in some countries to match. Language is another fault line, and the Arab world is not along in realizing what is gained and lost in language choice for higher education.

In an ideal education, bilingualism might be the aspiration, but in practice this is a hard goal to attain.

The chapters in this volume succeed in offering the multiple perspectives that go into the rapidly evolving infrastructure of the region in which education is like the canary in the mine shaft. Behind seemingly technical issues such as health care infrastructure or education in science and engineering loom the larger issues of national and religious identity, leadership, and the pragmatic issue of what actually works. By approaching these concerns from multiple perspectives, we hope to have advanced awareness of the importance of looking beyond the day-to-day challenges of making higher education work and fostering an awareness of longer-term objectives. Fernand Braudel's *longue durée* may be too long a time span, but we can all benefit by asking not only what works today, but what is likely to work for the next generation.

Notes

1 http://home.moe.gov.om/english/module.php?module=pages-showpage&CatID=4&ID=7
2 Sheikha al-Misnad, *The Development of Modern Education in the Gulf* (London: Ithaca Press, 1985).

1

Building Universities that Lead: The Arabian Peninsula

Dale F. Eickelman

Higher education in the Arabian Peninsula has existed for thousands of years. There have long been centers of Islamic learning in Mecca, Tarim in the Hadhramawt, and—just at the peninsula's edge—the island of Qeshm off southern Iran. Most of the Western-style institutions in the Arabian Peninsula are less than half a century old. Saudi Arabia's College of Petroleum and Minerals—today the King Fahd University of Petroleum and Minerals, had a hundred students when it opened in 1963. Kuwait University followed in 1966, United Arab Emirates University (1976), and Oman's Sultan Qaboos University (1986), to name only several of the state universities It is only in the last 15 years that private higher education institutions have been authorized, beginning with the United Arab Emirates and the Sultanate of Oman in 1995, with most other countries following in the present century. In Kuwait, for example, the decree authorizing private higher education dates only from 2000 and the first private university opened its doors in 2003.

The range of educational models followed by private universities ranges from stand-alone institutions to branches of foreign universities that offer studies only in selected subjects. All private universities are required by national laws to partner with foreign institutions and these include established Arab, American, British, Dutch, Australian, Indian, and German universities. Some places, such as Education City in Qatar, aggregate the branch campuses of established foreign institutions, and Qatar University, the state institution, which began a major reform program in 2003, offers the most comprehensive on-line analysis of its activities (http://www.qu.edu.qa/offices/oipd/) of any of the region's state institutions.

For many states of the region, accreditation agencies within the ministries of higher education license and accredit private universities, and sometimes impose more rigorous review standards than international accrediting agencies can provide. The United Arab Emirates' Commission for Academic Accreditation (www.caa.ae) accredited 79 academic institutions as of 2016, by far the largest number of post-secondary institutions in the region. The Oman Authority for Academic Accreditation (OAAA), as the Oman Accreditation Council (www.oaaa.gov.om) was renamed by royal decree on April 5, 2010, encompasses

48 higher education institutions, of which eight are universities, six of which are private. The Oman Authority is the only one in the Arabian Peninsula to provide online audit reports of the reviewed institutions. Kuwait's Private Universities Council (PUC) (www. puc.edu.kw), established in 2000, has licensed seventeen institutes of higher learning as of 2016, eight of which are accredited. As of 2010, the PUC was joined by the National Bureau for Academic Accreditation and Educational Quality Assurance (NBAQ) (www.nbaq.edu. kw), although as of 2016 the PUC continued to assume all accreditation functions.

All the accreditation agencies are bilingual in Arabic and English, since private institutions operate primarily in English. Language choice is a key issue. Both private and state universities in the GCC region and elsewhere, like the regional accreditation agencies, share information on "quality assurance" and "best practices."[1]

The impetus for the rapid growth in higher education in the Arabian Peninsula, and private higher education in particular, is not unique to the region. The exponential increase in the number of students graduating from secondary school institutions has created a demand for higher education that far outstrips the ability of existing state institutions to absorb them. As a stopgap measure in Oman in June 1999, for example, the Council of Ministers abruptly ordered the state university to double its intake of students for the 1999-2000 academic year. By 2001, the year that Oman announced the creation of the state-run Accreditation Council, the Ministry of Higher Education stated that Omani institutions could absorb only 32 percent of the estimated 27,000 school-leavers per year. By the academic year 2007-2008, Oman had 66,301 high school leavers, of whom 75 percent, or 49,856, applied to Oman's various higher education institutes. Only 19, 815, or 40 percent of these applicants were absorbed.[2] In Saudi Arabia, the number of state universities increased from 8 to 20 from 2003 to 2009, and new universities continued to open through 2015. The Saudi Minister of Higher Education, Khalid al-'Anqari, announced the goal of institutions of higher learning absorbing no fewer than 86 percent of secondary school graduates: "In most countries," the minister said, "a maximum of only 50 percent secondary school graduates get to universities."[3] This aspiration to extend post-secondary education to include the majority of secondary school graduates increase is a major change from the latter half of the twentieth century. To take only Oman as an example, in 1975-1976 a mere 22 students were enrolled in secondary school education within the country. By 2005, the number reached 293,000, and Oman is only one example among many.

The Saudi Minister's comments underscore the shift to mass higher education throughout the Arabian Peninsula, a phenomenon basic to reshaping notions of self and society. We know a lot about basic statistics—the numbers of pupils, teachers, the near-elimination in recent years of the numerical gender gap in higher education between women and men. We know less about how the shift to mass higher education changes people's thinking about self and society. Before the 1950s, being a secondary school graduate made one a member of the elite in many countries of the region. When large numbers have advanced diplomas, the quality and social context of higher education shifts dramatically.[4]

On the plus side, mass higher education creates large numbers of people able to participate in wide-ranging public debates and whose concerns rise above the question of making an adequate living. In January 2008, Dubai's Shaykh Muhammad bin Rashid said that education and entrepreneurship are the twin underpinnings for building a safer world, themes echoed throughout the Gulf Cooperation Council countries and elsewhere.[5]

On the negative side, one also recognized by Shaykh Muhammad bin Rashid and echoed in several many reports on higher education, the massification of higher education has also led to a quality deficit in which the quest for credentials and sinecures contributes to what sociologist Ronald Dore terms the "diploma disease."[6] This "disease" is especially pronounced in GCC countries where many graduates, especially male, prefer government sinecures to employment in the private sector.[7]

The leadership of all the GCC states is committed to a knowledge-based society. The issue is how this aspiration translates into building institutions of higher education. Qatar has been perhaps the most forthcoming in identifying the quality deficit at all educational levels, and in 1996 began making preparations for major educational reform. A Qatari-commissioned Rand Corporation survey carried out in 2001-2002, the most thorough publically available for any GCC state, that at the K-12 level there was a "lack of vision or goals for education" and an "outmoded, rigid," and "unchallenging curriculum."[8] A structure had to be put into place that supported quality. The curriculum in its judgment was unmotivated and over-regulated, the system lacked performance indicators, and qualified teachers were short in numbers. The post-secondary pre-reform structure was equally bleak.[9] A subsequent 2015 report on K-12 education in Qatar was equally incisive but assessed concrete ways in which teaching at this level might be improved.[10] Even with relatively open checkbooks, the various branch campuses in Qatar and the United Arab Emirates have been challenged in recruiting sufficient numbers of qualified students. New York University's Abu Dhabi campus flew 320 student applicants from around the world to Abu Dhabi in April 2010. Only four local students attended the initial recruitment session; the entering class had 120 students.[11] Other universities in the GCC states recruit locally and invest heavily in pre-university preparatory courses to prepare local students for university entry.

Learning to Think Locally and Globally

The drive for improved higher education is global. For decades, business leaders, university administrators, and educational policy-makers worldwide have focused on how higher education can best produce new generations of workers with a knowledge base and an aptitude for critical thinking to allow them to flourish in an increasingly demanding economy. In the United States, the dynamic tension between managing universities to achieve a utilitarian education for "proficiency in some gainful occupation" and a pursuit of "higher learning," to use the terms of sociologist Thorsten Veblen (1857-1929), has been endemic.[12] The problem is not simply one of adapting to changing technologies, nor even anticipating where technology is headed. The core problem has been defined as training young people to succeed in a world where they face unanticipated changes in technology and organization. The solution to this challenge has been to understand knowledge as rooted in problem solving and critical thinking.

Jamil Salmi, coordinator of the World Bank's Tertiary Education Thematic Group, described the challenge this way:

> The learning process now needs to be increasingly based on the capacity to find, access and apply knowledge to problem-solving. In this new paradigm, where learning to learn, learning to transform information into new knowledge, and learning to transfer new knowledge into applications, are more important than memorizing specific information, primacy is given to information seeking, analysis, the ability to reason, and problem-solving.

The concept of a "knowledge economy" resets the conceptual boundaries for how learning occurs. Clearly, knowledge generation is not—and never has been—entirely a local phenomenon. The argument about success in a knowledge economy now hinges on several inter-related points. Thanks to new communications technologies and the greater ease of travel, knowledge travels more quickly and widely than it ever has. Nonetheless, those at the point of origin of new knowledge have a significant advantage in having been there first and in having produced an educational infrastructure capable of generating this valuable knowledge. In this sense, and despite the reality of globalization, the ability to generate knowledge confers a local advantage. In turn, this heightens the value of knowledge-building capacity in all places connected to the knowledge economy.

Reflecting high aspirations, some GCC countries have announced massive investments in higher education and in institutions that aspire to be research and educational leaders. At the research end these institutions include the King Abdullah University of Science and Technology (www.kaust.edu.sa), aggressively recruiting for new faculty in the fields of science (www.kaust-aea.cam.ac.uk/). In the liberal arts, New York University Abu Dhabi (NYUAD), describes itself as a "research university with a fully integrated liberal arts and science college."[13] NYUAD is a entirely funded by Abu Dhabi.[14] It certainly has a diverse student body. Its class of 2019, with 299 students, is from 85 different nationalities, including dual nationals. Emirati students composed 14 percent, or 43 of the class.[15]

The American term "liberal arts" is not widely understood in the region, and the term "liberal" (Arabic, _liberali_) often has negative connotations because of its association with autocratic, secular, and military regimes. The term "critical thinking" (Arabic, _al-fikr al-naqdi_) is often used instead to encompass the skills associated with the liberal arts. Local cultural knowledge, skills, discernment, good judgment, pride in one's own society and the ability to live and appreciate others have long been a part of Muslim majority societies, and many of these skills, especially those of writing and thinking critically and in public, built into education at all levels, can jump start the transition to knowledge-based societies.

A Changing Educational Ecology

India and China, countries that two decades ago had closed economies and trailed badly in the relevant higher education indices, are instructive benchmarks for educational innovation. Both these countries have revamped their educational systems to the point that they are producing numbers of knowledge workers in the technology fields—and many others—far beyond what the US and other western countries are producing. Both India and China have much larger populations than the US, but this fact in itself leads to no inevitable conclusion. Numbers speak to demand, but they do not guarantee a conversion of students into effective cohorts of globally valued workers.

As a consequence of global dynamics, the priority is for workers who can produce knowledge and participate fully in what has been called "a global system of innovation." Students and their families are demanding an education that provides access to this global system, a demand that is making change within national university structures. One indication of this demand is the overwhelming choice of English as the language of instruction. The author was present at the first meeting at the American University of Kuwait with the parents of students in December 2004. The University's first president opened the meeting in Arabic but was quickly asked by a large numbers of parents to switch into English. Many in the older generation were uncomfortable with speaking in English about their children's education, but their choice of an English-speaking university for their children was unquestioned.

At the University of Nizwa, in the Sultanate of Oman, the story is much the same. The University's Chancellor, Dr. Ahmad al-Rawahi, explained to new students in Arabic in 2007 that a "private" university (Arabic, *jami'at khassa*) does not necessarily mean a profit-making entity for its shareholders, but a non-state institution (*jamia'at 'amma*) in the public sphere and for the common good (*al-maslaha al-'amma*)—a phrase with strong resonance in the Muslim-majority world.[16] Instruction, however, is in English even if most students at Nizwa, as at other schools throughout the region, need pre-university English instruction in order to follow university courses.

The preference for English as the language of choice is deliberate. In September 1980, the author, then in Oman conducting anthropological field research, accepted an invitation from Oman's Council of Ministers to outline the questions that the Council should discuss in deciding whether to establish a national university. One alternative proposed was to make Arabic the primary instructional language, with qualified instructors recruited from elsewhere and allowed a set number of years, as in the Netherlands, to learn the national language. However, with the exception of Islamic and Arabic studies, the language selected when Sultan Qaboos University opened in 1986 was English.

Recent developments in Indonesia allow an external perspective for gauging both the growth in student demand and changes in educational expectations worldwide. In 2004, there were 80,000 places in Indonesia's top-tier state universities and 344,000 applicants for these places, meaning that fewer than one in four Indonesian high school graduates could be placed. Other state-funded alternatives provided some relief; overall, 900,000 Indonesians received higher education in the state system. But three million Indonesians students were at a post-high school level of study, meaning that more than two-thirds of Indonesian higher education was in the hands of private universities of one kind or another with wide variations in quality, focus, and religious affiliation. The demand in Indonesia is not likely to decrease. Several years later, in 2007, 3,755,000 students were enrolled in post-secondary education, and 74 percent of these students were in private universities.[17]

This dramatic increase in student numbers is a global phenomenon. In China in 2015, 26.2 million students entered the country's universities, nearly eight times the number who did so in 1998. In 2007, 10.1 million secondary school graduates took the entrance examination for higher education, but only 5.67 million, or 56 percent, were enrolled, leaving the rest of the applicants without an option to continue their studies.[18]

The global growth in demand covers not only recent secondary school graduates, but growing numbers of older workers who return to higher education to improve their career opportunities. In the United States, for example, the number of students in higher education who are more than 22 years old was 45 percent in 1970. This percentage – of a larger pool of students – was estimated to grow to 57 percent by 2010. This increase speaks to the practical appeal of the idea of life-long learning, but it also raises the question of where and how these non-traditional students are going to be educated. Some of this demand is for periodic in-service training. In this respect, the short-term courses offered by many military organizations, health care institutions, and the judiciary in some locales complement conventional degree courses.

In the United States, standard public institutions have not grown quickly enough to keep pace with the expanding demand for higher education. Globally, a variety of expert surveys project a similar phenomenon: the demand for higher educational opportunity by older workers that goes beyond the narrow scope of job retraining. Some of this demand is fueled by demands for certification that often are linked to salary increases or promotions. But much of the demand for higher learning goes beyond the search for credentials or status alone.

The global growth in higher education – extending beyond the original capacity of existing structures and institutions – has produced a variety of responses, including the creation of new kinds of institutions and adaptation of the old. State systems have been expanded, but demand has outpaced this expansion. Non-profit institutions have grown as well, but again not in numbers that match the increased number of students. Consequently, for-profit higher education plays an increasingly important role in providing life-long learning opportunities, particularly for those already in the workforce.

A brief profile of a for-profit American university gives a flavor of who is being served by these developments. Centered on on-line learning, the University of Phoenix grew from 10,000 students in 1999 to 458,600 full-time equivalent students as of 2010, although by 2014 the number fell back to 213,800 and was expected to drop to 200,000 by 2015.[19] The average age of the student is 34 and tuition for an undergraduate degree is just more than $30,000. In more than half the cases, employers provide at least partial reimbursement of tuition costs. The university may be American, but the student body is not – it includes students from 91 countries.

The global characteristics of relevance to the Arabian Peninsula may be summarized as follows:

- The need of employers globally for problem-solving based education. As one Saudi businessman observed, the need in his companies is not for graduates trained in narrow specialties that quickly go out of date, but for graduates capable of critical thinking in a wide range of fields and able to rapidly learn new skills and regularly to renew their learning to new issues.

- The transnational character of this need; students are judged increasingly by their skills, not their origins, even where local employment laws privilege citizens.

- The consequent demand of students for an education that will provide these skills.

- The development of new institutions—including private, for-profit universities—to meet this need.

While the appeal of a critical thinking approach in higher education has been widespread, individual adaptations of the idea have been shaped by local circumstances. Censorship often restricts the books available to student and how regional history can be taught. This is not a problem limited to the Arabian Peninsula or to Arab countries. Some U.S. states insist on teaching creationism alongside evolution and some localities restrict what books can be used. Other constraints reflect resource availability and social mores.

Starting with a common commitment to critical thinking as a part of higher learning, educators have arrived at a diversity of models for its implementation. The most important variable is the relationship with outside university partners in institutional development. In many cases, the partners include American universities, with institutions from England, Australia, Canada, and Lebanon also seeking to participate in GCC educational growth. The terms of the partnerships vary, but several common factors contribute to university development in the GCC region:

1) Experience with English language instruction, both for native speakers and English as a Second Language (ESL) students, based on the perception that English is the door to global competence. Throughout the Arabian Peninsula,

as in North Africa in the Arabic-speaking world, language training is both a prerequisite for higher learning and an end in itself.

2) An established tradition of broad-gauge, critical thinking instruction, based in the liberal arts tradition of American universities or its equivalent elsewhere.

3) GCC-based educational policy-makers who value their own American (or English-language) educations and wish to see local students exposed to similar approaches.

4) A demonstrable link between this style of instruction and successful integration into both the local and global economies.

5) An aspirational goal for local students who may not have the social or financial means to study abroad, but who still want this style of education.

6) These common elements figure prominently when universities describe themselves to prospective students.

A survey of website mission or value statements reveals a striking similarity of language. This discourse has become central to the institutional identity of universities—both the state universities and their private counterparts—in the Arabian Peninsula. Sultan Qaboos University in Oman describes itself as "an institution that makes student learning its central focus." Kuwait University offers an education "challenging minds, inducing critical thinking and encouraging creativity." The American University of Kuwait is "dedicated to providing students with knowledge, self-awareness, and personal growth experiences that can enhance critical thinking, effective communication, and respect for diversity." Zayed University in the UAE "seeks to prepare Emirati students for a meaningful and successful twenty-first century personal and professional life." The American University of Sharjah "integrates liberal studies, professional education, and co-curricular and extracurricular learning experiences to provide its graduates both breadth and depth of knowledge."

Built around this conceptual core, university development has followed a number of tracks. It remains uncertain which of these approaches best delivers on the the promise defined in the mission statements.

Education City, Qatar

Coordinated by the Qatar Foundation, Education City includes satellite campuses of six American universities, each offering a particular disciplinary specialization: the Georgetown University School of Foreign Service in Qatar (international relations), Northwestern University in Qatar (journalism and communications), Carnegie Mellon University in Qatar (computer science), Virginia Commonwealth University in Qatar (design), Texas A&M University at Qatar (engineering) and the Weill Cornell Medical College in Qatar. In addition, HEC Paris offers executive education for mid-career and senior executives, and the University College of London has offered courses in archaeology, the environment, conservation, and Information Science.

The Qatari selection criteria for university partners emphasized strong, specialized bachelor's degree programs from top-tier American schools, reflecting the stated Qatari goal of offering degrees in subject areas of greatest interest for national development. One program, the Qatar Faculty of Islamic Studies, has no foreign partner. Within each of the internationally affiliated programs, the parent university establishes academic standards in principle along the general lines offered on their home campuses, and the campuses share an Academic Bridge Program that provides regional secondary school graduates with English and math instruction and the study skills needed for university success. The branch campuses do not currently have large enrollments: there was a total of 1,124 students enrolled in 2007-2008. 51 percent of whom were Qatari nationals (www.qf.org.qa), Qatari officials say that they are deliberately focusing on high-performing students. This strategy is intended to produce a well-trained cadre of Qataris with international certification in important disciplines, and also demonstrate at the societal level the impact of quality education.[20]

During the development of Education City, policy-makers also developed a program of reform for Qatar University, a public institution with more than 7,000 students, so that that the mass higher education of Qatar University would not be left behind by the establishment of Education City.[21] At the same time, the language of instruction at Qatar University shifted to English from Arabic, and the university reforms, as mentioned earlier, are strongly linked with the wider challenge of reforming primary and secondary level education. Although there cannot be perfect consistency between reform efforts of such different scales, both initiatives are marked by a concern with improving educational and admissions standards, faculty development, student access to advanced knowledge and research, and the autonomy of the educational program. In the social sciences, including history, the branch campuses of North American universities often face local restrictions on course content. Both language competencies and censorship—textbooks commonly require approval by administrators and in some countries access is restricted to books pertaining to local society—limit what local branches can do.[22]

The American University of Kuwait (AUK)

Established by Amiri decree in 2003, AUK is a Kuwaiti institution whose mission is "based on the American model of higher education . . . designed to prepare students for the contemporary world where critical thinking, communication skills, and life-long learning have become imperative."[23] In practice, AUK has developed a broad-based liberal arts curriculum that allows for specialized majors—such as business management—but also requires that students meet General Education guidelines including humanities and language instruction. While offering instruction in English, as do a number of other newer universities in the region, AUK is particularly attentive to the link between command of English and the importance of connecting different fields of knowledge.

From its inception, AUK has been a Kuwaiti institution owned by a local holding company. However, it maintains a strong relationship with Dartmouth College, one of America's "Ivy League" universities. Thus, the development of administrative, faculty, and curricular initiatives has reflected Kuwaiti priorities, shaped by ongoing consultation with Dartmouth administrators and faculty. Education at AUK is the product of an ongoing exchange between local leadership and its American university partner, but with an emphasis on building AUK and enhancing its autonomy. AUK admits both men and women as full-time students, but since January 2008 like other Kuwaiti universities has been obliged to maintain complete classroom gender separation (Arabic, _man'a al-ikhtilat_, literally, "prevention of mixing"), something that did not exist earlier in higher education in Kuwait. Earlier normal practice since the foundation of Kuwait University in 1966 was for women and men to share classroom space, but with students customarily sitting separately. Practical exigencies have led to informal accommodations of the "prevention of mixing" requirement at virtually all public and private universities in Kuwait.

University of Nizwa, Sultanate of Oman

A private university, Nizwa (in the northern interior of central Oman) presently enrolls more than 6,500 students, 95 percent of whom are Omani. Originally situated in temporary facilities—a former secondary school campus for students from remote areas in Oman—Nizwa University has built a new campus to accommodate 15,000 students.[24] Opened in 2004 in the wake of the Sultan Qaboos' call for the creation of private universities in Oman in 1999 (and a grant of 17 million Omani rials, or US $44 million), the University of Nizwa has a technical orientation in its curriculum, which emphasizes the mastery of various computer and technology skills as well as specialized training in nursing and pharmacy; economics, administration, and information systems; engineering and architecture; as well as arts and sciences. A high degree of technology certification is one of the requirements for graduation. The required course emphasis on English language and presentation skills and computer literacy (in addition to Arabic language and Islamic civilization) indicates that one of the university's key concerns is producing graduates who can enter smoothly into the Omani economy, particularly those sectors which interact with international partners. Not all universities in the region succeed in achieving this balance.

The University of Nizwa has cooperative relationships with American and other English-language universities, but lacks a privileged foreign partner in its development. The school is described as modeled on "the North American system." This requires an ongoing marketing effort with the Omani public, which like other publics in the region is not broadly familiar with this style of education. Nonetheless, Omani families are beginning to shop for new university alternatives and visit the campus in order to evaluate claims about course offerings, language instruction, and the social environment. Women comprise 88 percent of the students, and many live in residential housing on campus, having chosen the University of Nizwa over other universities in the Sultanate.

The Implications of Contrasting Approaches to Higher Education

These three examples differ considerably on the particulars of their structure and approach to higher education. A number of questions emerge for further consideration:

- How does the relationship with an American (or foreign) university partner shape a GCC-based university? What factors determine how local universities structure these relationships? Are these relationships driven by economic opportunity by the foreign counterparts or by the search for mutual benefits?

- To what extent do social factors determine student preferences among universities? How does gender segregation or its lack influence these choices?

- Many of the countries of the region are state-centric. How does that influence the autonomy of the educational sphere and foster the open exchange and development of ideas and research?

- How do marketing campaigns for the universities treat questions of educational approach and gender separation?

- How do the different universities explain their missions and purposes to their local publics?

- How do universities frame the introduction of curricula based on critical thinking as a central element for students who aspire to social and economic leadership but who also want immediate entry into the job market?

Explaining Choice

Many universities in the region emphasize how they serve as a gateway to particular educational styles. Thus an American-style education is widely understood as acutely attuned to the demands of the global economy, incorporating command of the English language, technical and subject mastery, a learning style that incorporates critical thinking, and flexibility that promotes life-long learning. These elements are not always easily achieved in the Arabian Peninsula because of the lack of strong educational reform at the pre-university level. Various institutional approaches have been attempted, but "American style" education asserts these three key elements at least aspirational as an essential offering to prospective students. Hence the importance of the institutional partners.

Although educational visa numbers for regional students in the US have returned roughly to their pre-2001 levels, the significant drop-off over the intervening years gave a strong push to local efforts to create new universities and to seek educational opportunities elsewhere. Local universities offering an American-style education have often targeted students who are reluctant for cultural or security reasons to go to the US, students who may not be competitive for entry into higher-ranked American universities, and students who see value in getting an American education locally for substantially lower tuition rates.

A growing middle class in the region has also given voice to parents who prefer that their children—particularly their daughters—be educated at home but in ways that meet their test of quality. In the United Arab Emirates, Kuwait, and Oman, meetings with focus groups of students confirm that these factors influence choice.

Emerging Trends

Competing Models

The new universities in the GCC have grappled with curricular and institutional issues that we would recognize as directly related to providing a quality education: private versus public; profit versus non-profit; independent versus affiliated or branch. In many cases, state universities, once thought of as preferable because low cost or free tuition for those who gained entrance, experience increasing competition from private universities and are obliged to modify their own institutional presentation and services. Some governments offer students portable scholarships, allowing them choice among institutions and fostering competition where before there was none.

Despite American policy failures in the Middle East, American higher education remains the gold standard, a model to be emulated and adapted to local purposes. This reflects the impact of higher education on America's economic success—the current economic crisis notwithstanding—as well as the impact of generations of Arab students who studied in the US. The internationalization of US higher education is not, however, immune from economic reversals. In 1989, at the height of Japanese economic growth, 21 "branch" campuses of US universities were operating in Japan. Today only one such branch campus remains. In May 2009 George Mason University closed its branch campus in Ras al-Khaima because its local subsidy had been cut, and in July 2010 Michigan State University shut down most of its operations in Dubai.[25]

It is far from clear that American policymakers even today recognize the appeal of the American university model in the Middle East, its significance, or its potential impact on the aspirations of a new generation of Arab students who seek to study in American-style institutions of higher education in their own countries. Over time, much greater attention to the development of these universities – their structures, their curricula, their accreditation, and the values they espouse – could produce a strong counter-current to anti-American sentiment in the region and to anti-Muslim and anti-Arab prejudice in the US. At present, other countries, such as lower-cost Australian education for middle class Omanis frustrated with navigating the US visa system and the high cost of U.S. institutions, offers a growing and competitive alternative.

Gender Relations

To varying degrees, universities in the Arabian Peninsula are under pressure to maintain gender separation on campus. Doing so sometimes adds considerable costs in the form of the duplication of efforts and facilities, and may undermine the preparation of students for jobs in the gender-integrated global market. Paradoxically, gender segregation may work to the disadvantage of male students. A 2007 McKinsey study suggests that gender segregation hurts the educational opportunities of male students more than their female counterparts at all educational levels.[26] In at least one country in the region, it is illegal for instructors to grade male and female students using the same scale, and in most countries females must score higher than their male counterparts to gain access to free education at state institutions. Many private universities now have large majorities of women students (88 percent at Nizwa University versus a near gender parity at the American University of Kuwait). The consistently higher performance by women over men can only in part be explained by the greater ease with which men can pursue studies outside the GCC region. Gender separation also raises the question of why higher education seems to be more important to Arab women at this time rather than to Arab men.

Sometimes the different approaches are highly local. One important difference between Qatar's Education City campuses and Qatar University is that Education City integrates both genders in the classroom; Qatar University separates them. Gender separation varies significantly throughout the region. In Kuwait, the consequence of introducing classroom gender separation for the first time in January 2008 was to increase teaching loads from an average of 7.5 per instructor per year (with course overloads) to 11.5 courses, a teaching load that cannot be sustainable in the long run if one is to attract quality faculty members. In other countries, men and women learn together and the trend is toward eliminating gender separation.

Critical Thinking

Acknowledged as the aspirational basis of American higher education, this concept is not always well understood, and runs the risk of being perceived to subvert well-established mores. Islamic education has its tradition of critical thinking, and many beneficiaries of Islamic education themselves apply critical thinking to issues of faith and heritage. For example, a former Kuwaiti civil servant writing in his private capacity, used sayings (*hadith*) of the Prophet Muhammad to argue that early Islamic tradition never limited interaction between women and men, even in mosques, for the purposes of learning, so that gender separation as currently understood is an innovation (Arabic, *bid'a*) that contravenes a properly understood Islamic tradition.[27]

It is through public local discussions of such issues that educational practices will become transformed in the GCC region. In the United Arab Emirates, a new Islamic studies (Arabic, *dirasat islamiyya*) curriculum was introduced in 2009) in government schools at the primary and secondary levels. This curriculum, the equivalent of civics education elsewhere, is intended to foster a spirit of active, critical inquiry into the reading of religious texts and an understanding of public life.[28] This is entirely a local initiative, but one that integrates the best of critical inquiry in a combined local and global perspective.

Combining local and global perspectives is the great challenge that faces higher education at this time – in the Arabian Peninsula and around the world. US President Barack Obama has said that higher education is the great civil rights issue of this century. In the United States, civil rights have traditionally meant providing equal access to all of society's institutions. In the new world of higher education that confronts us, civil rights could mean providing the world with access to the ideas and the aspirations of our young people. Critically educated young people are, as we all know, our greatest natural resource.

Notes

An earlier version of this chapter was first presented (with Clifford Chanin, conference co-organizer) at the conference, "University Development and Critical Thinking: Education in the Arabian Peninsula for a Global Future," American University of Kuwait, March 10-12, 2009. We gratefully acknowledge conference funding from the American University of Kuwait.

1   Hollings Center for International Dialogue, "Quality Assurance in Higher Education: An International Dialogue on Progress and Challenges," July 10, 2010 (www.hollingscenter.org).

2   Rawya Saud Al Busaidiyah, Minister of Higher Education, "Actively Encouraging E-learning," *Oman Vistas* 2008, available at: http://tinyurl.com/z5r675f

3   Khalid al-'Anqari, "Saudi Varsities to absorb 86% high school grads," *Arab News*, June 27, 2008.

4   Dale F. Eickelman, "Mass Higher Education and the Religious Imagination in Contemporary Arab Societies," *American Ethnologist* 19, no. 4 (November 1992): 643-55.

5   Mohammed Bin Rashid Al Maktoum, "Our Ambitions for the Middle East," *Wall Street Journal*, January 12, 2008, A9.

6   Ronald Dore, *The Diploma Disease: Education, Qualification, and Development* (Berkeley: University of California Press, 1976); United Nations Development Programme/Arab Fund for Economic and Social Development, *Arab Human Development Report 2003: Building a Knowledge Society* (New York: United Nations, 2003); Michael Barber, Mona Mourshed, and Fenton Whelan, "Improving Education in the Gulf," *McKinsey Quarterly* (Special Edition, March 2007: 39-47, online at: http://tinyurl.com/jdmod8g) (accessed 29 June 2016).

7   See, for example. Cathleen Stasz, Eric R. Eide, and Francisco Martorell, *Post-Secondary Education in Qatar* (Doha: Rand Qatar Policy Institute, 2007), 46.

8   The survey of the existing educational system was carried out in 2001-2002. Dominic J. Brewer, Catherine H. Augustine, Gail L. Zellman, et al., *Education for a New Era: K-12 Education Reform in Qatar* (Doha: Rand-Qatar Policy Institute, 2007), 37-42.

9   Joy S. Moini, Tora K. Bikson, Richard C. Neu et al., *The Reform of Qatar University* (Doha: Rand-Qatar Policy Institute, 2009). The Rand-Qatar publications are available online at: www.rand.org/qatar

10 Asmaa Alfadela, *K-12 Reform in the Gulf Corporation* [sic] *Council (GCC) Countries: Challenges and Policy Recommendations* (Doha: WISE, n.d. [2015]).

11 Andrew Mills, "NYU Populates a Liberal-Arts Outpost in the Middle East," *Chronicle of Higher Education*, April 11, 2010; available online at: http://tinyurl.com/jh3yxwb.

12 Thorsten Veblen, *The Higher Learning in America: A Memorandum on the Conduct of Universities by Business Men* (New York: Huebsch, 1918).

13 www.nyuad.nyu.edu

14 Mills, "NYU Populates"

15 http://tinyurl.com/hwskhwy

16 Ahmad Khalfan al-Rawahi, remarks at new student orientation, University of Nizwa, February 18, 2007.

17 UNESCO Institute for Statistics, *Global Educational Digest 2009: Comparing Educational Statistics Across the World* (Montreal: UNESCO Institute for Statistics, 2009) (www.uis.unesco.org).

18 Uwe Brandenberg and Jiani Zhu, *Higher Education in China in the Light of Massification and Demographic Change* (Gütersloh, Germany: CHE Centrum für Hochschulentwicklung, 2007, 22 (available at: http://tinyurl.com/h3q97g5); Javier C. Hernández, "China Tries to Education to the Poor, Igniting Class Conflict," *New York Times*, June 12, 2016, A1.

19 *Chronicle of Higher Education, Almanac of Higher Education 2010-2011*, August 27, 2010, 29: http://tinyurl.com/qx6xfng

20 http://tinyurl.com/hb7dsta

21 See Moini, Bikson, and Neu, *Reform of Qatar University*.

22 For example, a faculty member teaching early Islamic history at Qatar University was told that he would lose his job if he continued to mention the early struggles for leadership that immediately followed the death of the Prophet Muhammad in 632. Interview with the faculty member, Doha, February 24, 2008.

23 http://tinyurl.com/z33rd4f, accessed June 29, 2016.

24 www.unizwa.edu.om

25 Tamar Lewin, "University Branches in Dubai are Struggling," *New York Times*, December 29, 2009; Melanie Swan, "Michigan State University Shuts Most of Its Dubai Campus," *The National* (Abu Dhabi), July 6, 2010, available at: www.thenational.ae

26 Barber, Mourshed, and Whelen, "Improving Education in the Gulf," 43-44.

27 Imad Alatiqi, "Male-Female Encounters in Early Islamic Society—Examples and Case Study." Paper presented at the conference, "University Development and Critical Thinking," American University of Kuwait, March 10-12, 2009.

28 For example, see the teacher's guide to the fourth grade, part 1, United Arab Emirates, Ministry of Education, *Dalil al-mu'allim ila* kitab "al-tarbiyya al-Islamiyya al-saff al-rabi'a al-jiz al-awwal." Abu Dhabi: Abu Dhabi Company for Printine and Distribution, 2006 (ISBN 9948-09-137-X).

2

Western and Islamic Models of
Higher Education in Saudi Arabia and Iran

Keiko Sakurai

In recent decades, the Gulf countries have invested enormous efforts in providing university education, particularly in science, technology, and business. The purpose is to make the economy sustainable by reducing dependency on mineral resources, diversify economic structure, and replace foreign workers with nationals.

Countries such as the United Arab Emirates (UAE) and Qatar have made tremendous investments to create higher-education hubs by attracting foreign branches of world-class universities based in the United States and Western Europe as well as inviting Western provosts, professors, and consultants to their national universities.[1] By 2012, Qatar had opened eight branch campuses of foreign universities.[2] The UAE's component emirates have competed over the number of foreign university branch campuses they host. As of 2012, Dubai had opened 25 branch campuses, while Abu Dhabi had five and Ras al-Khaimah, seven.[3] The majority of foreign university branch campuses in Qatar and the UAE were opened in the 2000s, and have successfully attracted foreign students.[4] Together with the application of Western education and administrative models, they have promoted English as the medium of instruction, especially for the sciences, technology, and business.[5]

In contrast, Iran and Saudi Arabia are more cautious of foreign influence on higher education and significantly restrict the operation of foreign universities within their territories. However, they are not indifferent to the idea of creating "world-class" universities that can attract overseas students. They are eager to create leading universities, especially in the field of science and technology, with their own initiatives. Iran and Saudi Arabia have developed two types of university; one is a "modern" university focused on the teaching of modern sciences. A majority of government universities fall into this category. The other is an "Islamic university" dedicated to the training of 'ulama'. Most of the traditional Islamic seminaries were replaced by the Islamic universities and some of them have even developed into "world" centers of Islamic higher education.

These different approaches originate in the historical relations between the state and the religious establishments in each country. As the rulers of the UAE and Qatar do not derive their legitimacy from religion, their educational policies are not mediated by the religious establishment. In contrast, Iran and Saudi Arabia, as "religious states," claim their legitimacy by the enforcement of Islamic law in public affairs. The Iranian regime, known as "the government of the jurist" (*vilāyat-i faqīh*), was established as the result of the 1979 revolution led by Ayatollah Khomeini. The national constitution guarantees high-ranking Islamic jurists supervision of state affairs. Saudi Arabia's present government dates back to the 1745 religio-political alliance of the house of Saud and 'Abd al-Wahhab. This ensured the Al Sa'ud monopoly in politics, but its legitimacy depends on religious authority.

Additionally, both Iran and Saudi Arabia have a long-standing history of Islamic scholarship. Cities such as Isfahan, Mashhad, and Qom in Iran, and Mecca and Medina in Saudi Arabia, serve as centers of Islamic learning, attracting international scholars and students. The existence of these centers ensures the 'ulama's strong influence in educational affairs. Although the contemporary 'ulama acknowledge the Western university system as a "universal model," they question the universality of Western curricula, classroom arrangements, and ideas of academic freedom, claiming that these aspects require amendment to better align with Islamic norms. Accordingly, Iranian and Saudi Arabian universities employ locally relevant classroom arrangements and curricula.

By focusing on Iranian and Saudi models of higher education, this chapter explores why and how these countries attempt to maintain their religio-cultural norms despite their acceptance of the institutional characteristics of Western universities.

First, we describe the current landscape of higher education in Iran and Saudi Arabia, including mission statements and agendas, as described by the ministries of higher education and the universities. Special attention is given to issues where transmission of Islamic values is deemed essential. Second, we discuss how Iran and Saudi Arabia try to ensure Islamic norms while adopting the institutional characteristics of Western universities, by focusing on gender policy and curricula.

Third, the chapter examines how the two nations seek to enhance the international prestige of their universities by focusing national universities dedicated to the teachings of non-religious sciences. Fourth, the chapter sheds light on Islamic universities' attempts to modernize the training of 'ulama by adopting the Western university model and produce a new generation of religious experts who serve to protect and promote "official Islam," as defined by the state. Fifth, it describes Iranian and Saudi global strategies to make Islamic universities "world centers" of religious education. Finally, this chapter argues how the interplay between the Western and Islamic models produces new models of universities in both countries.

Higher Education in Iran and Saudi Arabia

Iran's modern higher education began in 1851 when the Dar al-Fonun (The Academy of Applied Sciences), modelled after the French Polytechnic, was established. The ministries later established several colleges to train experts and bureaucrats. In 1934, the University of Tehran was founded as Iran's first modern university, adopting the French model. Originally it had faculties of arts, sciences, medicine, engineering, and law, and later added theology, fine art, and agriculture. After World War II, government universities were constructed in major provincial cities such as Tabriz (1947), Mashhad (1949), Shiraz (1949), Isfahan (1950), and Ahvaz (1955).[6] Additionally, three private universities were opened, Pahlavi University in Shiraz (1949), Melli University (1960) and Aryamehr University (1966) in Tehran. Due to a sudden increase in oil revenue, nine additional government universities were established in the mid-1970s.[7]

The 1979 Islamic Revolution transformed the landscape of higher education. In response to Ayatollah Khomeini's speech "The Meaning of Cultural Revolution" (April 1980), the Headquarters of the Cultural Revolution (reorganized into the Supreme Cultural Revolution Council in 1984, as the highest authority in educational affairs) was established to purge Iranian universities of Western influence.[8] All universities were closed in June 1980, and both faculty and students, especially left-wing supporters who defied the consolidation of clerical rule, were accused of being anti-Islamic and expelled from campuses. Clerics revised the curriculum and textbooks, especially the humanities and social sciences, to reflect Islamic values.[9] All the private universities were converted into government institutions and placed under strict state surveillance.

When universities were reopened in 1983, ideologically committed staff filled most faculty posts, and students were selected for both academic performance and ideological commitment. The loss of qualified faculties and overemphasis on ideology, along with the eight-year war with Iraq, affected the quality of Iranian higher education. However, since the 1988 ceasefire with Iraq, Iran has witnessed a rapid development of universities in both the government and private sectors. The higher-education system is highly centralized, with the Ministry of Science, Research and Technology (until 2000, it was called the Ministry of Culture and Higher Education) supervising human affairs and syllabi. The highest authority in higher education is the Supreme Council of the Cultural Revolution, founded in 1984 by Khomeini's decree. The council members, appointed by the supreme leader, are responsible for ensuring that all aspects of education are Islamic.

Every province of Iran has tuition-free government universities. An alternative to full-time, government universities is Payam-e Noor, a distance-learning government university founded in 1988, which offers less expensive tuition than private universities. It has more than 500 local study centers and campuses scattered across the country, administrated by 31 provincial centers.[10] Payam-e Noor underwent unprecedented growth during the mid-2000s, under the slogan of "higher education for all," with enrollment increasing from approximately 380,000 in 2005, to 1,000,000 in 2011-2012.[11]

Demand for higher education increased in the mid-1990s and crucial in meeting this demand was the Islamic Azad University (IAU), established in 1982 by the state's clerical leaders as a non-profit organization. At first, IAU utilized existing buildings without its own campus. Following the Iran-Iraq war, it grew to be one of the world's largest private universities by absorbing students who, although excluded from highly competitive government universities, can afford tuition fees.

In 2012, Iran's higher education institutes numbered over 2500. Among them, 318 are government universities under the direct control of ministries, 344 are private universities, and 408 are branches of IAU.[12] Among Iran's population of about 80 million (2014 census), about 4,435,000 students are enrolled at higher education institutes (2012/13); 35.7 percent were enrolled at IAU, and about 87 percent were studying for an Associate or Bachelor's degree.[13]

The growth of Iranian higher education is remarkable. Gross tertiary enrollment ratios rose from about 3 percent (4 percent male, 2 percent female) in 1970 to 10 percent in 1990 (13 percent male, 7 percent female); 18 percent (19 percent male, 16 percent female) in 2000 to 37 percent (36 percent male, 38 percent female) in 2009; and by 55 percent (both males and females) in 2012. This demonstrates the universalization of higher education in the 2000s.[14]

Currently, Saudi Arabia has twenty-five[15] government universities and nine private universities, along with numerous colleges. Most premier government institutions were established in the 1950s to the early 1980s, while all private universities were established in the last two decades. King Saud University,[16] established in 1957 in Riyadh, is the oldest university in Saudi Arabia. It began with 21 students and 9 staff, but soon grew to 66,174 students;[17] it is currently ranked the highest among Saudi universities.[18] In the 1960s, the Islamic University in Median (1961), the University of Petroleum and Minerals in Dhahran (1963), and the King Abdulaziz University[19] in Jeddah (1967) were established. In the mid-1970s, the Imam Muhammad Ibn Saud Islamic University and the King Faisal University in Riyadh were opened, coinciding with the establishment of the Ministry of Higher Education.[20] In 1981, the Umm Al-Qura University in Mecca was opened. Established by royal decree, they subsequently became the country's top government universities for education and research.

Among these universities, the Al-Imam Muhammad Ibn Saud Islamic University, the Islamic University of Medina (IUM), and the Umm Al-Qura University are dedicated to Islamic sciences, while the others focus on secular subjects such as science, engineering, and humanities. The 2000s saw a boom in new government universities. Most were created as regional universities by amalgamating the pre-existing technical colleges or adding new colleges.[21] Due to the increased in the number of universities in the 2000s, now each of Saudi Arabia's 13 regions has at least one university, and students receive free education at government universities.

Prince Sultan University was the first private institution, established in 1999. Private universities were a feature of the 2000s. Most opened in major cities to offer undergraduate courses emphasizing marketable knowledge and skills, including accounting, marketing, finance, business management, information technology, engineering, and English. Most accept male and female students in separate departments. The exception is Effat University, which is exclusively for females. It opened in Jeddah in 2008, and offers undergraduate education in business, engineering, social science, and the humanities. Students at private universities are entitled to receive scholarships and "soft" loans.[22]

Government universities depend entirely on government funds, and the government also provides considerable financial support to private universities. All universities are controlled by the Ministry of Higher Education, which is responsible for implementing the rules, policies, and decisions made by the Council of Higher Education.[23] The government's tight control is considered necessary to ensure educational standards and monitor educational activities, but this leads to inflexibility in governance.

In Saudi Arabia, the King Abdullah University of Science and Technology (KAUST) was opened in 2008 as an autonomous research-oriented university for graduate and postgraduate students. Supervised by its own Board of Trustees, it introduced innovative policies, such as co-education, not possible under the Ministry of Higher Education. Since its establishment, KAUST has attracted both male and female students from throughout the world.[24]

In 2013, Saudi Arabia's population was about 20 million (non-Saudi citizens excluded), and about 1,360,000 students were enrolled at universities and colleges—95 percent at government institutions.[25] Saudi Arabia's higher education has developed rapidly in the last few decades. Gross tertiary enrollment ratios grew from 10.3 percent (10.8 percent male, 9.7 percent female) in 1990 to 58 percent (56 percent male, 59 percent female) in 2013, and female students outnumbered male students at domestic universities for the first time in 1999.[26]

The Dual Mission of Higher Education

Higher education in Iran and Saudi Arabia has two missions. The first is to elevate its world reputational ranking. The second is to instill in the younger generation a strong belief in Islam and loyalty to the ruler, who holds ultimate responsibility for enforcing Islamic law. These simultaneous pursuits characterize these countries' educational policies in two ways. The policies promote tertiary education in non-religious sciences without compromising Islamic values, and update the content and teaching style of religious sciences by adopting the Western degree-issuing system. In both aspects, increasing the number of foreign students is vital.

In Iran, the _vilāyat-i faqīh_ has decisively influenced the character of higher education. The Cultural Revolution was launched in 1980 as a program to realize revolutionary ideals, end cultural and economic dependency on the West, and restore the nation's dignity, based on Islam. The Supreme Council of the Cultural Revolution was established in 1984 by Ayatollah Khomeini to become the decision-making body in science, culture, and education.

The council remains active in "eliminating the undesirable atmosphere in the society that was devoid of revered human values" and "promoting independent Iranian and Islamic culture in the light of Islamic precepts."[27]

Educating youth with a strong commitment to an officially recognized Islam that regards the *vilāyat-i faqīh* as an ideal form of government until the resurrection of the hidden imam of the Twelver Shi'ism, is the fundamental mission of Iran's Islamic regime. This mission is upheld from primary to tertiary education, and even officially recognized religious minorities must be loyal to the *vilāyat-i faqīh*. The Iranian regime reaffirmed this mission when facing widespread political protest known as the "Green Movement" after the 2009 Iranian presidential election. The protests were suppressed, and thousands of participants, including university students, imprisoned.

After the Green Movement was quelled, the Supreme Council declared that the content of social sciences and humanities taught in schools and universities was un-Islamic and should be revised. However, clerical leaders were not entirely at odds with the Western model of higher education. They acknowledged the advantages of bureaucratic management, a standardized curriculum, and the grading system of degree-issuing universities. They were eager to introduce these initiatives even for the training of religious experts, formerly the responsibility of individual 'ulama.

Ironically, the regime's strong commitment to popularizing degree-issuing university education went too far, aggravating the social illness of a disproportionate emphasis on academic achievements. Apart from promoting Islamization, Iranian universities value science and technology on the ground that it is value neutral and serves the interests of Muslims around the world. Many ideologues of the Islamic Revolution, including Ayatollah Khomeini, claim the advancement of science and technology ensures Muslim independence from Western colonial powers. These examples demonstrate how Iran has been selective in adapting modern forms of higher education, though there are considerable differences regarding to what extent it can or should be introduced.

Saudi Arabia shows similar trends, though it seeks a different way of balancing the two aims. Article 13 of the Basic Law of Government, legislated in 1992, states that "The aim of education is to implant the Islamic Creed in the hearts of all youths, to help them acquire knowledge and skills, to qualify them to become useful members of their society, to love their homeland and take pride in its history."[28] This strong commitment to Islamic values also appears in Saudi Arabia's "Education Policy," and these guidelines must be followed to the highest levels. Furthermore, the Statute of the Council of Higher Education and Universities, Article 1, declares, "Universities are academic and cultural institutions that operate in accordance with Islamic Sharee'ah precepts."[29]

These statements are evidence of the religious establishment's strong, persistent influence in education. On the other hand, the kings of Saudi Arabia have strived to promote academic education. This goal is implicit in the official documents of the

Ministry of Higher Education, which states, "The higher educational system plays a pivotal role in meeting development requirements by securing a scientifically-qualified human force with high-profile technical expertise and good ethics within the framework of the Islamic law."[30] The Ministry of Higher Education has funded projects and initiatives to enhance the quality of university education. For instance, it announced a program to promote excellence in university education in 2009. The program aims to elevate the rank of at least five universities in the Times Higher Education World University Rankings and at least three universities in the Shanghai ranking by 2015.[31] Thus, Saudi Arabia seeks to elevate the world rank of its universities by promoting non-religious sciences.

Ensuring "Islamic" Values While Adopting the Western University System

It is a matter of legitimacy for both Iran and Saudi Arabia to ensure the Islamic character of higher education, but there is no determinate answer regarding how they will make higher education culturally relevant. To understand how these countries try to ensure the Islamic nature of education, we examine two factors.

Gender Norms

Muslims worldwide debate the correct interpretation of Islamic gender norms and their application in educational institutions. Even in Muslim-dominant societies, the interpretation and application of gender norms varies. Accordingly, Iran and Saudi Arabia have applied different rules in the treatment of female university students.

In Iran, gender segregation has been the rule in primary and secondary education since the 1979 revolution, but not in higher education. Although the possibility of gender segregation in higher education was discussed during the Cultural Revolution, it was not implemented due to a lack of resources and teaching staff. Some universities created single-gender spaces by dividing classes with a curtain, but this practice soon fell into disuse. Thus, most universities have maintained gender-mixed campuses. However, a strict dress code, especially for female students and faculty, is compulsory. Dress inspections at the university entrance gate by security officers are common practice, and women are required to wear at least a tight head cover and a loose-fitting long sleeve coat in a monotone color, normally black, gray, or dark brown.

Furthermore, gender-based restrictions were applied to some courses. For instance, departments such as geology and agricultural engineering were closed to women because these professions are regarded as unsuitable. Entry quotas for women were also introduced in medical, para-medical, and some engineering fields. However, the removal of major gender-based restrictions in the late 1980s helped boost the proportion of female students in government universities.[32] Female students outnumbered male students in all departments except engineering in 2005.

In 2009, the Minister of Science, Research and Technology, Kamran Daneshjoo, publicly questioned co-education at universities. In response, some universities introduced single-sex undergraduate classes, asking professors to teach the same subject separately to each gender. In 2012, the Ministry of Science, Research and Technology re-introduced gender-based restrictions, but it allowed each university to decide the disciplines to which the policy would apply. Consequently, women were barred from 77 academic fields, such as mining and forestry.[33]

Based on Article 155 of the Education Policy, Saudi Arabia is one of the few Muslim countries that enforces strict gender segregation at all levels of education except nurseries and kindergartens. Top universities as well as provincial institutions accept both male and female students, but female students must study in a separate branch of the university. Women typically have access to fewer departments and courses because certain fields run counter to women's innate nature. For instance, at King Saud University, female students are excluded from physical education, architecture and planning, teacher training, engineering, and agriculture. At King Abdulaziz University, women are excluded from engineering, geochemistry, marine science, metrology-environmental science, arid zone agricultural science, and teacher training. On the other hand, male students are excluded from domestic science. Thus, teaching subjects are differentiated based on gender.

Some Saudi universities are single gender. King Fahad University for Petroleum and Minerals in Dhahran is dedicated to the training of male experts in science, engineering, and management. Princess Nora bint Abdulrahman University in Riyadh, established in 1970, was originally the first all-women's college. In 2004, under the supervision of the Ministry of Higher Education, it became a university by amalgamating existing colleges in Riyadh. In 2008, its name was changed in honor of Princess Nourah bint Abdulrahman, the sister of the country's first king, King Abdulaziz. It moved to a large campus in 2011 and became the world's largest female university. It offers education in the fields of health, science, and humanities in 15 colleges.[34] In the private sector, Effat University is another women's university.

Female enrollment in higher education has grown rapidly since 1961-1962, when the Saudi government allowed women to study as irregular "part-time" students at the Colleges of Arts and Administrative Sciences of King Saud University.[35] The number of female students at Saudi universities increased steadily, and female students now outnumber male students. In 2010-2011, female students represented 61 percent of total undergraduate enrollment. However, female students proceed to postgraduate studies in much smaller numbers than their male counterparts do. As mentioned, the distribution of courses differs between male and female students. About 37 percent of Saudi university graduates in 2010-2011 specialized in humanities and Islamic studies, but this was 43 percent for female graduates. Graduates with an engineering major accounted for 5 percent of all graduates, but only 0.2 percent of female graduates.[36]

Although strict gender segregation remains a basic policy in all levels of education, King Abdullah challenged this policy by opening KAUST, a co-ed university outside the supervision of the Ministry of Education, in 2009. Co-education relies on the idea of "putting the subject of total gender segregation into more of a cultural issue than a religious one."[37] "The campus now hosts 840 students from 69 countries, including 246 from Saudi Arabia and 302 women."[38] However, the religious establishment has strongly criticized KAUST's gender policy,[39] and achieving consensus will take time.

Disciplines and Subjects

The arrangement of faculties and departments in Iranian and Saudi universities is similar to Western universities. Likewise, the universal values of higher education, such as the development of critical and analytical thinking are in principle well recognized in Iran and Saudi Arabia, and students are encouraged to acquire research skills to produce rigorous academic papers that contribute to university rankings. However, the religio-political establishments of both countries are fully aware that if critical thinking is applied to the area of social sciences and humanities, students might challenge the legitimacy of the state's religio-political authority. Here lies the dilemma of promoting the universal values of higher education, and preserving Islamic values.

Both Iran and Saudi Arabia face this dilemma. Iran's religio-political authority was confronted by the Green Movement after the 2009 presidential election. At first, the target of criticism was the election result, but it soon moved to the very legitimacy of the state. Confronted by student demonstrations that demanded freedom of speech and human rights, the Iranian regime concluded that the content of humanities and social sciences courses had misguided the students. The supreme leader of the state, Ayatollah Khamenei, stated, "Many of the humanities and liberal arts are based on philosophies whose foundations are materialism and disbelief in godly and Islamic teachings." The state news agency reported his warning to professors and students that "Science leads to the loss of belief in godly and Islamic knowledge."[40] He especially showed deep concern about philosophy and sociology.

The religio-political leaders' hostility toward Western humanities and social sciences dates back to the Cultural Revolution, when Khomeini criticized intellectuals who were serving the interest of the West. This hostility was again publicly expressed when the reformist political scientist Saeed Hajjarian was coerced to testify that he was misled by Western social scientists such as Max Weber and Jürgen Habermas.[41] Based on these experiences, three decades after the Cultural Revolution, Iran has again launched the Islamization of social science and humanities curricula to eliminate an atheistic worldview.

Similar to Iran, Saudi Arabia facilitates the study of sciences and technology to elevate its universities' international rankings. Massive investment in the creation of universities dedicated only to the sciences and engineering, such as the King Fahd University of Petroleum & Minerals, is evidence of this trend. In addition to that, the Saudi Ministries of Education and Higher Education have deliberately excluded subjects that might question the basic values and principles of Islam. For instance, teachings on religions other than Islam, non-Islamic civilizations, evolution, and anthropology are carefully avoided. Books on music, philosophy, other religions, and other civilizations are difficult to find in bookstores, since the Ministry of Information prohibits their publication.[42]

Although social sciences are widely taught in Saudi universities, including three Islamic universities, according to the College of Social Sciences at Umm Al-Qura University, they must remain "within the Islamic scope of thoughts and beliefs."[43] Moreover, social sciences must defend the values of Islam. The Department of Media at the College of Social Sciences at Umm Al-Qura University states, "the discussion of academic issues in this department is noted for including criticism, analysis, and defending the verified Islamic creed."[44] According to Prokop, "in departments such as art, history and administration, approximately 40-45 percent of teaching hours are dedicated to religious teachings and Arabic classes." Even in the King Fahad University of Petroleum and Minerals, Islamic and Arabic studies make up "approximately 10-15 percent of the curriculum."[45]

Furthermore, Saudi universities have sought the Islamization of social sciences. As part of this effort, King Abd al-Aziz University introduced the Department of Islamic Economics, and Imam University established the Departments of Islamic Psychology and Islamic Sociology.[46]

Enhancing International Appeal

Iranian universities are predominantly domestic-oriented, with mostly Iranian staff, though some attract students from neighboring countries. Until recently, students from Afghanistan were the largest group of foreign students. However, due to the recent political instability in Iraq and Syria, and the Memorandum of Understanding that Iran concluded with Iraq, students from Iraq and Syria are now the largest groups of foreign students.[47] Among the government universities, the University of Tehran, the Amir Kabir University of Technology, and the Ferdowsi University of Mashhad have the most foreign students. The University of Tehran accepts around 1,000 foreign students from 44 countries. Seven percent of these study in a undergraduate program, 74 percent in Master's, and 19 percent are PhD students.[48] The Ferdowsi University of Mashhad accepts foreign graduate students, and these are mainly from Central Asia and neighboring countries.

Alongside these efforts to attract foreign students to government universities where courses are taught in Persian, Iran created an international college town on Kish Island, a resort island in the Persian Gulf, which is a designated free-trade zone. Kish University was the island's first university. It started as a small school offering an Associate degree in Accountancy and a Bachelor's degree in Business Administration in 1996. From 2003 to 2007, it offered an undergraduate co-operative program in Electrical and Computer Systems Engineering together with Monash University in Melbourne, Australia.[49] Students who completed the first four semesters of the Monash Bachelor of Engineering program at Kish University could proceed to higher levels of study in Melbourne. In 2005, the Sharif University of Technology, Iran's premier university in technology, opened an international campus on Kish Island and agreed to take over the management of the university by 2009. The international campus of Sharif University of Technology provides Bachelor to PhD courses in engineering and sciences, and a Master's course in management. All courses are offered in English. To facilitate the internationalization of the MBA program, the international campus of Sharif University of Technology launched an online MBA course in partnership with the Multimedia University, a private university in Malaysia.

The University of Tehran also opened an international campus in Kish in 2007, to facilitate the enrollment of foreign students. It provides education from Bachelor to PhD levels in English and offers courses in engineering, science and biotechnology, economics, fine arts, law, and management, among others.[50]

The creation of international campuses in Kish is strategic. As Kish Island is a free-trade zone, its laws are more relaxed than the mainland, so it can attract foreign investment and tourists. In Iran, all women have to observe a dress code, but this is less strict in Kish. However, international campuses in Kish have failed to attract a meaningful number of foreign students or talented Iranian students. This is attributed to Iran's unwillingness to compromise its ideological mission and cultural exclusionism. Deep-rooted suspicion against Western cultural influence discourages the participation of foreign scholars in teaching and the development of partnerships with foreign universities.

Despite the inclination toward cultural exclusionism, Saudi universities have heavily depended on foreign academic staff, although the numbers are decreasing. According to statistics from 1998, there were 8925 staff members at seven government universities and about two-thirds were Saudi nationals (63.3 percent); the others were Arab nationals (27.5 percent), Asian and Sub-Saharan African nationals (5.6 percent), and Western nationals (2.7 percent). Among non-Saudi faculty members, Egyptians were the largest group. The high percentage of foreign academics compensates for the lack of qualified nationals, rather than facilitate internationalization. For this reason, foreign faculty members are not entitled to claim tenure or citizenship, and are under strict surveillance.[51] According to the Ministry of Civil Service, about 15,000 non-nationals teach at various levels in Saudi higher education. However, to facilitate their replacement with Saudi nationals, a process called "Saudaization," "the Ministry of Higher Education recently issued instructions to universities not to renew the contracts of expatriate professors who have passed the age limit."[52]

Although Saudaization is a general policy, leading universities are eager to attract top academics by introducing incentives such as salaries and grants. KAUST attempted to create "partnerships with foreign universities through which they will jointly hire professors who will split their time between the partners."[53]

KAUST has challenged the dominant idea of being "Islamic." Due to the growing influence of liberal elites who "have pushed for privatization and international partnerships that diminish the control of the ulema in the sphere of education"[54] and the initiatives of King Abdullah, KAUST has become the champion of internationalization. It was designed by American consultants and built by the Saudi national oil company, Saudi Aramco, to operate outside the supervision of the Ministry of Education. It only provides postgraduate courses in science and engineering and "The curriculum is entirely secular, with no required courses in religion or Arabic."[55] Many world-class scientists who teach there were invited from abroad, and students from more than 60 countries study tuition-free. The campus is isolated from the rest of society by a wall to create a "free-zone" where women can study and engage in research with men without wearing the *'abaya* (head and body covering). They enjoy sports and drive cars within the campus. When Sheikh Saad Al-Shethri, a member of the Council of Islamic Scholars, criticized KAUST's policy of co-education, King Abdullah removed him from the council.[56]

However, despite the fact that cooperation with foreign universities and scholars, and that English as the language of instruction are recognized as indispensable to developing world-class universities, deep-rooted criticism and suspicion of Western influence stands in the way of reform. In sum, despite their desire to elevate the prestige of their universities internationally, Iran and Saudi Arabia are not ready to risk their religious legitimacy based on Islamic norms and values.

The Islamic University: Teaching Islamic Sciences Within the Framework of the University

The training of 'ulama is of vital importance for both Iran and Saudi Arabia. Before the introduction of modern education, Islamic knowledge was transmitted by a mentor to a disciple, without state interference. Lack of institutional formality and dependence on the mentor-disciple network were characteristics of traditional Islamic learning.

However, the introduction of modern education has changed the style and nature of Islamic education. In Saudi Arabia, the traditional study circles in the mosques and small institutions of Riyadh, Buraydah, Unayzah, and Hail where replaced by colleges and universities.[57] Currently, three Islamic universities engage in the production of 'ulama, including religious teachers, preachers, and scholars entitled to issue legal opinions on matters not explicitly addressed in the Quran (*mujtahids*). Among them, the Islamic University of Medina (IUM) was the first Islamic university, opened in 1961. Though it recently added non-Islamic faculties, the university at its core comprises the Faculties of Shari'a, the Holy Quran and Islamic Studies, Noble Hadith and Islamic Studies, and the Arabic Language.[58] The Umm al-Qura University in Mecca was established in 1981. It originated from the College of Shari'a in Mecca, Saudi Arabia's first higher education institution, which opened in 1949.[59] The College of Shari'a and Islamic Studies, the College of Da'wa and Usul al-Din, and the Higher Institute of Promotion of Virtues and Prevention of Vices at Umm Al-Qura University offer advanced Islamic education. Graduates are expected to serve as religious experts in various organizations. Umm Al-Qura University also has non-Islamic colleges of engineering, applied sciences, medical sciences, and education.

The origin of the Imam Muhammad ibn Saud Islamic University dates back to 1949, when King Abdul Aziz opened the Riyadh Sharia Institute. It became the foundation for Sharia Institutes in various parts of the country. The Colleges of Sharia and the Arabic Language were opened in Riyadh in 1951 and 1952, respectively, and they were integrated into a university when the Imam Muhammad ibn Saud Islamic University was officially established in 1974. Currently, the university has 61 affiliated institutions providing Islamic studies across the country. The university has non-Islamic colleges, but maintains its strong Islamic identity. Of the three Islamic universities, Imam Muhammad ibn Saud Islamic University has been "especially important in the training of the Saudi judges."[60]

The development of religious studies within the university framework has allowed new groups to conduct religious debates. Historically, Wahhabi study circles trained 'ulama to be "problem-solvers" and jurists. However, university religious education produces 'ulama and religious intellectuals who have sufficient knowledge of Islamic traditions to express opinions and interpretations.[61]

As opposed to Saudi Arabia, where the traditional circle of Islamic learning was replaced by university religious education, Iran has maintained a dual education system in which a considerable number of religious seminaries still operate outside the control of the Ministry of Science, Research and Technology. However, to perpetuate the _vilāyat-i faqīh_, it is essential to educate 'ulama and bureaucrats to be skilled in both religion and politics. Therefore, the state's clerical leaders designed an institution to teach seminary and university subjects. Imam Sadiq University was opened in Tehran in 1983 by Ayatollah Mahdavi Kani, who was a disciple of Ayatollah Khomeini and one of the most powerful clerical figures of the Islamic Republic. At Imam Sadiq University, "students are to take courses in Islamic studies next to their major in humanities."[62] The male section offers Master's and PhD courses in theology, political science, law, management, economics, and culture and communication. Imam Sadiq University has produced many bureaucrats who serve in high government positions.

The Imam Khomeini Education and Research Institute, founded in 1991 by Ayatollah Mesbah-Yazdi, has also produced many bureaucrats who dominate high positions in the regime. Though it teaches mainly non-religious subjects such as economics, psychology, Western philosophy, and Western law from Bachelor to PhD level, students must have completed a basic level of seminary education and continue seminary studies after admission. Students from this institution have attended graduate schools in Western countries.[63]

Baqir al-'Ulum University in Qom was founded by the Islamic Propagation Office of the Qom Seminaries in 1992, and recognized as a university in 2003. It offers Bachelor's to PhD courses in six departments, including political science, Islamic history, and Islamic philosophy and theology. The entry requirements include a basic level of seminary education. The significance of these institutions is their hybrid nature they provide 'ulama with academic education and with seminary training.

The Global Strategy of Islamic Universities

Historically, centers of Islamic learning were meeting places for scholars, which attracted students from different regions. However, once the modern state monopolized education, these centers were divided by political boundaries, and Islamic education was aligned with state interests.

Until the early 20th century, the most prestigious center of learning for Twelver Shi'i was in Najaf, Iraq. At the turn of the century, there were about 20 seminaries, which attracted students and scholars across political boundaries. However, the creation of the Iraqi state and restoration of the Faydiyya seminary in Qom marked the decline of Najaf and the rise of Qom as a new center of Shi'i learning. As opposed to Najaf, Qom had mostly Iranian students attending its various seminaries, and the number of foreign students was limited until the 1979 revolution.

The 1979 revolution decisively influenced Shi'i scholarship. Qom witnessed an influx of students, especially from neighboring Afghanistan and Pakistan. Most were Shi'ite youths fascinated by the victory of Iran's revolution, who came to learn from Iran's experience. Confronted by this phenomenon, the state's clerical leaders established the Council for Supervising Non-Iranian Seminary Students to develop a training program for potential non-Iranian preachers. The council was reorganized as the International Centre for Islamic Studies (ICIS) in 1986, an umbrella organization that supervises seminaries and institutions for non-Iranian students. Its responsibility is to develop seminaries and curricula including Persian language training for non-Iranian students and facilitate the systematic recruitment of foreign students. As the Supreme Leader of the Islamic Republic, Ayatollah Khamenei was interested in establishing his religious authority outside Iran, and, for this purpose, he gained direct control of ICIS to centralize the management of non-Iranian student affairs.

Khamenei also sought to modernize seminaries under the supervision of ICIS, which adopted the modern university system of credits and semesters and provided five levels of education equivalent to university degrees. Although seminaries operating under ICIS supervision retain their basic religious identity, their certificates are confirmed by the Ministry of Science, Research and Technology. The ICIS constitution stresses its mission is to train non-Iranian preachers, trainers, teachers, researchers, interpreters, *mujtahids*, and administrators who are refined, aware of the important issues of the day, able to run scientific and cultural magazines, and learned in Islamic sciences, humanities, and Ahul al-Bait studies. This statement implies the scope of education extends beyond religion to the realm of public affairs.[64]

The management of foreign seminary students in Qom was strengthened when Al-Mustafa International University (MIU) was established in 2008. MIU took over the organization and activities of ICIS as well as the Organization for Overseas Seminaries and Schools, founded in 1991/92 to supervise schools and seminaries outside Iran for non-Iranian students. According to MIU's 2009 prospectus, it had about 18,000 non-Iranian students, 10,000 of whom were studying in Iran, while the remaining 8,000 were in affiliated institutions across the world.[65] The name change from "center" to "university" signifies the determination to create a new model of the Islamic university in which humanities subjects are taught from an Islamic perspective, together with Islamic science. The initiative also aims to improve graduates' social status and work opportunities by providing them with a "university" degree.

Although MIU is a private university, drawing its budget mainly from the profits from factories that it owns, as well as investments, religious endowments, and government funding, its education policy reflects the interest of *vilāyat-i faqīh*. MIU calls itself a "mission-oriented" university that trains preachers in "disseminating Islamic viewpoints and divine teaching and expanding Islamic culture as well as moral and spiritual traits". The prioritization of training for Islamic propagation distinguishes MIU from the traditional Shiʿi seminaries, whose ultimate goal is to train *mujtahid* who are entitled to issue legal opinions—although advancement to the status of *mujtahid* is open to MIU students. MIU's progress reveals the global strategy of Iran's Islamic education is to expand Iran's scope of denominational influence through Islamic teaching within the framework of modern higher education.[66]

The Islamic University of Medina (IUM) is another mission-oriented university whose aim is to disseminate globally the Saudi version of Islam, known as "Wahhabism,"[67] through non-Saudi students. According to IUM's official website, IUM is "a global Islamic Institution" aiming to educate "Muslim students from various parts of the world, and make them scholars specialized in Islamic and Arabic Sciences." The mission of graduates is to "call, advocate and invite people to Islam, to solve the problems of Muslim bothering on their religious and worldly affairs in light of the guidance of Quran and Sunnah and the work of our righteous predecessors."[68]

IUM has distributed generous scholarships to students globally.[69] In its early period, most students originated from Muslim-majority countries, especially the Arabic-speaking regions. However, in 2011, there were 13,000 students from 160 countries.[70] Over 3,000 applicants were accepted for the 2014 academic year; and the highest percentage of applicants were from sub-Saharan African countries (39 percent), followed by Southeast Asia (12 percent), the Middle East and South Asia (9 percent each).[71] Thus, the trend is for non-Arabic speaking students to comprise the majority of foreign students.

When it was established, the IUM was expected to counterbalance the growing influence of "Nasserist and other brands of radical republicanism."[72] In addition, the founding of IUM was a part of the Saudi royals' effort to gain support from clerical elites by allowing them tight control of Islamic education. Therefore, IUM's presidency was in the hands of the Saudi's Grand Mufti until 1975.

The dramatic rise in oil prices in the wake of the third Arab-Israel war (1973) boosted IUM's budget "nearly fivefold in the space of just two years,"[73] and it added more colleges. IUM's budget grew again in 1979 when oil prices increased following the 1979 Iranian revolution. This time, IUM assumed a mission to counter the influence of the anti-monarchical Shi'i revolution. Thus, IUM's development is influenced by the Saudi political situation within and outside the state. IUM depended heavily on non-Saudi teaching staff in its early period, including members of Islamic organizations, such as the Muslim Brotherhood. The majority originated from Egypt, Sudan, and other Middle Eastern countries. However, following the Saudi effort to minimize the influence of political Islam, the percentage of non-Saudi teaching staff decreased by the early 1990s. IUM taught Islamic sciences exclusively until, for example, the establishment of new non-Islamic colleges of computer sciences and engineering, approved by the Higher Education Council.[74]

MIU and IUM's policies of providing Islamic education to large numbers of foreign students is unique in Iran and Saudi Arabia, and to date there is no equivalent in other Gulf countries. MIU and IUM are controlled by religious establishments, which are closely allied with the state.[75] Their primary responsibility is to strengthen the religious foundation of the state through the missionary activities of their graduates.

Conclusion

As opposed to Western countries, where modern higher education developed in tandem with the emancipation of education from religious domination, higher education in Iran and Saudi Arabia is influenced by non-secular states whose legitimacy rests on the enforcement of Islamic law. As a result, higher education has been instrumental in imposing religious values on knowledge rather than liberating it from religiosity.

While securing the religious credentials of universities, Iran and Saudi Arabia have attempted to create universities that attract foreign students by offering courses in English or relaxing gender segregation. However, currently, these innovations are restricted to isolated universities. This represents a clear manifestation of the priority for religion concerns by these countries.

In the case of Islamic universities, we observed a different trajectory. In the process of popularizing a Western framework of higher education, Iran and Saudi Arabia extended state control over the 'ulama-led private circles of Islamic education or Islamic seminaries and re-arranged their curricula in conformity with state interests. The transformation of traditional study circles or seminaries into an Islamic university enhanced their appeal to younger generations, and helped Qom and Medina become world centers of denominational education. Significantly, a majority Shia anti-Monarchical Iran is a political rival of the Saudi monarch, the self-proclaimed leader of the Sunni world. Against this backdrop of political rivalry between the two nations, MIU and IUM's mission is to expand their global influence through their graduates.

Notes

1 "UAEU has invested heavily in US consulting teams, obtaining advice from them on curricular revisions and other changes that would qualify major fields of study for accreditation by US professional associations." http://tinyurl.com/jbwuwh6, (accessed 29 June 2016). In case of Qatar, RAND Cooperation, played an important role for the reform of Qatar University. Matthew Gray, _Qatar Politics and the Challenges of Development_, (Boulder, CO: Lynne Rienner Publisher, 2013), 138.

2 Arwa Lois Dou Ibnouf and Jane Knight, "The Evolution of Qatar as an Education Hub: Moving to a Knowledge-Based Economy" in _International Education Hubs: Student, Talent, Knowledge-Innovation Models_, ed. Jane Knight (Dordrecht: Springer, 2013), 51-52.

3 Warren Halsey Fox and Sabha al Shamisi, "United Arab Emirates' Education Hub: A Decade of Development", in Knight, 67-71.

4 Romani distinguishes market driven cases in UAE and Qatar from state driven case in Saudi Arabia. Vincent Romani, "The Politics of Higher Education in the Middle East: Problems and Prospects," _Middle East Brief_ no.36 (2009), 4.

5 As for the language of instruction, Qatar's sole National University changed the language of instruction from English to Arabic, for law, media studies, business administration, and international affairs, although the language of instruction for the sciences and technology remained English. Maha Ellili-Cherif and Haitham Alkhateeb, "College Students' Attitude toward the Medium of Instruction: Arabic versus English Dilemma", _Universal Journal of Educational Research_ 3, no.3 (2015), 207.

6 Keiko Sakurai, "Making Qom a centre of Shi'i scholarship: al-Mustafa International University," in Masooda Bano and Keiko Sakurai, _Shaping Global Islamic Discourses: The Role of al-Azhar, al-Medina and al-Mustafa_, (Edinburgh: Edinburgh University Press, 2015), 58-59.

7 David Menashri, _Education and the Making of Modern Iran_ (Ithaca, NY: Cornell University Press, _1992_), 213.

8 Imam Khomeini, _Islam and Revolution: Writings and Declarations_, trans. Hamid Algar (Berkeley.CA: Mizan Press, 1985), 295–99.

9 Keiko Sakurai, "Iran: Three dimensional conflicts," in _Education in West Central Asia_, ed. Mah-E-Rukh Ahmed (London: Bloomsbury Academic, 2013), 60-61.

10 Official website of Payam-e Noor University, http://tinyurl.com/hnrwtkv (accessed 29 June 2016).

11 Official website of Payam-e Noor University, http://tinyurl.com/h5o9evf (accessed 29 June 2016).

12 Iranian Students' News Agency, 18 November 2013, http://tinyurl.com/guwrmwk (accessed 10 May 2015).

13 Statistical Centre of Iran, _Iran Statistical Yearbook 2012-2013_ (Iran: Statistical Centre of Iran 2013), 656.

14 UNESCO online statistics, http://data.vis.unesco.org/ (accessed 29 June 2016).

15 World Education News & Reviews, 3 November 2014, http://tinyurl.com/jg9occf (accessed 12 September 2016).

16 This university was called Riyadh University from 1967 to 1981.

17 The portal of the Ministry of Education (accessed 5 May 2015; no longer available).

18 Andrys Onsman, "It is better to light a candle than to ban the darkness: government led academic development in Saudi Arabian universities," _Higher Education_ 62, no.4 (2011), 522-23.

19 It was first established as a private institution in 1967 and changed to a government university in 1971. Mahmoud Abdullah Saleh, "Development of Higher Education in Saudi Arabia," _Higher Education_ 15, nos 1-2 (1986), 20.

20 The Ministry of Education established in 1953 had supervised higher education until the establishment of the Ministry of Higher Education in 1975. However, the Ministry of Education and the Ministry of Higher Education have merged by the King Salman's royal orders issued in February 2015. Al Arabia News, 29 January 2015, http://tinyurl.com/zoanco4 (accessed 29 June 2016).

21 Onsman, 521.

22 Larry Smith and Abdulrahman Abouammoh, "Higher Education in Saudi Arabia: Reforms, Challenges and Priorities," in _Higher Education in Saudi Arabia: Achievements, Challenges and Opportunities_, ed. Larry Smith and Abdulrahman Abouammoh (Dordrecht: Springer, 2013), 3.

23 Einas S. Al-Eisa, and Larry Smith, "Governance in Saudi Higher Education", Smith and Abouammoh, 30.

24 *Ibid.*, 31.

25 UNESCO online statistics, http://data.uis.unesco.org/ (accessed 29 June 2016).

26 *Ibid.*

27 Official Webpage of the Supreme Council of Cultural revolution, http://en.farhangoelm.ir/SCCR/ Introduction (accessed 29 June 2016).

28 Online translation of Saudi Arabia's Basic Law of Governance: http://tinyurl.com/zxm8cuh (accessed 12 September 2016).

29 Kingdom of Saudi Arabia, Council of Higher Education, Secretariat General, *The Statute of the Council of Higher Education and Universities* (1994). http://tinyurl.com/gwzrrha (accessed 29 June 2016).

30 Ministry of Higher Education, Deputyship for Planning & Information, General Department for Planning & Statistic, *Ministry of Higher Education's Plan to Achieve Excellence in Science and Technology*, 2010, http://tinyurl.com/gvr2rtf (accessed 29 June 2016).

31 Abdulhalem Mazi and Philip G. Altbach, "Dreams and Realities: The World-Class Idea and Saudi Arabian Higher Education," Smith and Abouammoh, 24.

32 Keiko Sakurai, "University Entrance Examination and the Making of an Islamic Society in Iran: A Study of the Post-Revolutionary Iranian Approach to 'Konkur'," *Iranian Studies* 37, no.3 (2004), 398-99.

33 Tabnak, 9 August 2012, http://www.tabnak.ir/fa/news/264141/ (accessed 29 June 2016).

34 Official webpage of The Princess Nora bint Abdulrahman University, http://tinyurl.com/zpkuffo (accessed 29 June 2016).

35 Fatima B. Jamjoon and Philippa Kelly, "Higher Education for Women in the Kingdom of Saudi Arabia," Smith and Abouammoh, 120.

36 Arab News, 6 April 2014, http://www.arabnews.com/news/551356 (accessed 29 June 2016).

37 Arab News, 4 February 2013, http://tinyurl.com/zm3lhq8 (accessed 12 September 2016).

38 *Nature* 518, issue 7537 (2015), http://tinyurl.com/hm2es3t (accessed 29 June 2016).

39 *Saudi Gazette*, 29 May 2015 (accessed via Internet 21 May 2015; no longer available).

40 *New York Times*, 1 September 2009, http://tinyurl.com/hrjjzb4 (accessed 29 June 2016).

41 *The Chronicle of Higher Education*, 1 November 2009, http://tinyurl.com/jdjj346 (accessed 29 June 2016).

42 Thomas W. Lippman, *Saudi Arabia on the Edge: The Uncertain Future of an American Ally* (Washington D.C.: Potomac Books, 2012), 131. Kindle edition.

43 The official website of Umm Al-Qura University, accessed via https://uqu.edu.sa on 20 May 2015; no longer available.

44 The official website of Umm Al-Qura University, https://uqu.edu.sa/social-sciences-en/en/1250 (accessed 29 June 2016).

45 Michaela Prokop, "Saudi Arabia: The Politics of Education," *International Affairs* 79, no.1 (2003), 79.

46 Stéphane Lacroix, *Awakening Islam: The Politics of Religious Dissent in Contemporary Saudi Arabia*, trans. George Holoch (Cambridge, MA: Harvard University Press, 2011), 47.

47 Mehr news, 24 Aban 1393, http://www.mehrnews.com/news/2418984/8 (accessed 12 September 2016).

48 Official website of the University of Tehran, http://tinyurl.com/jywnv72, (accessed 29 June 2016).

49 Official website of the Department of Electrical and Computer Systems Engineering (ECSE), Monash University, http://tinyurl.com/jz73asu (accessed 29 June 2016).

50 The official website of the University of Tehran Kish International Campus http://kish.ot.ac.ir (accessed 12 September 2016).

51 André Elias Mazawi, "The Academic Profession in a Rentier State: The Professoriate in Saudi Arabia" *Minerva* 43, no. 3 (2005), 229-30, 237.

52 Arab News, 4 January 2014. www.arabnews.com/news/503261 (accessed 29 June 2016).

53 Zvika Krieger, "Saudi Arabia Puts Its Billions Behind Western-Style Higher Education," *Chronicle of Higher Education* 2007, September 14, 6.

54 Leigh Nolan, "Liberalizing Monarchies? How Gulf Monarchies Manage Education Reform," *Brookings Doha Center Analysis Paper* 4 (2012), 15.

55 *Ibid.*, 18.

56 Thomas W. Lippman, *Saudi Arabia on the Edge: The Uncertain Future of an American Ally* (Washington D.C. Potomac Books 2012), 142-44. Kindle edition.

57 Madawi Al-Rasheed, *Contesting the Saudi State: Islamic Voices from a New Generation* (Cambridge, MA: Cambridge University Press, 2006), 63.

58 Official web page of the Islamic University of Medina, http://iu.edu.sa/ (accessed 12 September 2016).

59 Official Webpage of Umm Al-Qura University, https://uqu.edu.sa (accessed 29 June 2016).

60 Robert W. Hefner and Muhammad Qasim Zaman (eds.), *Schooling Islam: The Culture and Politics of Modern Muslim Education* (Princeton, NJ: Princeton University Press, 2007), 252.

61 Madawi Al-Rasheed Madawi, *Contesting the Saudi State-Islamic Voices from a New Generation,* (Cambridge: Cambridge University Press, 2007), 63.

62 Official web page of Imam Sadiq University. http://www.isu.ac.ir/ (accessed 12 September 2016).

63 Official website of Imam Khomeini Education and Research Institute, http://edu.iki.ac.ir/ (accessed 29 June 2016).

64 Sakurai 2015, 48.

65 International and Public Relations Office, al-Mustafa International University, *An Introduction to al-Mustafa International University* (Qom: MIU, 2009).

66 For further details of MIU, please see Sakurai 2015, 41-72.

67 Saudi Arabia prefers to call it "Salafism." See Hefner and Zaman, 253.

68 Official website of the Islamic University of Madina: http://iu.edu.sa/ (12 September 2016).

69 Mike Farquhar, "The Politics of Religious Mission and the Making of a Modern Salafi Pedagogy," in Bano and Sakurai, 25.

70 *Saudi Gazette,* 7 February 2011, http://tinyurl.com/jazxp47 (accessed 29 June 2016; no longer available).

71 http://tinyurl.com/j3enzx6 (accessed 29 June 2016; no longer available).

72 Farquhar, 22.

73 Farquhar, 23.

74 *Saudi Gazette,* 27 August 2010, http://tinyurl.com/hb39e2r (accessed 29 June 2016).

75 Hefner and Zaman, 263.

3

Higher Education and the Changing Aspirations of Women in Saudi Arabia

Namie Tsujigami

This study explores Saudi Arabia's ongoing projects on higher education and job creation for women, and is based on fieldwork conducted in December 2013 at a University that I call "Anonymous." This chapter highlights the changing priorities of Saudi women in their academic and career goals in the last decade. Government expenditure on education in the fiscal year 2014 has risen to 25 percent, and this trend appears likely to continue.

The establishment of Anonymous incorporated six women's colleges in 2011. It has been a Saudi flagship project, providing further evidence of Saudi Arabia's rapidly growing commitment to women's higher education. The massive 800-hectare campus requires a metro for transport within the campus.

By expanding educational opportunities, the Kingdom is responding to the acute need for educational institutions at all levels due to rapid population growth. Saudi Arabia's population mushroomed from 5.7 million in 1981 to more than 30 million in 2014.[1] With the economic expansion based on oil price increases in the 2000s, the Saudi government expanded its budgetary allocation on education. The number of universities in the Kingdom, which remained at a one-digit level in the 1990s, grew to the current sixty universities plus many colleges. According to the annual report of the Saudi Arabian Monetary Agency (SAMA), Saudi Arabia allocated SAR 216 billion (= US $580 billion) to education and human resource development, which comprised 25.1 percent of the total budgetary appropriations for 2015.[2] The total number of students registered in higher education was 1.5 million as of 2014.

What Natasha Ridge calls the "reverse gender divide" is the case in Saudi Arabia. Paradoxically, women are less likely to be employed than men despite their higher achievements in education. In the past, Saudi Arabia has lagged behind in terms of women's empowerment in general and women's education in particular. Until the 1990s influential clerics and officials were not willing to approve women's education and labor participation. Now that they have given as de facto green light to women's participation in the labor force, what are the implications for gendered power relations?

A Move Beyond Segmented Feminism?

Women in the Middle East have long been viewed as discriminated against and oppressed.[3] Scholars have searched for the reasons of the impediments of female labor force participation in the Middle East. R. Inglehart and P. Norris insist in their sensational book, *Rising Tide*, that "an Islamic religious heritage is one of the most powerful barriers to the rising tide of gender equality."[4] In challenging Inglehart and Norris, Michael Ross argues that oil wealth, not Islamic tradition, discourages women from participating in the labor force, thus leading to gender inequalities. Ross argues that the "resource curse" reduces not only economic opportunities for women, but also leads to women's diminished political influence and educational attainment.[5]

Ross's assumption that oil production leads to less education for girls is drastically changing due to the undergoing significant transformation as a result of modernization programs introduced in the GCC. John Willoughby refutes Ross's argument by illustrating the investment of oil-rich countries such as Qatar in female education. As s a result, the GCC labor market is increasingly witnessing "segmented feminization,"[6] whereby highly educated women compete successfully for professional jobs while others of lower educational attainment have more difficulty in replacing the male, expatriate workers.

The level of divide between highly educated women and less educated ones varies among the rentier states. For example, it is more prominent in Qatar than in Bahrain, for example, where oil resources are largely exhausted. Willoughby claims that the feminization of education and labor is taking place among the daughters of the elite families. Although I agree with Willoughby on the persistent divide based on class (or on tribe-based stratification), gender, and race in the Gulf, this chapter suggests that the current inclusive Saudi educational program, which provides both male and female students with educational opportunities with generous allowances and other entitlements, may contribute to closing such gaps among the female nationals.

Expanding Girls' Education and Higher Education in Saudi Arabia

Despite massive modernizing efforts in Saudi Arabia since its establishment in 1932, girls' public education was not formally established until 1960. The introduction of girls' public education was initially controversial. Alyamani documented that the education of women in the 1950s was believed to lead to immorality by corrupting their minds and turning their valued priorities away from their roles as good wives and mothers.[7] Girls' public schools were established during the reign of King Faisal - seven years after the founding of public schools for boys. King Faisal is known to have played a critical role in allaying conservatives' worries about female education as contrary to the teachings of Islam. Queen 'Iffat Al Thunayan, King Faisal's wife, also greatly contributed to advancing education. She established the Ta'if Model School for Boys and Girls in 1943, where boys and girls were educated separately in the same school, and she initiated the establishment of the Dar Al Hanan, the first private school for women in Saudi Arabia in 1955.[8] King Faisal placed girls' education under the supervision of a board of *'Ulama* as well as the Presidency for Girls' Education, to reassure people who held conservative attitudes. By doing so, the King was able to make them understand that their attitudes against girls' education were not rooted in Islam but in tradition. At the onset of the girls' education, the board of *'Ulama* are said to have claimed to limit girls' education to subjects that suited women's "nature"[9] in accordance with their gendered identity as good wives and mothers. However, girls' schools had almost the same curriculum as that of boys except for physical education and home economics.[10] The gendered gap was bridged in middle school and high school levels by 1994, and the female college and university students outnumbered their male counterparts by 2000.[11]

The Saudi education system and its curricula has been condemned for "breeding extremists" and the need for reforms were spotlighted particularly after September 11, 2001. For example, Cordesman contends that the heavy focus on religious studies resulted in under-valuing career-related skills and vocational training.[12] The Ministry of Education responded to the criticism by "re-training" as many as 2,000 extremist teachers.[13] Despite the government's efforts to improve their reputation, another incident occurred—a fire at a girl's school in Makkah in 2002. In the incident, members of the Hai'a, the Committee for the Promotion of Virtue and the Prevention of Vice, are reported to have prevented fire rescue because girls were not properly dressed, an action that claimed the lives of fifteen school girls. The government quickly closed down the General Presidency for Girls Education, the administration organization of girls' education that is closely associated with the Hai'a, after the incident. The fact that the administration of girls' education was transferred to the Ministry of Education demonstrates the Hai'a's diminished control over education.[14] Nonetheless, the quality of Saudi Arabia's education is often criticized for being unaltered, and critics claimed that the Saudi textbooks remain mostly untouched, despite fierce foreign criticism.[15]

Although women's education began slowly, it witnessed a rapid quantitative growth in recent years. Notably, women entering university quickly increased in the last few decades. Natasha Ridge offers two insightful reasons why women's higher education became paramount. First, Ridge acknowledges "the marriage of the human rights discourse on education for marginalized populations such as women and girls."[16] With the emergence of international organizations for the promotion of human rights, women's rights came to be recognized as important part of human rights. It was further supported and developed by global feminists whose slogan was "women's rights as human rights." With this international atmosphere, Ridge emphasizes that women's education came to have a symbolic value in any policy discussion.[17] The other reason for women's advancement in educational attainment is because teaching was deemed to be an "appropriate career" for women due to the sex-segregated nature of schools."[18] It makes sense that a woman needed to obtain bachelor's degree to become a teacher. In this way, Ridge explains that there emerged a reverse divide between two sexes, which is often unaddressed.

It should also be noted that the adverse gender divide in education is not reflected in employment opportunities. Ridge also recognizes this point, saying that "paradoxically, however, despite national males having less and lower-quality education, they are more likely to be employed than females."[19] Ridge says that there are job opportunities for the boys even if they are not university graduates, which makes the adverse gender divide even worse. Diane Zovighian looks at the reasons for this paradox. Her paper looks into the persistent wage gaps between genders and less diverse occupational positions among women in Kuwait and Bahrain. She is convinced that female workers tend to occupy technical and professional positions including teachers, whereas they have limited access to managerial positions as management remains a male domain. In her argument, women's access to the labor market is limited because their access to education is restricted in terms of study fields despite their high levels of educational attainment. Although a younger female cohort tends to enter new economic sectors, which timidly diversify the women's occupational positions, marriage and family life tend to eliminate women from the labor market.[20]

The Saudi government has tried to create more job opportunities for young women as well as young men through the program of *nitaqat*,[21] introduced after the Arab Spring, and women's economic participation has been expanded throughout the last decade. Nonetheless, women's economic participation still remains low by international standards. Ironically, the feminization campaign within the *nitaqat* program that attempts to boost job opportunity creation for women is often abused. Companies hire Saudis as ghost workers to increase and satisfy the level of Saudization simply for form's sake. Female ghost workers are reported to be more problematic than men, partly because women accept lower salaries than men.[22] Steffen Hertog clarified that women have lower wage expectations than men in all sectors. Indeed, women receive less salary than men; the average salary for male directors and managers are over 7000 SAR while female directors and managers are paid only 5000 SAR. The most significant gap is detected within the agricultural workers; men receive 6000 SAR in average vis-à-vis less than 2000 SAR for women.[23]

Trajectories of Female Labor

Modernization theory assumed a linear-development model in which women's educational attainment and labor force participation would expand in hand with modernization. In the case of Saudi Arabia, this model did not work. In Katakura's striking anthropological work in Wadi Fatima in the 1960s, Bedouin women's roles in everyday life and rituals were vividly portrayed.[24] The women in Wadi Fatima at that time were not educated, so that Katakura played a role of teaching female children how to write the Arabic alphabet and count their livestock. Although these women were not educated or employed, Katakura showed how women contributed to their pastoral society. A meticulous related study by Al-Baadi discloses how women in pre-oil era were engaged in economic, familial, and other activities whether they are farmers, Bedouin, or townswomen.[25] Women farmers took charge of milking animals, pressing dates, and grinding grain in addition to other domestic chores. For Bedouin women, milking goats and sheep, preparing dried milk and butter, and weaving tents and carpets not only satisfied household needs but also goods for sale in the market. In Al-Baadi's work, the only economically inactive groups are implied to be upper- and middle-class urban women. Yet, these unban women were in a minority, since in the pre-oil era most Saudis were farmers and pastoralists.[26]

Women's economic roles and the economic value of their labor witnessed a major transformation in recent decades. According to Alyamani, Saudi women constituted only 4.16 percent of total labor force in 1979-1980.[27] According to Rehemi, who conducted an attitudes survey of both Saudi men and women in the early 1980s, a large majority of the population (72 percent) had reservations about women working. They were concerned that having women work outside the home would lead to family disagreements.[28] His survey demonstrated that as many as 74 percent believed that Saudi women should work only when in need of money. Among those who answered the questionnaire, all Saudi women studying in the United States believed that teachers were the preferable kind of occupations that Saudi women should hold.[29]

*Fatwa*s also advised women to remain at home. Al-Atwaneh argues that the Saudi Dar al-Ifta, the official Saudi religious establishment for issuing fatwas, considers home as the natural place for a woman, where "she is expected to devote her efforts to raising and educating the next generation."[30] His study further explains that the Saudi Permanent Committee for Scientific Research and Legal Opinion allows women to work outside the home only when three interrelated preconditions are fulfilled: a woman's work is appropriate for her nature; there is no mixing with unrelated males; and she should wear modest clothing.[31]

However, the *'ulama*'s claims of education in accordance with women's nature got quickly out-of date. Currently, Saudi women constitute 10.2 percent of the total labor force,[32] a number that still remains low by international standards. The Central Department of Statistics and Information's Labor Force Survey shows that unemployment is more problematic among less educated people. According to the table "Distribution of Saudi Labor Force (15 years and above) by Education Status," 66.2 percent of the unemployed do not have a bachelor's degree. Although it should be noted that those who have a bachelor's degree constitute 31.9 percent of the unemployed, less educated people are even more likely to be unemployed.[33] The same report gives the data that unemployment rate is higher among women (32.8 percent) than men (5.9 percent).[34] The data shows that a big female population is out of work. More importantly, the data imply that a large number of women are in need of paid work.

Female Students' Aspirations for Education and Career

How should we understand women's aspiration for education and career, especially younger women? This study is mainly based on a one-week visit in December 2013 when I escorted students from the University of Tokyo who studied Arabic at Anonymous University. Staying at the Saudi students' accommodation enabled me to informally discuss career aspirations with twenty-one students living in the dormitory. I asked the same questions of all the students and grouped their responses into tables. The students, aged between eighteen and twenty-three, were all Saudi. My questions mainly explored the motivations of those who left their family to study in dormitories on campus. All of the residential students came from distant places such as cities of Eastern Province, Jidda, Hafr al-Batin, or those who lived on the outskirts of Riyadh but were unable to commute daily. All students except one were not married. What was striking about them is that only one student said that she was interested in getting married, whereas twelve students preferred either to study in a master or doctoral course, eleven were interested in studying abroad, ten wanted to start working, and two to start businesses—multiple answers were allowed. Although the sample is limited and it is not considered improper for a young, unmarried woman to express interest in getting married to an outsider woman such as myself, it can be concluded that the students preferred to continue their studies after graduation. Even the student interested in marriage also showed interest in continuing to study. It is no wonder that students are attracted to pursuing an academic path, considering the generous government allowances for education, including scholarships abroad.

The other question asked was the importance of marriage. Among the four alternatives of "very important," "relatively important," "not very important," and "not important at all," none answered "very important," eight answered "relatively important," ten said "not very important," and three chose "not important at all." Here, I reflect on the aspect of the reflexivity between the researcher (the author) and the researched (dormitory students). Because I am a female university professor, many Saudi students imputed a career-orientedness to me, and this imputation may have influenced their answers. It is clearly shown in the answers to the question of "When you get married, how many children do you want?" Thirteen answered between three to five, three answered one or two, while the remaining five answered none. Some respondents' answers were conflicting between marriages and having children. For example, a student answered that marriage is not very important, although she wanted five children. The apparent discrepancy is demonstrated in her opinion unless she wishes to be a single mother, which is unlikely. What is inferred from the discrepancy is that she may get married and have children in the future although she cannot think of marrying right now. However, we should not overlook the fact the four respondents who answered that marriage is not at all important didn't want any children. It is a surprising result considering that marriage has long been thought to be a very important rite of passage for everyone in Saudi Arabia.

A recent survey that claims 33.45 percent of the women aged over 30 remain unmarried was treated with alarm in Saudi Arabia.[35] It stirred a heated debate on the reasons for delaying marriage such as the high cost of wedding ceremonies, dowries, low tolerance, and social status of the potential spouse's family.[36] These are the critical factors that delay marriage, but the outcome of my de facto survey infers the changing attitudes of the young girls towards marriage and career also delay marriage.

To the question of "What do you want to be in the future?" four students answered "medical doctor" and two answered "researcher." Other students said entrepreneur, architect, social worker, accountant for a large enterprise, and one student hoped to establish a hospital for people in need. In marked contrast to the survey conducted by Rehemi in the early 1980s, all female students who answered my question hoped to either work or continue studying after graduation. No one answered "teacher" as their favorable profession, nor they seems to believe that women should work only when in need of money. Rather, they valued career more than marriage for the near future.

To understand students' economic background, I asked about the sources of financial support from their family, and if any, the amount. Seventeen students answered that they receive family financial support. Three received less than 500 SAR (1 USD is equivalent to 3.75 SAR) per month, seven received between 501 and 1,000 SAR, five received 1001 and 1500 SAR, and one respondent received between 2001 and 3000 SAR (another respondent avoided specifying the amount). Three students did not receive any financial support, and one revealed that her family receives financial support from the government because of economic hardship. Her mother is the second wife of her father, who cannot afford two big families, so that they receive 2,000 SAR per month from the government. Because students are receiving around 1000 SAR per month from the government and the university covers most of the living expenses, they can survive without family support. But here, I would argue that no one receives lavish amounts from their family for conspicuous consumption.

The other question was whether students had domestic helper(s) at their family home. Eleven out of twenty one answered "yes," and said that they have only one domestic helper. Again, we cannot judge their economic background by merely counting their family domestic helpers, but it demonstrates a strong contrast to my previous study on Saudi female employers of domestic helpers in Riyadh, where as many as 92 percent of the respondents had domestic helper(s), and it was not uncommon to have hired more than two.[37]

Frequency of their return visits to home helps understand their lifestyles and networks. Five students went home every weekend, six every month, and eight only during vacation periods. In general, it has been uncommon for Saudi girls to live away from home. But their answers show that a considerable number of them got opportunities to expand their social networks through university accommodations. Dormitory residence allowed them to build up personal connections with their classmates, dorm mates, and dormitory supervisors, most of whom were outside their kin or family networks.

The opportunity to live away from family and kin is a significant aspect of modern education that facilitates women's networks, considering that their networks had often been limited to their kin in the past. For example, Soraya Altorki discusses the role of *wafa'* in Saudi society. *Wafa'* denotes the ties that women forge in extending their social world beyond the limits of their household through social visits. Until the 1950s, these social visits were limited to married women, while single girls were exposed only to close friends and kinswomen in the western part of Saudi Arabia.[38] Women in the cities nowadays enjoy higher level of mobility compared to the situation in the 1980s, when Altorki's work was published, because of the spread of vehicles and expatriate chauffeurs hired by each household. Yet as Doumato explains, public education at any level helps alter the gender paradigm, as public education provides the students with opportunities to form "empowering personal connections outside the family network"[39] by attending schools, colleges and universities.

To the question on the pupose of work, fourteen students answered to realize their dreams, nine answered to serve the society, while seven aspired to financial independence. Another seven aspired to become leaders in the society. Students say that they want to realize their dreams and serve society. Slightly less emphasis was put on financial independence and becoming leaders in society. This is partly attributed their interpretation of the Qur'an, in which men are supposed to have a degree of responsibility over women.

Generous Financial Support and High Security on Campus

To understand female students' aspiration for education and career in the context of Saudi Arabia, it is important to grasp their living conditions. When compared to university students elsewhere, students in Anonymous University accommodations generally enjoy indirect and direct government economic support. They do not have to pay tuition fees like other university students in Saudi public universities. In addition, they receive a generous 1000 SAR monthly benefit. Every room in the university accommodation is fully furnished. Each student is provided with a daily free meal. With these benefits, some students can survive without family financial support. Therefore, it is essential for parents to send their daughters to the dormitory if they have financial difficulty.

On the other hand, students have limited mobility inside the campus. The Saudi government proudly advertises the university as the biggest women's university in the world. They need the internal metro not only because the campus is huge, but also to keep the campus under high security control. The campus is divided into several parts by cemented walls. All students must register their names before they take metro from the accommodation to the classroom, and they are checked again when they return from classes. Within this high level of security, dormitory students are not allowed to leave the campus freely. Their supervisor takes them out every other week, which is the only chance for them to buy necessities. High security may be seen as keeping young women's sexuality under control, which is definitely the unspoken part of the national project.

The outcome of these discussions with students suggests that going to public university is a low-risk investment for Saudi girls and their parents. Considering the higher unemployment rate of women in Saudi Arabia compared to their male counterparts, and severe unemployment problems among lesser-educated women, as well as free-of-charge lectures, accommodation, and generous benefits for public university students, it is simply more strategic and profitable for a woman to go to university. It shows a strong contrast with their male counterparts, who are likely to be employed without higher education. Sending a daughter to college is an investment without risk for parents. Not only does the Saudi government cover tuition costs, it also provides free accommodation on well-guarded college campuses that protects their reputations. It may also serve to expand the future prospects of marriage, considering the fact that more and more Saudi men prefer working women as wives.[40] Although men are still viewed as breadwinners and responsible for maintenance, intensive consumerist social settings as well as the rise in the nuclear family requires more cash inflow to households.

This need for cash inflow is particularly true for students from the countryside, where job opportunities are scarce and people's living standard is not as high as in the cities. For example, the girl whose family receives financial support from the government may have been simply unemployed if she did not go to university. In addition, she would have been without the benefit given to all public university students if she did not go to the university. This generous support gives a great incentive for the people from humble social strata, who might not have sent their daughters to the universities far away without the benefits, free accommodation, free tuition fees, and high campus security.

Values Produced to Meet the Needs of the Labor Market

Female students at the university are ambitious. All are interested in either working or studying after graduation. It seems that they do not care much if their career delays their marriage, which means that they prioritize career over marriage. Colleges also meet their needs. Anoynmous University consists of Colleges of Humanities,[41] Colleges of Science,[42] and Colleges of Medicine.[43] The composition of the colleges emphasizes practical studies such as colleges of science and medicine, and there is no college intensively teaching Islam. Anoynmous University is also highly conscious about the practicality of its degrees. Its website contains the following appeal:

> The education of women in the Kingdom of Saudi Arabia has received a great deal of attention and this has allowed Saudi women to make definite strides towards achieving their ambitions and unveiling their uniqueness in different fields.
>
> The Saudi woman has emerged, not only at the local level, but at the international level as well. We see examples of Saudi women in the fields of culture and specialized research, examples who are respected and acknowledged in international arenas and in the various fields of science, proving their success and their worthiness that rivals that of their peers in other advanced countries.[44]

Remarkably, there is no reference to Islam, religion or fostering good wives and mothers. Rather, the website emphasizes success, competitiveness and achievement in various fields, including science. It is a strong sign of a philosophical departure from Islam-oriented academism. Both the students and the university recognize the need of practical skills and trainings that will attract prospective employers.

Conclusion

The discussions with residential students at Anonymous University sufficed to pose broader questions and allow at least tentative findings. First, new universities like Anonymous University at least ideally aim at fostering successful and competitive students in scientific fields. They provide educational and material support to students, including those from modest social backgrounds. Studying at public universities for these girls is strategic and profitable. The fact that unemployment is more problematic among less educated people indicates the advantages of a university education, which are now widely recognized. These students are not only studying to avoid unemployment, but in order to take professional positions such as medical doctor, researcher, entrepreneur, architect, social worker, and accountant. These values show a clear contrast to the attitudes toward women's labor participation in the 1980s, in which there was the fear that women working outside home would create conflict within the family.

Second, the current mass higher education for Saudi nationals signals a gradual departure from what Willoughby called the "segmented feminization," in which highly educated women compete successfully for job professionals while women of lower educational attainment have more difficulty replacing male expatriate workers. Michael Ross argues that oil wealth, or the "resource curse," contributes to reduce women's educational attainment and labor participation. In contrast to this view, Saudi Arabia is spending the oil wealth to prepare for a post-rentier economy. With the shrinking oil wealth per capita, along with rapid population growth, Saudi Arabia took a step forward to educate both male and female young population and aims at leading them to enter into the labor market. Although there should be pros and cons for the inclusive higher education system that is fully embraced by the government, this is perhaps the only solution to educate women from the lower-middle or lower strata of the society for the time being, because they would otherwise be left less educated and subsequently unemployed.

Lastly, these female residential students step out of an earlier tradition of women remaining at home or going outside only when accompanied by a related male (*mahram*). Although their movements are controlled on campus, students enjoy an autonomy outside of their family and kin networks, building personal connections throughout their four years of study. Whether such change is pushed by the external pressures of human rights organizations or the more practical demand that women need higher education to participate in the labor market, people's attitudes toward women's education and labor participation is steadily changing.

The paradoxes of an adverse gender divide in higher education and male preference in the labor market may remain or become worse if three factors fail to change. First is the educational system. One of the failures of the higher education system in Saudi Arabia in the past was that it produced too many female schoolteachers. Teachers have long been the most preferred occupation for women among Saudis. But this value has created a redundancy in teachers when nationalization of school teaching has been completed. Saudi universities have tried to depart from religion-oriented education to match the needs of the labor market. This trend must be accelerated to meet the need of labor market sustainably.

The second factor is the labor market. Private companies are currently obliged to hire a certain percentage of Saudis according to the size of their enterprise. The feminization campaign within the program boosts job creation for women. However, many "fake nationalizations" occur, and women have lower wage expectations than men. The justifications offered for paying women less is that the men are the breadwinners and responsible for maintaining households. One concern here is the rapid transformation into intensive consumerism, including conspicuous consumption, and the emergence of households with nuclear families in the cities. These transformations require more cash inflows, thus necessitating dual-income households. Will women continue to play a mere supplementary role in the household, even though their educational attainment is higher than their partner?

The last factor is persistent gendered values and norms. One of the findings of the discussions with the dormitory students was that students indeed hope to realize their dreams and to serve the society. In the meantime, they put slightly less emphasis on financial independence and becoming leaders in society. This is partly due to their religious tradition and women's heavy responsibility towards marriage and family life. One may object that Saudi women are not burdened with domestic chores, because most of the Saudi households hire live-in domestic helpers. They have helpers who clean, cook, and do other domestic chores. But again it is mostly Saudi women who train and manage the domestic helpers, many of whom arrive in Saudi Arabia without proper training.

It is often argued that women in the Middle East prefer bargaining within patriarchal systems rather than liberating themselves from them. The skewed patriarchy may persist as long as both men and women wish it to continue, even though acknowledging it is a mere illusion for both genders. The rapid spread of higher education may further foreground these inequalities and lead to new public roles.

Notes

1   World Bank Indicator http://tinyurl.com/y2a2l6l (accessed June 29, 2016).
2   Saudi Arabia Monetary Agency, "Fifty First Annual Report," Saudi Arabia Monetary Agency, 120: http://tinyurl.com/h4y853d (accessed June 29, 2016).

3   For example, Lila Abu-Lughod, *Do Muslim Women Need Saving?* (Cambridge, Massachusetts & London: Harvard University Press, 2013), critically argues that women in the Middle East are portrayed as innocent victims in male-dominant society.

4   Ronald Inglehart and Pippa Norris, *Rising Tide: Gender Equality and Cultural Change around the World* (Cambridge: Cambridge University Press, 2003), 71.

5   Michael Ross, "Oil, Islam and Women," *American Political Science Review* 102, no. 1 (February 2008): 107-23. Ross's argument came under the spotlight, which led the journal, *Politics and Gender*, to feature a special issue on the topic in 2009. A. Kang, for instance, suggested that political institutions, particularly gender quotas, should be accounted for, whereas M. Charrad argued kinship/politics nexus is at work. Alice Kang, "Studying Oil, Islam, and Women as if Political Institutions Mattered," *Gender and Politics* 5, no. 4 (2009): 560-68, and Mounira Charrad, "Kinship, Islam or Oil: Culprits of Gender Inequality?" *Gender and Politics* 5, no. 4 (2009): 546-53.

6   John Willoughby, "Segmented Feminization and the Decline of Neopatriarchy in GCC Countries of the Persian Gulf," *Comparative Studies of South Asia, Africa and the Middle East* 28, no.1 (2008): 184-99.

7   Abdulrahman Alyamani, "Women's Higher Education, and Women's Employment in Saudi Arabia," PhD dissertation, University of Illinois at Urbana-Champaign, 1985, 106.

8   Mohammad Younus, "Women and Education" *History of the Middle East* (Teaneck, NJ: Fairleigh Dickinson University, 2012): 15-25: http://tinyurl.com/zt986sh

9   For example, prominent clerics such as Uthaimeen commented that a women's education is sufficient if she can read and write, and understand the Qur'an and Sunnah. Another cleric, Jibreen, is worried about the ideological side effects of women learning computer. See Namie Tsujigami, *Gender and Power in Contemporary Saudi Arabia: A Discourse Analysis from the Perspective of Foucaudian Theory of Power* (Tokyo: Fukumura Shuppan, 2011) (in Japanese), 90-91.

10   According to Doumato, the only exception in school curricula was that girls study home economics whereas boys take physical education. Eleanor Doumato, "Education in Saudi Arabia," in *Gender, Women and Globalization in the Arab Middle East: Gender, Economy, and Society*, ed. Eleanor Doumato and Marsha Posusney (Boulder and London: Lynne Rienner Publishers, 2003), 245.

11   Male female ratio differs depending on the statistics. SAMA's statistics shows that male students constituted 54.4 percent of total newly enrolled students, while female students accounted for 45.6 percent. Saudi Arabian Monetary Agency, *Fifty First Annual Report*, 35-36.

12   Anthony Cordesman, *Saudi Arabia Enters the Twenty-First Century: The Political, Foreign Policy, Economic, and Energy Dimensions* (Westport: Praeger Publishers, 2003), 175-77. His book, published in the early 2000s, argues that the Saudi government has long neglected the quality of education, and focused only on the quantity. He also expresses discontent about women's status. He sees women in Saudi Arabia as "part of the problem, rather than part of the solution" and carefully criticized practices of marriage, divorce and sex segregation, while recognizing women's agency in political and economic fields.

13   Eman Nafjan "Teaching Intolerance," *Foreign Policy*, April 23, 2012: http://tinyurl.com/hhm2z52 (accessed June 29, 2016).

14   Saudi Arabia accelerated its political and social reforms including educational reforms particularly after the Riyadh compound bombing in 2003, as it was a real threat to the kingdom.

15   See Center for Religious Freedom of the Hudson Institute with the Institute for Gulf Affairs, *2008 Update Saudi Arabia's Curriculum of Intolerance: With Excerpts from Saudi Ministry of Education Textbooks for Islamic Studies* Washington, DC: Center for Religions Freedom, 2008), and Nina Shea, "This Is A Saudi Textbook," *Washington Post*, May 21, 2006.

16   Natasha Ridge, *Education and the Reverse Gender Divide in the Gulf States: Embracing the Global, Ignoring the Local* (Amsterdam: Teachers College Press, 2014), 63.

17   It should be noted that global feminism is often criticized as imperialist and reductionist.

18   Ridge, *Education and the Reverse Gender Divide in the Gulf States*, 54.

19   *Ibid.*, 105.

20 Diane Zovighian, "Gulf Women's Participation in the Labor Market: Paid Labor, Care and Social Protection in Patriarchal Systems," in *National Employment, Migration and Education in the GCC*, ed. Steffen Hertog (Berlin: Gerlach Press, 2012), 183-230.

21 The *nitaqat* program is a new Saudization program introduced in July 2011, which evaluates private companies based on their nationalization performance.

22 Ibrahim Naffee, "Heavy Penalties for Hiring Female 'Ghost Workers'," *Arab News*, September 21, 2014 (http://www.arabnews.com/news/633201).

23 Steffen Hertog, "A Comparative Assessment for Labor Market Nationalization Policies in the GCC," in *National Employment*, 71.

24 Motoko Katakura, *Bedouin Village* (Tokyo: University of Tokyo Press, 1977).

25 Hamad Al-Baadi, "Social Change, Education and the Roles of Women in Arabia," unpublished PhD dissertation, Stanford University, 1983.

26 *Ibid.*, 35-40.

27 Abdulrahman Alyamani, "Women's Higher Education, and Women's Employment in Saudi Arabia", unpublished PhD dissertation, University of Illinois at Urbana-Champaign, 1985, 75.

28 Madani Rehemi, "A Survey of the Attitudes of Saudi Men and Women toward Saudi Female Participation in Saudi Arabian Development," unpublished PhD dissertation, University of Colorado at Boulder, 1983, 88.

29 Rehemi, *Attitudes of Saudi Men and Women*, 85.

30 Muhammad Al-Atawneh, *Wahhabi Islam Facing the Challenges of Modernity* (Leiden: Brill, 2010), 99.

31 *Ibid.*, 101.

32 Central Department of Statistics and Information, *Labor Force Survey 2014-Round 2* (Riyadh: Central Department of Statistics and Information, 2014), 15.

33 *Ibid.*, 17.

34 *Ibid.*, 23.

35 "Alarm over Rising Rate of Saudi Spinsterhood" *ArabNews*, January 19, 2015: http://tinyurl.com/jabx58u (accessed June 29, 2016).

36 Habib Toumi, "6 Reasons Why Two Million Saudis Are Not Married," *Gulf News*, April 30, 2015: http://tinyurl.com/ho29gye (accessed June 29, 2016).

37 Namie Tsujigami, "Exploration of Vulnerability/Agency of the Female Migrant Domestic Workers: An Analysis on Employers' Narratives in the Gulf States," *Hakusan Review of Anthropology* 16 (2013) (in Japanese): 55-73.

38 Soraya Altorki, *Women in Saudi Arabia* (New York: Columbia University Press, 1986).

39 Eleanor Doumato, "Education in Saudi Arabia: Gender, Jobs, and the Price of Religion," in *Women and Globalization*, 250.

40 "Majority of Young Saudi Men Prefer Working Women for Brides: Survey," *Al Arabiya*. June 22, 2014: http://tinyurl.com/z7jrdr4 (accessed June 29, 2016).

41 Colleges of Education, Arts, Social Services, and Languages and Translations.

42 Colleges of Science, Computer and Information Sciences, Business Administration, and Arts and Design.

43 Colleges of Nursing, Pharmacy, Health and Rehabilitation Science, Dentistry and Medicine.

44 Website of Anonymous University (accessed June 29, 2016).

4

Making a Branch Campus "Work": Georgetown University's School of Foreign Service in Qatar

Daniel C. Stoll

Over the past 10 to 15 years, the Middle East generally and the Arab Gulf specifically have witnessed a dramatic increase in the number of higher education institutions (HEI) that have been established in the region, many with assistance from or with connections to HEIs in other parts of the world. According to a recent report, there were over 260 HEIs in the Arab Middle East in 2007—up from on 10 in 1940 and just 140 in 2000.[1] In the Gulf alone, there are now over 100 public, semi-public, and private colleges and universities, while in 1990 there were fewer than 10 public universities. Another report estimates that over 50 per cent of the universities founded in the Arab Middle East since 1993 are branches of Western universities, mainly from the United States.[2] Overall, the form and composition of these newly established institutions range from new national universities to for-profit schools to branch campuses of institutions in other countries, particularly North America and Western Europe. The latter are often smaller-scale replicas of the home institution outside of the Gulf. While the circumstances surrounding the establishment of such branch campuses vary, the decision to build such an institution has generally involved a calculation that addresses a range of existential or "foundational" questions. These questions include: the overall rationale for embarking upon such a significant undertaking; the identity and philosophy that would define the new campus; and the relationship between the new campus and its host country, as well as the branch campus and its home institution. In addition, the home institutions must address a host of logistical and administrative issues when deciding to establish a branch campus. These include, but are not limited to: how faculty will be recruited and retained; how the student body will be recruited and retained; and what support services will be provided to students as well as faculty and staff.

This chapter examines the creation of one such branch campus—Georgetown University's School of Foreign Service in Doha, Qatar (SFS-Q), which was launched in 2005. It outlines a number of the questions or issues university leaders addressed before agreeing to accept the invitation from the Qatari government to launch the school. It also examines the subsequent administrative, governance, and financial structures put into place by University leaders in order to support the delivery of the Bachelor of Science of Foreign Service (BSFS)—the degree program brought from Washington DC to Doha's Education City, the location of SFS-Q. The questions with which Georgetown's faculty and administrative leaders grappled before launching the campus, as well as the subsequent challenges confronting those leaders in ensuring that the campus would thrive, often confront leaders at other institutions contemplating a similar decision. Consequently, this chapter serves as a kind of lens through which the phenomenon of international branch campuses can be understood.

The Globalization of Higher Education

Although branch campuses have proliferated in recent years, there is no single accepted definition for such an institution.[3] Most simply, an international branch campus is an:

> Entity pertaining to a university whose primary location is in one country, which operates in another and offers its own degree in that country. Upon successful completion of the course program, fully undertaken at the unit abroad, students are awarded a degree from the foreign institution.[4]

The Cross-Border Education Research Team at the State University of New York at Albany offers a different definition:

> An entity that is owned, at least in part, by a foreign education provider; operated in the name of the foreign education provider; engages in at least some face-to-face teaching; and provides access to an entire academic program that leads to a credential awarded by the foreign education provider.[5]

Finally, Stephen Wilkins of the University of Bath provides yet another definition of such an institution:

> An international branch campus may be defined as an educational facility that has its own premises (which normally include teaching rooms, a library, and a refractory, and sometimes also recreational facilities and student accommodations) where students receive face-to-face instruction in a country different to that of its parent institution. The branch operates under the name of the parent institution and offers qualifications bearing the name of the parent institution.[6]

Just as there are varying definitions of what a branch campus is, there are also different motivations and rationales for launching such campuses. Often referred to as the "second wave" in the globalization of higher education (the so-called "first wave" being the increase in the number of study abroad, exchange or other student mobility programs), branch campuses are sometimes regarded as a mechanism for generating badly needed revenue for the home institution.[7] Also, as Ben Wildavsky notes in his comprehensive analysis of contemporary trends in international higher education, a home institution could be motivated by a desire to improve its position in international rankings, while at the same time creating a global education network and burnishing its reputation as a leader in higher education innovation.[8] Still other institutions want to enhance their stature as universities with a global footprint.

The motivations compelling host countries to support or sponsor a branch campus are equally varied. For some, a branch campus gives young citizens entering tertiary education access to a high quality education at a cost lower than if the students had studied abroad; this can be a particularly compelling argument if the host government underwrites the education of its citizens attending university in another country.[9] Still other host countries regard higher education as an engine for economic growth by developing human capital. As noted by Donn and al-Manthri, "there has been a tendency in the Arab Gulf States… to respond to the impact of economic and social changes by tailoring education, in the curriculum especially, to immediate economic needs." In such a scenario, welcoming a branch campus of a leading Western university is less a way of developing critical thinking skills and instilling humanitarian principals than it is to close a real or perceived development gap.[10]

Still other observers believe that hosting a branch campus is a means for enhancing a country's so-called "soft power", a concept defined by Joseph Ney and other political theorists as, "the ability to affect others to obtain the outcomes one wants through attraction rather than coercion or payment."[11] By encouraging the creation of a branch campus, a host government not only provides access to Western education to its own citizens, but also extends this opportunity to students from other countries—thereby enhancing the host country's reputation and creating a favorable impression of the host government among these students and their families. Of course, the country in which the home institution is based also enjoys a similar kind of influence and "power" when a branch campus is established abroad.

More fundamentally, the presence of a branch campus of a Western university is many times regarded by a host government as a means to address the often parlous state of higher education in the Arab Middle East. As outlined in sobering detail by the *Arab Development Report* issued by the United Nations Development Program in 2003, higher education in the Arab world is characterized by: low research productivity; low quality research; redundancy in disciplines deemed attractive or prestigious (e.g., medicine and engineering), while little attention is given to other disciplines (e.g., information technology or molecular biology); and the almost complete lack of vocational training. As the Report notes, the "data…tell a story of stagnation in certain areas of knowledge productivity, especially in the field of scientific research," with scientific research suffering from "miserly" R&D expenditure and "poor institutional support and a political and social context inimical to the development and promotion of science." In other, non-scientific fields such as the social sciences and humanities, productivity remains low by international standards. Overall, "the most important challenge facing Arab education is its declining quality."[12] This characterization of education generally in the region is echoed by the World Bank, which notes that

> Evidence demonstrates that school systems in MENA are generally of low quality. Basic skills are not being learnt, a fact most clearly captured by international standardized tests, whose results reveal that the Region is still below the level expected given MENA countries' per capita income.[13]

Acutely aware of this under-developed state of higher education in their countries, successive governments within the Arab world, particularly in the Gulf countries, have established branch campuses of major Western universities both as a means of diversifying their economies and enhancing social and economic development, and as a means to "change Arab academe from a site of knowledge *reception* to one of knowledge *production*."[14]

Finally, it should also be noted that in at least one instance, a host government has looked beyond the immediate economic and educational needs of its own population and has aspired to create an enterprise with a more global reach. The invitation in 2004 by the government of the Abu Dhabi in the United Arab Emirates to New York University to open a branch of the NYU system in that Gulf emirate stemmed from a desire to create a university capable of producing global leaders, not just educated citizens of the United Arab Emirates. With the intention of establishing "a fully connected global network university," the government of Abu Dhabi seeks to create a "new paradigm in higher education for a global world," that reaches beyond the Gulf by recruiting students, faculty and staff from around the world. While students from Abu Dhabi and the Emirates also benefit from NYU's presence in the Emirates, NYU Abu Dhabi aspires to become an engine for global education and development.[15]

Laying a Foundation for a Branch Campus

As a university begins to consider establishing a branch campus in another country, it must address a number of foundational questions about the form and nature of the institution to be created, while articulating a compelling rationale for an ambitious endeavor. These questions often range from the practical (how will operations be funded?) to the pedagogical (what subjects or degree programs will the branch campus deliver?) to the philosophical (how will the identity or ethos of the campus be formed?). Will this new entity strive to be an exact duplicate of the home campus, or will it adopt the home institution's values and identity to conditions within the host country? As answers to these questions take shape, the university must address a range of operational questions. How will the faculty be formed and what governance structures will be put in place? How will students be recruited and what admissions standards will be used when evaluating applications?

How will a "community" made up of faculty and staff be created and sustained, and what kind of infrastructure will be established to support what will, for the most part, be a cadre of expatriate employees? Finally, the complex, multi-dimensional question of how the branch campus structures its relations with the home campus, the host country, and the offices or organizations sponsoring the new venture must be answered.

To understand how a major US research institution engages with this range of questions, we will investigate how Georgetown University in Washington DC established SFS-Q. While no two universities follow exactly the same path in deciding to launch a branch campus in another country, Georgetown's example can provide a useful guide for understanding the challenges a university will face when considering such a project. In particular, it provides a perspective on the complex questions a North American university must answer when delivering an academic program for which it might have international renown in a setting that is often substantially different from that of the home campus. Such a study provides an important perspective through which this trend in global higher education can be examined.

In 2003, the Qatar Foundation approached Georgetown about the possibility of opening a branch campus in Doha.[16] In particular, the Foundation wanted Georgetown, the oldest Catholic and Jesuit university in the United States, to bring its internationally-ranked School of Foreign Service to Qatar and deliver the School's undergraduate degree in international affairs. Georgetown's School of Foreign Service would become part of a growing constellation of US universities located in Qatar's Education City, a venture which by that time had attracted campuses from four other US universities: Texas A&M, Virginia Commonwealth, Carnegie-Mellon, and Cornell University. Like Georgetown, each of those institutions had been asked to deliver a particular degree program for which it had recognized expertise: engineering (Texas); fine arts and design (Virginia Commonwealth); medicine (Cornell); and business and information technology (Carnegie-Mellon). When inviting Georgetown to Education City, it asked that the School of Foreign Service deliver its Bachelor of Sciences in Foreign Service (BSFS) program exactly as it did in Washington DC, using the same curriculum, maintaining the same academic standards, and the using the same faculty whenever possible.[17]

Although Georgetown had a well-established reputation for expertise in international affairs and related fields and offered a robust array of study abroad and exchange programs, the Foundation's proposal initially caught many senior administrators by surprise. At the time, the university had no plans to undertake something as complex and time-consuming as establishing a campus outside of the United States; other institutional priorities demanded attention, including the aftermath of its decision to sell its teaching hospital to a health care company. There were also concerns among some faculty and university administrators that creating such a campus would take vital resources away from the University's established programs. The Foundation's proposal, however, drew the support of certain key administrative leaders within the university and, over time, there began a discussion among the university's leadership about whether or not the School could and should embark upon such an ambitious effort.

Central to this discussion were issues questions related to the project's financing as well as whether or not establishing a campus abroad fit into the university's overall mission. Over a period of several months, however, proponents of the proposal assured Georgetown's Board of Directors, the university's governing body, that a number of key considerations would be addressed: the Foundation's commitment to provide full financial support would reduce the financial burden on the university; Georgetown's history of engagement with and expertise in the Middle East meant that the university had a high degree of familiarity with that part of the world; establishing a campus abroad was very much in keeping with Georgetown's desire to be a globally-engaged university; and locating a campus in the Middle East would be in keeping with many of Georgetown's most deeply held values, including a desire to foster greater interfaith dialogue. Once the decision was made to work with the Foundation in establishing a campus in Doha, the process unfolded with remarkable speed: after the initial discussion in 2003, a delegation of senior administrators, members of the Board of Directors and faculty visited Doha in February 2004 for a site visit; the final agreement between Georgetown and the Foundation was signed in May 2005; and in August of that same year Georgetown welcomed the first class to the School of Foreign Service-Qatar (SFS-Q).[18]

Building the Faculty

Georgetown's decision to begin operations and accept its first class of students in August of 2005 meant that it had to move quickly in pulling together a faculty. Here, the University's considerable expertise in Middle East studies gave it access to faculty members, who were both extremely knowledgeable about the region and willing to relocate to the Gulf. Initially, the focus of SFS-Q was on delivering the BSFS program, which has a strong emphasis on the liberal arts. Faculty came from Georgetown's campus in Washington D.C., and included both senior, tenured professors as well as adjunct faculty. During the initial years of operations, the primary responsibility of the faculty was to deliver the undergraduate program: while faculty often pursued their existing research agendas, the focus in Doha was very much on teaching and instruction, rather than on research and publication.

In time, however, particularly as the School's student body grew and as SFS-Q began to expand its curriculum, the need for a larger, more research-focused faculty with established governance structures became apparent. In attempting to address this need, Georgetown confronted many of the challenges branch campuses in the Gulf and beyond face when building the faculty. As research into effective academic institutions highlights, creating an environment in which academic staff feel satisfied and motivated,

> involves a reciprocal relationship in which faculty members are treated with fairness and respect, experience those essential elements in their work, and are accorded some measure of security in return for their contributions to the work of the institution.[19]

Creating such conditions in a US or North American environment is difficult enough. Exporting the US model of higher education abroad and replicating an environment familiar to many US-trained faculty (and many expatriate faculty in branch campuses in the Gulf are indeed products of US universities), can be doubly challenging.

Recent scholarship on the role of faculty at branch campuses in the Gulf has explored a number of concerns that faculty members often have related to their work in the region. This research has tended to highlight three primary and often interrelated concerns around such employment: a lack of the kind of governance structures commonly found in US institutions of higher education; limits on academic freedom; and a lack of job security and stability. As Romani and others point out, most branch campuses lack a faculty senate or a similar governing body that gives faculty a voice in the governance of the institution. Such an absence, in turn, contributes to the perception of faculty in many institutions that decision-making is opaque at best, and is generally driven by the senior administrative leadership with little input from the faculty. Many faculty report a sense of detachment from or a lack of involvement with key decisions about the direction of their institution and how it is run, while others note the impression they are merely employees or "cogs" of the institution and not integral parts of its operation.[20]

Intricately linked to this sense of detachment is the perceived lack of job security. Many countries in the Gulf still maintain the so-called *kafala* system, which requires all expatriate employees to have a local employment sponsor and which often limits the length of employment to 3-year periods. As Noori and others have noted, this sponsorship system makes it impossible to create the kind of tenure system found at many US colleges and universities—which in turn heightens the concern that a faculty member could be dismissed at any time.[21] Since termination of an employment contract under the *kafala* system results in the termination of a worker's right to remain in the country, the threat of dismissal means more than just unemployment—it means the faculty member (and any dependent family members) must also leave the country often within as little as two weeks. Concerns about the draconian nature of the *kafala* system are compounded by legal systems and employment laws in the host countries that are often very different from those of the United States—all of which contributes to the sense of insecurity reported by many expatriate faculty at these branch campuses.[22]

A third, related concern often expressed by expatriate faculty working in the Gulf relates to the principle of academic freedom. Many faculty report feeling constrained in the kinds of issues or topics they can discuss in class or focus on in the research they can pursue. In recent studies, faculty report a kind of self-censorship with regards to issues involving religion, sexuality, and political and social structures within the host country, citing a fear of dismissal if class discussions or research on such topics is perceived as somehow offensive to governing elites or even subversive to the established governing structures.[23] Even when faculty report that they enjoy considerable academic freedom *inside* a classroom, they believe the same cannot be said *outside* of their classes, which causes them to be more circumspect with their involvement in public discussions or limit the topics they pursue in their research.[24]

SFS-Q's answer to these challenges has been two-fold. First, it has drafted documents defining the roles and responsibilities of faculty at the Doha campus and outlining certain governance structures. These documents include the SFS-Q Faculty By-laws, as well as the SFS-Q Faculty Framework. The latter document came together over the course of several years, and reflects input from a variety of parties both in Doha as well as on Georgetown's campus in Washington, D.C. Participants in the drafting process included: senior faculty leadership at both SFS-Q and the School of Foreign Service (SFS) in Washington; the deans of both SFS and SFS-Q; academic deans at both campuses; the Office of the University Counsel; as well as representatives from the Provost's Office in Washington. The document, which was reviewed and approved by the SFS-Q faculty as well as the SFS Faculty Council, not only outlines the composition of the faculty in Doha, but also delineates the procedure by which research leaves are granted, defines the faculty governance structure, and details the process by which faculty are reviewed and promoted. The complex and lengthy process required to bring a final version of the Framework to fruition speaks to the challenges branch campuses face in establishing a system of faculty governance similar to those found in US institutions.

Also contained within the document is a description of "core faculty status," Georgetown's answer to the instability caused by the *kafala* system and the lack of tenure available to faculty at SFS-Q. As the Framework notes: "The Core Faculty appointment framework is designed to respect three defining features of core academic appointments in the system of American higher education (i.e., academic freedom, peer review, and shared governance)."[25]

The Framework outlines a review and promotion process similar to the process used in most US colleges and universities for granting tenure: junior faculty with a core appointment are reviewed annually; they undergo a more comprehensive review in the third year of their appointments in order to gauge their progress towards promotion to senior core status; and then generally undergo review for senior core status in their sixth or seventh year of their appointment. Much like a faculty member at a U.S. college or university undergoing tenure review, the SFS-Q junior faculty member assembles a dossier demonstrating evidence of scholarly research and documenting her/his teaching and service records. A review committee comprised of tenured faculty from Georgetown's Washington DC campus as well as members of the SFS-Q Senior Core Faculty solicits external reviewers, who provide their evaluation of the dossier. Members of the SFS-Q Senior Core Faculty then vote confidentially as to whether to advance the candidate to the appropriate title and membership in the Senior Core Faculty. The SFS Dean, SFS-Q Dean and Dean of Georgetown's Graduate School all provide letters to the dossier, which is then reviewed by Georgetown's Provost. Appointment or advancement to Senior Core status will be recognized in several ways, including:

- Three-year rolling, automatically renewing contracts;

- Contract terms signaling long-term continuing of employment and explicit acknowledgement that the award of Senior Core Status expresses an intention of containing employment; and

- A salary adjustment.[26]

While employment at SFS-Q for faculty and administrative staff alike can be affected by a variety of factors (including changes in the level of funding provided by the Qatar Foundation, as well as political conditions within the Gulf), the existence of the Framework and of Core Faculty Status should provide a considerable degree of stability and certainty for SFS-Q faculty.

One additional question for branch campuses (and indeed national universities in the region) involves the source of the faculty they want to recruit. Will faculty, for example, come from the home campus or will they be recruited from the host country—or through international searches? As a recent study highlights, many campuses in the Gulf (especially in the UAE, Qatar and Saudi Arabia) have a sizeable number of expatriate faculty, in large measure because the pool of qualified national faculty is limited.[27] Indeed, this paucity of qualified national faculty is often one reason why a branch campus has been invited to the host country in the first place: the campus will become one means by which such qualified national faculty are to be developed. Hence, most branch campuses often utilize two means for identifying and recruiting faculty: bringing faculty from the home campus, and recruiting qualified expatriate faculty locally or through international searches.

In its initial years of operation, Georgetown looked to tap the extensive faculty resources of its home campus; as noted earlier, the faculty brought to Doha in the first year of operation came exclusively from the Main Campus in Washington, and the same was true to a large extent for the second cohort. Using faculty from the Washington DC campus was seen as a way of bringing Georgetown's values and ethos to the branch campus—a crucial component of a Georgetown education. In time, however, it became necessary to look beyond the home campus, and recruit more broadly. While SFS-Q continues to emphasize the desirability of bringing senior, tenured members of the Washington campus to Doha (both for the reasons cited above, and in order to help mentor and develop junior faculty), the majority of faculty searches in recent years have resulted in attracting faculty from other North American and European institutions, many at the junior level. Most have a doctorate from a US institution and hence are familiar with the US model of higher education. Although many come to SFS-Q from a similar educational background, the reasons they seek an appointment to SFS-Q vary. Some are drawn by the prospect of working on a new and exciting educational initiative, one that could contribute to the host country's development. Others come because of the proximity of the branch campus to their research or the possibility of professional development. Still others are attracted by the salaries that are generally higher than in the

United States, as well as what are often generous benefit and allowance packages. Once at a branch campus, faculty often cite the small class size and opportunity to work with students who are often highly motivated as reasons for remaining at the campus.[28]

Creating the Student Body

Just as SFS-Q has worked to develop a world-class faculty with appointments similar to those found in US higher education, so also has the campus worked to recruit and retain students capable of thriving in an academically rigorous program and who also reflect the diversity of the region. In doing so, Georgetown had to answer a number of questions that most branch campuses must also address. Should, for example, the same admissions requirements be used, or should they be adjusted to local circumstances? What level of English language proficiency will be required, and should the School provide remediation for prospective students in need of assistance? Should the School require standardized test results and, if so, should the scores be similar to those required by the campus in Washington? And, as any family with college-bound children knows, issues of financial need are often paramount in the minds of students and family when deciding where to enroll. Would SFS-Q have access to financial aid in order to ensure that students from all socio-economic backgrounds matriculate? Answering these questions was complicated by the fact that each of the US institutions in Education City follows very different admissions and financial aid policies and has very different tuition levels—which means there is no consistency among the institutions on these fundamental policies.[29]

Recruiting and retaining a diverse student body has been a particularly important goal for Georgetown. In doing so, SFS-Q has been guided not just by its own admissions policies as well as core values, but also the vision of Qatar Foundation. As noted above, Qatar Foundation created Education City in order to foster social and economic development both within the country and the region generally. "Human Development" is one of the four "pillars" of *Qatar National Vision 2030*, Qatar's plan for the "economic, social, human and environmental development of the country in the coming decades." A strategic goal of this particular "pillar" is an "educated population," which initiatives like Education City are designed to achieve.[30] Hence, unlike campuses such as NYU Abu Dhabi (which is focused on developing the next generation of leaders from around the globe), SFS-Q and the other schools within Education City are intended to help educate and develop the country's next generation of leaders, while also contributing to development within the Gulf more broadly. As a result, SFS-Q sees itself as an integral part of the country's overall development strategy and, as such, seeks to recruit as many qualified Qatari students as possible.

At the same time, a diverse student body—including in terms of gender, country of origin, and socio-economic background—is a key component of the vision SFS-Q has articulated for itself. Hence, SFS-Q seeks to expand its pool of scholarship funds in order to academically qualified students, who might not be able to afford the tuition of a private institution; while Qatar Foundation supports non-Qatari students with a generous program of interest-free loans, there continues to be a need for additional scholarships and grants. Having such funds is key to SFS-Q's goal of recruiting students from diverse economic backgrounds. In addition, and in keeping with the aims of Georgetown University in Washington, SFS-Q seeks to have students not just from the region but from around the world. As a result, in the 2015-2016 academic year, SFS-Q's students represent 45 different countries. Of the 253 students there, 103 are Qatari, and 174 are female, 79 are male.[31]

Of course, students do not only attend classes or conduct research or interact with faculty. There is a whole range of activities outside the classroom—social interactions through clubs and sports, academic support services, internship opportunities and the like—that students seek as part of their education at a branch campus. On the one hand, these services and activities are part of the overall experience provided over the course of a traditional US university education; on the other, these activities are often integral to the kind of educational experience a home institution wishes to deliver through the branch campus. For example, the goal of ensuring that SFS-Q perpetuates Georgetown's core values such as *cura personalis* (care for the whole person) and "Women and Men for Others," prompted the university to create a constellation of services and opportunities intended to give the SFS-Q students an educational experience similar to that enjoyed by their counterparts in Washington. Hence, SFS-Q has created a series of experiential learning programs designed to connect students with the broader community, programs ranging from English language tutoring for local workers to study tours allowing students to understand how societies cope with post-conflict reconstruction and development. In addition to offering a range of clubs and organized sports, SFS-Q also has brought a small number (three to four) recent graduates from the Washington campus to help the Office of Student Development in mentoring these student organizations and, in the process, create a Georgetown "identity" among the students. Over time, SFS-Q also established a number of offices, such as Counseling and Academic Support, to provide a range of support services to the students. In essence, a full-fledged Students Affairs operation has been created at SFS-Q as part of the effort to give students a university experience similar to what would be found on the Washington campus.

Creating a Community for Faculty and Staff

While the need to build a talented faculty, recruit qualified students, and create a rigorous academic program are of paramount concern to a branch campus, also important are considerations about how the campus will support the faculty and staff—and their families—that are recruited to fulfill the mission of the campus. Faculty and staff need places to live, must have a means of educating dependent children, and have access to reliable health care. When bringing on new faculty and staff, the branch campus needs to follow both local labor laws and also those of the United States—as well as the policies and procedures of the home campus. Help will most likely be needed for obtaining the necessary entry visas into the country as well as the residency permits allowing faculty and staff to work in the host country. And what support will the branch campus offer to spouses and partners of faculty and staff to find employment in the host country? In sum, a branch campus must often grapple with the challenge of creating a community and a support structure for faculty, staff and their families. The need for such support is often compelling, in light of how different the society and environment of the host country might be to that of the home institution.

In creating such a support structure, SFS-Q relied heavily on the assistance and expertise of several key offices on the Washington campus, particularly Human Resources, Finance, and Information Systems. Soon after SFS-Q began operations, it became clear that vital functions such as IT and human resources could not be handled solely from Washington: SFS-Q would need to establish similar offices in order to deal more effectively and efficiently with the day-to-day operations of the campus. At the same time, SFS-Q could not create these offices in a vacuum, but needed to ensure that the procedures and operations it was establishing in Doha meshed with and adhered to as much as possible those of the campus in Washington. Hence, a senior staff member from the University's Office of Human Resources was among that first cohort from Washington that came to Doha at the start of operations in order to help create the support infrastructure that was needed "on ground." It also became clear that SFS-Q would need local expertise to help it arrange appropriate housing for faculty and staff, and to deal with the complexities of Qatari visa and immigration procedures—which led to the hiring of the first locally recruited employee. The support SFS-Q gives faculty, staff and families on these issues is particularly necessary and valuable, since many SFS-Q personnel do not know Arabic and given the challenges of operating within a different legal system.

Faculty, staff and their families look for other forms of assistance and support as well. Dependent children, for example, need access to good schools and educational experiences as least equal to those found in the United States. In a country such as Qatar, this means that families often seek to place their children in one of the private international schools that have sprung up over time. Unfortunately, there is often greater demand for places in these schools than seats available, and families must sometimes put their children in schools that are perhaps not their first choice. Employment opportunities for spouses and partners can also be challenging, in part because of the nature of the *kafala* system but also because a general lack of jobs in some fields and industries. These challenges are, of course, not unique to a branch campus. International business, non-governmental organizations, and even diplomatic missions abroad often grapple with similar issues on behalf of their personnel. Unless a university has a history of or experience with operating outside its home country, however, it might be tempted to pay less attention to addressing these concerns and focus exclusively on delivering its core academic program. Given their centrality to the success of a branch campus, these issues should receive equal attention from senior administrators and faculty.

Maintaining Ties Between the Home Campus and Branch Campus

A challenge that many branch campuses encounter once they are operational involves the relationship they enjoy with their home campus. On the surface, it would seem that ties between the two campuses would be characterized by open communication and great collegiality; they are, after all, parts of the same institution. Indeed, the need for such strong and effective ties is paramount. As we have seen, a branch campus often relies on the support and expertise of important administrative offices on the home campus, even if parallel operations exist at the former. In addition, it is crucial that the academic programs at both locations are aligned and deliver the curriculum in the same way and with the same rigor. If, as many branch campuses will argue, the degree programs they are delivering are equal to those of the home campus, there must be close and on-going collaboration between the two campuses to ensure this is indeed the case. Also, if the faculty members at the branch campus are to be of the same caliber as those on the home campus, appointment procedures as well as the standards for advancing through the ranks must be aligned. Finally, faculty on both campuses should have the opportunity to collaborate on joint research projects and interact as colleagues within the same academic unit, regardless of the distance between the two campuses. By doing so, the branch campus will ideally become imbued with the same ethos as the home campus. In addition, an environment in which both campuses can benefit from engaging with each other develops organically and with as few obstacles as possible.

Achieving such collegiality and closeness is difficult, however. Factors such as geographic distance and differences in time zones can make communication and coordination challenging. Social, political and cultural conditions are often radically different between the two campuses—which, in turn, can create additional complications. A lack of familiarity on the part of the home campus with the often-unique challenges and circumstances of operating outside the home country can also create misunderstanding and miscommunication. Dealing with such a complicated and unknown environment requires creativity, open and frank communication, and considerable commitment of time, energy, and resources on the part of faculty and staff in both locations. Regular communication between faculty and administrative leaders on both campuses—either through site visits or weekly conference calls or emails exchanges—are essential. Site visits – in both directions – are particularly important, since they provide "first hand" exposure to representatives from the home campus to the often unique environment of the branch campus; in turn, they give personnel from the branch campus an opportunity to learn more about the institutional values and culture of the home institution, as well as a better understanding of the administrative processes they might be required to follow. Including senior members of the faculty from the home campus on search committees or promotion review committees for branch campus faculty will help ensure that the branch campus recruits and retains colleagues of equal caliber to those on the home campus. And, including senior faculty from the branch campus on similar committees on the home campus can help to improve ties between the two faculty bodies and correct any impression of a two-tier system.

Fostering close ties and clear communication between the home and branch campuses is essential not just for establishing the programmatic and administrative operations of the branch campus (and, hence, ensuring that it will be successful its overall mission), but also for helping shape its culture and identity. Since few US or North American universities have a long track record of establishing branch campuses abroad, the skills and expertise in managing such complex operations are often acquired "on the job," since many of the challenges and problems encountered in getting a branch campus operational are not found on the home campus. Even more challenging, however, is bringing clarity and a common understanding to what the branch campus is supposed to be: an exact replica of the home institution, a completely independent and distinct institution, or a campus that embodies the unique ethos and identity of the home campus while adapting to conditions in the host country. Achieving clarity on that issue often requires extensive and regular interactions among faculty and administrative leadership on both campuses. Anything less could undermine the ultimate success of the operation, while diminishing the students' academic experience.

Conclusion

As part of the so-called "second wave" of the globalization of higher education, the launching of branch campuses in regions such as the Middle East has created a host of new educational opportunities for bright, talented students. While many countries have sought to develop or improve their national institutions, many have also invited Western universities, particularly from North America, to set up campuses abroad to help achieve the development goals these countries have set for themselves. Several countries in the Gulf in particular (with the possible exception of Oman and Saudi Arabia), have been particularly receptive to the branch campus model. While the motivation for creating such institutions vary, university leaders are often confronted by similar challenges and problems as they strive to bring what are internationally-ranked academic programs to a new and very different kind of setting. These challenges are not just administrative or logistical in nature, but can also involve the very identity of both the home institution and the campus it establishes abroad. Understanding those challenges, as well as the need to clearly define the mission and ethos of the branch campus, will be key to the success of what ultimately is a significant undertaking.

Notes

1   Vincent Romani, "The Politics of Higher Education in the Middle East: Problems and Prospects," in *Middle East Brief* (Waltham, MA: Brandeis University, Crown Center for Middle East Studies, May 2009, 1).

2   Neema Noori, "Does Academic Freedom Globalize? The Diffusion of the American Model of Education to the Middle East and Academic Freedom," *Political Science* (July 2014) 609. See also Fatima Badry and John Willoughby, *Higher Education Revolution in the Gulf: Globalization and International Viability* (London, UK: Taylor & Francis Ltd, 2015).

3   The globalization of higher education, especially in the Middle East/North Africa (MENA) region has been the subject of considerable attention in recent years. Examples of recent research include: K.E. Shaw, editor, *Higher Education in the Gulf: Problems and Prospects* (Exeter, UK: University of Exeter Press, 1997); Christopher Davidson and Peter Mackenzie Smith, ed. *Higher Education in the Gulf States: Shaping Economies, Politics, and Culture* (London, UK: al Saqi Books, 2012); "The World is Going to University" *The Economist*, 28 March 2015, 3-11; Anna Kosmutsky and Rahul Putty, "Transcending Borders and Traversing Boundaries: A Systematic Review of Literature on Transnational, Offshore, Cross-Border and Borderless Higher Education," *Journal of Studies in Higher Education* (September 2015); Dale F. Eickelman, "Mass Higher Education and the Religious Imagination in Contemporary Arab Societies," *American Ethnologist*, 19, no. 4 (November 1992), 643-655; and *The Arab World Competitiveness Report 2013* (Geneva, Switzerland: World Economic Forum and the European Bank for Reconstruction and Development, 2013).

4   Philip G. Altbach, "The Branch Campus Bubble?" *Inside Higher Ed* (15 July 2011), http://tinyurl.com/j8sd8w7 (accessed 29 June 2016).

5   William G. Tierney and Michael Lanford, "An Investigation of the Impact of International Branch Campuses on Organizational Culture," *Higher Education* (August 2015), 287.

6   Stephen Wilkins, "Who Benefits From Foreign Universities in the Arab Gulf States?" *Australian University Review* (2011), 73.

7   Tierney and Lanford, "An Investigation," 284.

8   Ben Wildavsky, *The Great Brain Race: How Global Universities are Reshaping the World* (Princeton, NJ: Princeton University Press, 2010), 42-69.

9   Wilkens, "Who Benefits," 77.

10   Gari Donn and Yahya al-Manthri, *Globalization and Higher Education in the Arab Gulf States* (Oxford, UK: Symposium Books, Ltd, 2010), 105.

11   Joseph Nye, "Public Diplomacy and Soft Power," *Annals of the American Academy of Political and Social Science*, 616 (2008), 94. For a further discussion of the connection between soft power and the creation of branch campuses in the Gulf, see Osman Antiwi-Boateng, "The Rise of Qatar as a Soft Power and the Challenges" *European Scientific Journal*, 2 (December 2013); and Mehran Kamrava, *Qatar: Small State, Big Politics* (Ithaca, NY: Cornell University Press, 2013).

12   *Arab Human Development Report 2003: Building a Knowledge Society* (New York, NY: United Nations Development Program, 2003), 4.

13   *Education in the Middle East and North Africa* (Washington, D.C.: The World Bank, 27 January 2014), http://tinyurl.com/hes53gw (accessed 29 June 2016).

14   Romani, "The Politics of Higher Education," 4.

15   For a more complete description of NYU's campus in Abu Dhabi, see: http://nyuad.nyu.edu/en/about.html. In addition, see Elizabeth Redden, "Global Ambitions", *Inside Higher Education* (11 March 2013) http://tinyurl.com/je4uabr (accessed 29 June 2016). While NYU Abu Dhabi and the six US schools in Qatar (see below) continue to operate successfully in the region, other attempts to establish branch campuses in the Gulf have not been as fortunate. For example, both George Mason University as well as the Michigan State University have closed their operations in the Gulf (in Ras al-Khaimah and Dubai, respectively), often for financial reasons. See "US University Shelves UAE Campus Plan," *Gulf News*, (7 May 2007), http://tinyurl.com/hjldwwd (accessed 29 June 2016). See also "Teaching Troubles: Higher Education Hits a Low Mark," knowledge@wharton, (28 December 2010) http://tinyurl.com/j3vgxkq (accessed 29 June 2016); and "Collapsing Branch Campuses: Time for Some Collective Action?" *GlobalHigherEd* (9 March 2009) http://tinyurl.com/h892szy (accessed 29 June 2016). In addition, branches campus in the Gulf have met with considerable criticism, often focused on the conditions experienced by the workers building these campuses as well as concerns about possible limitations on freedom of expression and academic enquiry. For examples of such criticism, see: Zvika Krieger, "The Emir of NYU: John Sexton's Abu Dhabi Debacle," *The Atlantic* (13 March 2013) http://tinyurl.com/d4qtxq5 (accessed 29 June 2016); Ariel Kaminer and Sean O'Driscoll, "Workers at N.Y.U.'s Abu Dhabi Site Face Harsh Conditions," *The New York Times* (18 May 2014) http://

tinyurl.com/mbuqvfr (accessed 29 June 2016); Hugh Eakin, "The Strange Power of Qatar," *The New York Review of Books* (27 October 2011) http://tinyurl.com/5uvtcpb (accessed 29 June 2016); Human Rights Watch, "Building a Better World Cup: Protecting Migrant Workers in Qatar Ahead of FIFA 2022" (6 June 2012) http://tinyurl.com/h6blauk (accessed 29 June 2016); and Owen Gibson and Ian Black, "Qatar Still Failing Migrant Workers, Says Amnesty International," *The Guardian* (20 May 2015) http://tinyurl.com/mu4njeu (accessed 29 June 2016).

16   According to the Foundation's website, "Qatar Foundation for Education, Science and Community Development is a private, non-profit organization that serves the people of Qatar by supporting and operating programs in three core mission areas: education, science and research, and community development." The Foundation was created in 1995 by His Highness Sheikh Hamad bin Khalifa Al Thani, then Emir of Qatar, and Her Highness Sheikha Moza bint Nasser. http://www.qf.org.qa/about/about# (accessed 29 June 2016).

17   In addition to these five schools, a sixth US university has also created a branch campus in Education City: Northwestern University, which is delivering its undergraduate programs in communications and journalism. The Qatar Foundation has also supported the creation of a number of additional educational programs within the Education City framework, including: the Academic Bridge Program (a pre-college foundation program); and the Faculty of Islamic Studies. Qatar Academy, a K-12 school, is also located on the Education City campus.

18   This summary of the discussions leading up to Georgetown's decision to establish SFS-Q is based on interviews conducted with senior university administrators involved with the initiative. These include: James O'Donnell, Georgetown's Provost at the time; James Reardon-Anderson, founding dean of SFS-Q; and Junie Nathani, former Director of Human Resources and Chief Administrative Officer at SFS-Q. These interviews took place in a period between October 13 and November 2, 2015. Many of the factors shaping Georgetown's decision to establish a campus in Doha mirror those identified by researchers such as Tierney and Landford in their work on branch campuses, including "An Investigation," 295.

19   Ann E. Austin, David W. Chapman, Samar Farah, Elisabeth Wilson, and Natasha Ridge, "Expatriate Academic Staff in the United Arab Emirates: The Nature of their Work Experiences in Higher Education Institutions," *Higher Education*, 68 (2014), 545.

20   Romani, "The Politics of Higher Education," 5. See also Austin et al, "Expatriate Academic Staff," 550; as well as Michael H. Romanowski and Ramzi Nasser, "Identity Issues: Expatriate Professors Teaching and Researching in Qatar," *Higher Education* 69 (April 2015), 654.

21   Noori, "Does Academic Freedom Globalize?" 610.

22   Romanowski and Nasser, "Identify Issues," 664.

23   The issue of academic freedom at branch campuses in the Gulf continues to be the subject of considerable research. In addition to Noori and Romanowski, and Austin et al. cited above, see David Chapman, Ann Austin, Samar Farah, Elisabeth Wilson, and Natasha Ridge, "Academic Staff in the UAE: Unsettled Journey," *Higher Education Policy* 27 (2014) 131-51; Kristian Coates Ulrichsen, "Academic Freedom and UAE Funding," *Foreign Policy* (25 February 2013) http://tinyurl.com/zfr43d3 (accessed 29 June 2016); Phillip G. Altbach, *The Decline of the Guru: The Academic Profession in Developing and Middle-Income Countries* (New York, NY: Palgrave Macmillan, 2003); and Louis Menand, ed., *The Future of Academic Freedom* (Chicago, IL: University of Chicago Press, 1996).

24   Noori, "Does Academic Freedom Globalize," 610.

25   *SFS-Q Faculty Framework*, http://tinyurl.com/zmca5gx (accessed 29 June 2016).

26   Ibid, 12.

27   Austin et al., "Expatriate Academic Staff," 542.

28   Chapman et al., "Academic Staff in the UAE," 139.

29   For a more detailed discussion of the challenges confronting branch campuses in recruiting and retaining high-quality students, see: Angela Franklin and Khadeegha Alzouebi, "Sustainability of International Branch Campuses in the United Arab Emirates: A Vision for the Future," *Journal of General Education*, 63, no. 2-3, (2014) 121-37; Stephen Wilkins and Jeroen Huisman, "The International Branch Campus

as Transnational Strategy in Higher Education," *Higher Education*, 64, issue 5 (November 2012), 627-45; Stephens Balakrishnan Melodena, Stephen Wilkins and Jeroen Huisman, "Student Satisfaction and Student Perceptions of Quality at International Branch Campuses in the United Arab Emirates," *Journal of Higher Education Policy and Management* 34 (October 2012), 543-56; and "International Trends in Higher Education, 2015," University of Oxford International Studies Center (Oxford, UK: University of Oxford, 2015).

30   For the *Qatar 2030* document, see: *Qatar National Vision 2030*, http://tinyurl.com/poetn3r (accessed 29 June 2016).

31   Author's email exchange with SFS-Q, November 15, 2015.

5

Journalism and Scholarship: How One Learns in Qatar

Mary L. Dedinsky

In recent years, the nations of the Gulf Cooperation Council have established many campuses and programs of higher education sponsored by universities in the United States and Europe. Some of these programs in due course will produce a substantial body of scholarship that has been developed by individuals reared and trained in the Gulf States, applying the techniques of research and analysis acquired from their education in these foreign programs. This chapter examines the question whether this scholarship will be distinctive and, if so, what characteristics it is likely to have.

This chapter focuses only on part of the change occurring in Gulf States higher education. Certain changes occurring in Arabic higher education, such as a movement from memory to information management skill as a primary attribute of the learned individual,[1] are evident in Western universities as well. This chapter focuses specifically on the consequences of the Gulf States' initiatives to import Western higher education.

The evidence reviewed here suggests that the scholarship produced by graduates of Western universities in the Gulf States will be uniquely characteristic of the region. It will be based largely on the collection of facts about the Gulf States and it will seek to provide insights into, and develop strategies for addressing, challenges faced by the people of the region. The evidence, however, also suggests that this work will be useful to scholars worldwide. In time, scholars produced by these programs will contribute in a discrete way to the formal conversation pursued by a global community of scholars.

Qatar's Investment in International University Campuses

The evidence is derived from a journalism program of Northwestern University in Qatar (NU-Q). Qatar in recent years has established eight branch campuses of international universities, in a strategy pursued by other Gulf States as well. Qatar has been explicit about its goals in this initiative. Since his inauguration in 2013, Qatar's Emir, Sheikh Tamim bin Hamad Al Thani, has re-asserted the commitment of Qatar to move away from a petroleum-based economy and toward a "knowledge-based" one.[2] In this commitment,

Sheikh Tamim has perpetuated a policy adopted by his father and predecessor, the "Father Emir," Sheikh Hamad bin Khalifa Al Thani, and shared by the Gulf States generally. In pursuit of this policy, Qatar aspires to create a "world-class education system."[3] Part of this initiative has been the expansion of Qatar University, the national university, from a small college of education in the 1970s to seven colleges and several research centers with more than 15,000 students today, with plans to add colleges and expand the student body to 25,000 by 2019.[4]

Beginning in 1995, Qatar also began to establish campuses of international universities at a region in Doha called Education City, both to increase the available course offerings to Qatari students and to ensure high quality.[5] Sponsored by the Qatar Foundation for Education, Science and Community Development, Education City now includes Qatar campuses of six US universities, one UK university, and one French business school.[6] These campuses have developed collaborative relationships with each other and with Hamad bin Khalifa University (HBKU), also based at Education City and established by the Qatar Foundation in 2013 as a research institution. HBKU is home to the Qatar Faculty of Islamic Studies, established to promote an "intellectual plurality" that emphasizes the diversity of the Islamic heritage, and five other colleges.[7] Cross-registration arrangements permit students at one Education City campus to take courses at others, creating for the student a university of universities.

The US universities represented at Education City include Northwestern University, which offers degrees in communication and journalism. Sheikha Moza bint Nasser, Chair of the Qatar Foundation, has provided the following explanation for Qatar's decision to offer an American journalism program to its students:

> You cannot participate in the global knowledge economy without freedom of thought, freedom of speech and the freedom to challenge conventional thinking. . . . If we do not reform current practices and instead aim to transform today's adolescents into creative, productive and diligent contributors, our economies will not be able to compete internationally. . . . This is why we support the freedom of the press in Qatar and the wider Arab world through institutions like Al Jazeera, and it is why we are preparing a new generation of Arab journalists through programs at Northwestern University at Education City.[8]

There are limits on media freedom in Qatar, but the existence of the NU-Q Journalism Program is substantial evidence that the aspirations expressed by Sheikha Moza are genuine. NU-Q offers journalism and communication degrees in programs that develop the capacity for critical thinking on a broad foundation of liberal arts, with strong working relationships between faculty and students. As part of the nation's education strategy, the Qatar government and Qatar Foundation have allowed NU-Q substantial room to teach the skills and practices of American journalism, and the work of NU-Q journalism students is marked by vitality and an apparent sense of freedom.

Emerging Scholarship

The work of NU-Q journalism students suggests that future scholarship in the developing academic communities of the Gulf States will both reflect regional information, perspectives, and sensibilities and contribute substantially to a better understanding of transnational issues. In my experience, work undertaken by college journalism students resembles in certain respects the work of more seasoned scholars. The work reviewed here is a collection of news reports prepared by first-year college students. The proposition that there are substantial differences between these reports and the published work of scholars is obvious. Certain similarities between the two may not be so evident.

One similarity is this: like a piece of seasoned scholarship, each of the news reports assembled by these students has a central point (thesis) advanced in a school of thought (discipline) supported by facts, reliable authorities, and analysis. The school of thought in the field of journalism of course is the idea of news, the idea that certain information has immediate public interest and value. Certain factors contribute to the newsworthy value of information. As in any school of thought, these factors serve to focus the reporter's attention on certain kinds of information, screening out information that does not appear pertinent to the investigator's questions. Moreover, as in scholarship, newsgathering has developed systematic practices with professional standards to ensure accuracy, reliability and completeness.[9] And like any serious scholarship, journalism is built on a foundation of fact and reliable analysis.

Some sense of the substantial nature of the investigations pursued by college journalism students may be gained by reviewing the sources of facts and analysis they gather to prepare their news stories. The sample reviewed here are news reports developed in two years by first-year students in the NU-Q Journalism Program and published on the Internet.[10] These are not a complete set, or even an extensive sample, of the news reports prepared by NU-Q journalism students, but certain features of the reports reviewed here represent the broader body of work. These representative features provide the particular evidence I wish to review. The sample is a set of 18 news reports prepared and published in two years, 2012 and 2015, incorporating the work of 45 students.

In these two years of reports, the students cited eight Qatar government departments, 14 representatives of Qatar government departments, 14 representatives of Qatar government-related entities (e.g., public utility companies and public health institutions), 13 representatives of universities with Qatar campuses, 11 representatives of private enterprises in Qatar, nine representatives of Qatar charitable organizations, six international or foreign organizations and four scholars of Islam. They also cited a government-related entity (the nation's electricity transmission utility), two international universities with Qatar campuses, an independent news organization in Qatar, the representatives of two international or foreign organizations, the representatives of three private secondary schools in Qatar, and two Qatar charitable organizations. They also cited 37 individuals who related personal, illustrative anecdotes (see Appendix I for a chart listing these sources).

The students relied on some of these sources for purely factual information, including Qatar government departments and other organizations, and certain individuals, such as representatives of these organizations. They relied on authoritative individuals sometimes as sources of fact and sometimes as sources of analysis. Because they were preparing news reports, not works of scholarship, the students relied primarily on the oral statements of authoritative individuals rather than the citation of refereed and published works to provide analytical support for their conclusions. Authoritative analysis, however, was a key component of the students' work. The students largely refrained from personal analysis and instead collected the analysis of individuals who appeared to have sufficient knowledge to support the analysis provided.

As basic elements of newsworthy information, journalists and journalism schools in the US recognize several factors important to newsworthiness: timeliness, physical proximity to the reader, the presence of conflict, the public stature of individuals involved, the impact of the circumstances on the public, the unusual quality of the story, the human interest that may be found in the story, and the possibility of visual representations of the story through photography or video.[11] These factors are not applied consciously as a formula by working journalists, and often journalists recognize information as being newsworthy simply because it seems so. Indeed, journalists sometimes work to compensate for the attraction of stories containing the standard elements of newsworthiness, pursuing investigations of long-term developments that might escape notice in day-to-day stories. Nevertheless, the factors noted above do describe certain elements that journalists look for in potential stories, and the factors confirm that journalism is a school of thought, a discipline that organizes the development of reports based on fact and analysis.

With these factors in mind, it is not surprising the news reports prepared by NU-Q students all concern current circumstances in Qatar. Timeliness and proximity are important factors in the newsworthiness of information. It is also true the sources of information most available to NU-Q students were local individuals conversant with local conditions. The fact that these stories concerned conditions in Qatar does not alone make them specifically regional. The subjects chosen by the students and the issues that the stories raise also make these reports regional in their perspective.

The news reports prepared by NU-Q first-year students fell roughly into two general categories: (1) stories about adverse circumstances that Qatar residents believe could be alleviated in whole or in part by greater public awareness or by government action or both, and (2) distinctive features of Qatari society that raise issues of cultural tradition and development or are simply interesting. Both categories of reports contained information about positive features of Qatari government, culture or society, as well as challenges and unfavorable circumstances. Moreover, these categories are not precise; sometimes a news report encompassed both adverse circumstances and distinctive features of Qatari society. For example, one report featured an endeavor by Sheikha Al Mayassa bint Hamad Al Thani, the founder and chairperson of the Qatar Museums Authority, to persuade the

Qatar Supreme Education Council to reintroduce arts education into the public school curriculum.[12] The report was both a report of a deficiency in public education and story of cultural development. While such overlaps may be found in some of the reports, however, most fell into one category or the other. About two thirds of the news stories reported on adverse circumstances, while about one third focused on local culture.

As one examines the general topics chosen by the NU-Q students, it is apparent that most could be topics of news anywhere. Among the reports that addressed adverse circumstances, seven addressed perceived deficiencies in public services, three addressed environmental issues, and two addressed hardships faced by foreign workers. Among the news stories about public services, three addressed public education issues, three addressed public health issues and one addressed the availability of public transportation. Among the stories about local culture, two addressed changes in the roles of women in Qatar society, two addressed efforts to perpetuate traditional Qatar culture and two highlighted interesting features of Qatar society.

In the specific points made in the NU-Q student news reports, the reports are more local in immediate significance. An outline of the central ideas advanced in the stories is appended as Appendix II. Of the 18 reports in this sample, ten marshalled facts and analysis to assert that, while the Qatar government deserved credit for addressing certain national domestic problems, the Government could do more; four gave the Government credit without qualification; and three offered criticism, counterbalanced by some credit or praise. Six referred to Qatar's cultural tradition as a positive influence in present-day Qatar society, while one portrayed a particular feature of Qatar culture in a negative light. Of these reports, five were critical of Qatar present-day society and three offered both criticism and praise.

A report about waste management in Qatar, entitled "Throwing It All Away,"[13] has features that are broadly representative of the NU-Q news reports. It focuses on a specific adverse circumstance in Qatar: a relatively high level of waste material produced by Qatar residents. Although Qatar has been highly criticized by environmentalists, the story gives the Qatar government credit for having established a waste material processing facility in 2013 to process waste into compost and fuel for electricity. It also notes, however, that the facility on the day it opened was unable to process all of the waste produced in Qatar that day. The facility has a maximum capacity of 2,500 tons per day, leaving an excess of 700 tons that must be taken untreated to landfills, causing land pollution. The report also gives the Qatar government credit for having undertaken a public awareness campaign to encourage recycling of waste. The Government began this campaign among young school children, and, as the campaign seemed successful, the Government extended it to higher grades, with the plan eventually to extend it to the broader population.

The campaign highlighted the fact that recycling is a Qatar cultural tradition, prevalent when grandparents of present-day Qataris had limited income and regularly found new uses for old things. Government officials credited this reference to traditional culture for much of the campaign's success. The news report also invoked the nation's cultural tradition by noting a discrepancy between wasteful practices and the society's predominant religious tradition. The report quoted an educator and preacher at the Qatar Islamic Cultural Center who cited Islamic authority that was critical of the waste of resources and excessive spending.

While the news reports referred in positive ways to the nation's traditional culture as a general rule, there was an illuminating exception. One report described a Qatari Dressage Female Equestrian team, founded in 2013, whose members are quickly showing promise in international competitions.[14] The report highlighted generally the enthusiasm of the athletes and the satisfaction of their sponsor and their coach with their progress. The report, however, also noted that dressage was a sport in which women compete with men and that some Qataris were not pleased by this circumstance. They quoted comments of a Qatar Olympics official who said he and other Qataris did not approve of competitions between women and men or of the snug clothing that women wore in such competitions. The students presented this view respectfully, but they also noted the perception of the young female equestrians that most Qataris supported their activity and the participation of females in any sport. This presentation of disparate views placed the story in a context of change in the roles of women in Qatari society.

Local Facts and Global Significance

Examining the facts cited and analyses compiled by NU-Q students, it becomes apparent that the news reports' content is highly specific to the locale. For example, Qatar has only a two-day supply of water at any time and Qatar has the largest carbon footprint per capita in the world. One also finds the view of a UN climate change official that Qatar has the resources to lead the development of green technologies.[15]

One also learns that for every six women enrolled at a university in Qatar, there is only one male student. A Qatari family therapist opines that Qatari men have relatively little incentive to attend college in Qatar because they have attractive post-high-school options. Likewise, officials at two Qatar government departments express the view that the predominance of women pursuing higher education is reducing the marriage rate among Qataris.[16]

Each of these seemingly local circumstances, however, readily brings to mind conditions of global significance. While Qatar has a limited water supply, for example, the State of California recently curtailed water consumption by its residents for the first time because a long drought has caused its water in reservoirs to dwindle to a one-year supply.[17] These circumstances, together with the rate of CO_2 emissions by Qatar and the nation's developing capacity to lead the development of green technologies, highlight global challenges posed by climate and the potential in international collaboration to address a global concern.

Similarly, the predominance of women in higher education in Qatar corresponds to a similar phenomenon in the United States, where female enrollment in college has been growing since the 1970s and now between 55 and 60 percent of university students are women. Scholars do not have a settled view of the reason for this phenomenon in the United States, with some citing increasing career opportunities for women and others citing a higher incidence of behavioral problems in young men.[18] On this subject as well, a seemingly local fact in Qatar may have implications for a question of global interest or concern.

The interests and sensibilities of home-grown scholars in the Gulf States will not be far removed from the interests and sensibilities of NU-Q's journalism students as they have undertaken to report on subjects of public interest. For this reason, the evidence reviewed here suggests that the work of Gulf States scholars will draw upon local information but will have worldwide significance.

Fresh Perspectives

An additional subject that appears to have both local importance in the Gulf States and global dimension is the perception that loyalty to tradition and the demands of an advanced education are incompatible. Several commentators note that this perception among some in the Gulf States has posed challenges for the development of higher education.[19] Some Qatari interpretations of tradition do pose impediments to the gathering of facts and analysis by means that are accepted as normal in Western countries. The question remains whether the State's culture as a whole will leave enough room for the gathering of facts and analysis to allow a substantial body of scholarship to develop.

The work of NU-Q journalism students provides reason to believe that sufficient room for productive scholarship exists. The NU-Q student news reports are candid about adverse conditions in Qatar, neither ignoring such conditions nor treating them as insignificant. One report in 2012, for example, highlighted the plight of expatriate housemaids in Qatar who alleged that their employers subjected them to abuse. Students found more than 500 housemaids at a Qatar deportation center who had run away from their employers and a turnover rate at the center of about two months. The students reported that the center provided food and shelter for the housemaids while their reports were investigated, and the students noted other steps the Government was taking to protect vulnerable housemaids. The students, however, also reported views that the Government was not doing enough. In particular, the students noted that few employers were punished for abusing housemaids.[20] Although the students in their pursuit of the facts were unable for several days to gain access to the deportation center, a mother of one of them, a Qatari woman, told the center officials that they should talk to the students, and they did.

Even such a report of local misconduct may highlight an issue of transnational dimensions. A similar subject may be found in a recent *New York Times* series on nail salons in New York City, which reported that many New York manicurists work for unlawfully low wages and endure humiliation, financial abuse and even physical abuse, while salon owners are rarely punished.[21]

In the sample of news reports reviewed here, the reports are sometimes critical of Qatar society, and they sometimes note ways in which efforts of the Qatar government to address adverse circumstances could be improved. The stories, however, predominantly portray traditional Qatar culture as playing a positive role in present-day circumstances. This work is consistent with the expectations of the Qatar government in its endeavor to improve the State's educational system. In its Education and Training Sector Strategy, adopted in 2012, the Qatar Supreme Education Council expressed an intention of developing educational programs that both benefit from best international practices and "enrich and strengthen Qatari national values and Arab and Islamic Culture."[22] Sheikha Moza has articulated a perspective that reconciles Qatar's endeavor to achieve an excellent educational system with the Qataris' deep attachment to tradition.

> Spiritual values are strong in the Arab world and we are proud of our traditions. These values need to be nurtured and safeguarded; embedded within the context of family, these values are at the core of our reforms. Participation in the global knowledge economy is complementary with these values.[23]

Sheikha Moza has addressed the limitations of older forms of Arab education in the context of this perspective. "In general, the education system in Arab countries does not prepare young people for the global job market, as it neither encourages versatility nor enables students to apply a diverse range of abilities across a number of disciplines." For this reason, she said, "We are transforming our education system to better support the development of critical thinking and creative thinking skills." Qatar is seeking to develop citizens "who are able to think and act independently," while they are "seeking to do and decide things for themselves." The perpetuation of traditional Qatar culture, she said, is an essential part of this process. "We also must make sure our young people know the difference between right and wrong, and then trust them to make their own decisions."[24]

The work of NU-Q journalism students displays a capacity to examine adverse circumstances and to apply critical thinking skills to an endeavor to seek explanations and useful ideas for possible remedies. It also displays a respect for the region's cultural tradition. As the body of scholarship produced by graduates of international universities grows, it appears likely that commentators on higher education in the Gulf States will develop a more defined understanding of the relationship between Arab culture and the requirements of scholarship.

The Foundation: Primary and Secondary Education

One explicit goal of the Qatar government is to develop the State's system of higher education into a center for scientific research and development.[25] This goal may be distinguished from the continuing goal of Qatar and other Gulf States to develop a broad competence among their citizens to participate in the global knowledge economy. Science and other scholarly research require an intensive commitment to develop the skills of highly successful individuals to make contributions to emerging fields of knowledge. In Qatar, this is a mission of the recently established Hamad bin Khalifa University at Education City and of the National Qatar Research Fund. The Fund encourages collaborative research projects among scholars of multiple institutions and firms in Qatar and in other countries, expressing the Qatar Foundation's vision of Qatar as a "cosmopolitan nation that embraces scholarly excellence, innovation, creativity, inclusiveness and merit."[26]

Qatar and other Gulf States make significant contributions to scientific research and other fields of advanced scholarship by sponsoring the work of expatriates. Before the people of the region can begin to make significant contributions through the development of home-grown scientists and scholars, however, the Gulf States must address relative weaknesses in their systems of primary and secondary education.

The Gulf States have examined the performance their primary and secondary schools with the same unsparing perspective that NU-Q students have in their development of news reports. The states have sought reliable facts and analysis, participating in international testing and grading that have revealed that Gulf States students perform poorly comparison with students in other countries. In the most recent testing by the Organization for Educational Cooperation and Development (OECD), students in the United Arab Emirates among 76 countries placed 45th in math and science, Bahrain 57th, Saudi Arabia 66th, Qatar 68th and Oman 72nd.[27] Singapore placed first among the countries compared.

In test results from the 2012 OECD Programme for International Student Assessment (PISA), the most recent results available, Qatar's 15-year-olds placed in the lowest 15 per cent in reading among 64 participating countries and the lowest 10 per cent in mathematics and science.[28] UAE students placed in the lowest 10 per cent in reading and the lowest 5 per cent in science.[29] According to test results compiled in 2014 by the Brookings Institution, more than 40 per cent of primary and secondary students in Qatar were unable to demonstrate basic proficiency in literacy and numeracy, more than 35 per cent were unable to demonstrate such proficiency in Saudi Arabia and more than 25 per cent were unable in the UAE.[30]

Qatar is taking steps, sometimes apparently contradictory, to address deficiencies in its primary and secondary education programs. Qatar's financial investments in primary and secondary education placed Qatar second highest in the "quality of educational resources" among the 64 participating countries in the 2012 PISA survey.[31] Moreover, in his 2013 inaugural speech, Qatar's Emir said, "The measure of our success in education and development is not confined to what we invest in these domains, but also in the outputs," noting, "We'll be more tough and clear on the results."[32]

Qatar's public schools in 2012 switched their primary language of instruction from English to Arabic, addressing a factor in low student motivation and reversing a decision in 2001 to switch from Arabic to English in the teaching of math and science.[33] The Supreme Education Council in 2013 prescribed a system of penalties, penalties that barred students from certain exams, to address high rates of absenteeism.[34] The Council in 2015 adopted a more rigorous grading system than it had employed previously, having concluded that the earlier system failed to assess accurately whether a student was being prepared for higher education. Under the new system, about 28 per cent of the students did not pass the exams, while only 15 per cent had failed in 2014. While the Council urged students, teachers and parents to increase their efforts to improve academic performance, some dismayed Qataris were critical of the Council, attributing the scores to the Council's supervision of the public education system.[35] The Council itself, as well as other participants in the public education system, is being held to a higher standard of performance.

The Environment: Academic Freedom

The prospects for success in Qatar's goal of developing home-grown scientists and other scholars cannot be evaluated without consideration of the opportunities Qataris will have to entertain novel ideas and test these ideas through the collection and analysis of facts. As noted above, Sheikha Moza, who played a key role in Qatar's investments in higher education, has espoused the view that "you cannot participate in the global knowledge economy without freedom of thought, freedom of speech and the freedom to challenge conventional thinking."[36] Many who work in higher education, both in Qatar and elsewhere, agree.

There is no question that Qataris who pursue higher education and scholarship face challenges posed by certain characteristics of Qatar society. The Qatar government and the Qatar Foundation have sponsored the teaching of journalism at NU-Q as it is practiced in the United States, and NU-Q students have displayed a capacity to exercise the freedom of thought and expression that American journalists exercise as a matter of course. As NU-Q's journalism students have moved from campus to community in an endeavor to practice the skills they are learning, however, they have encountered a mixed reception.

The most common obstacle the students have found is a reluctance of Qataris to respond to requests for interviews. In the presentation of a 2015 news report at an NU-Q-sponsored public forum, a first-year Qatari student recalled the challenge of securing interviews: "Who can forget the classic, being-declined-an-interview after spending countless hours at a ministry or someone's office?" Upper-class NU-Q students who have returned to Qatar from journalism residency programs abroad have reported being taken off-guard when sources would respond immediately or within hours with information that would take days or weeks—if ever—to secure in Qatar. While NU-Q journalism faculty teach the same skills in Qatar that they teach in the United States, professors have had to adjust expectations about how quickly students can compile information for a satisfactory news report.

Another significant obstacle is uncertainty among Qataris about what is acceptable in their response to a journalism student's activities. When an NU-Q journalism professor sought permission from a local police station commander for students to interview shopkeepers in a poor neighborhood, the commander did not grant permission because he was uncertain that he could or should. A few students have been detained by police who thought the students were engaged in unlawful activity, although they were reporting stories that would be standard in the United States. One student reported being granted permission by one policeman to enter the site of a newsworthy event to take photographs and being detained afterwards at the site by a second policeman who thought the student's activity was unlawful. These circumstances bring to mind questions posed by a BBC News reporter arrested by Qatar police in May, 2015, while reporting on his own about the working and living conditions of migrant laborers. After two days in jail, he was allowed to join a press trip organized by the Qatar government to address the same subject. He asked, "Is it a case of the left arm not knowing what the right arm is doing, or is it an internal struggle for control between modernizers and conservatives?"[37]

Qatar has adopted a constitution that guarantees freedom of the press and freedom of expression "in accordance with the law," but Qatar law, without qualification, prohibits publication of that "all that may undermine the reputation of a person," and it forbids the publication of facts about trials "unless the competent court permits their publication."[38] While reports of court proceedings and reports of criticized public figures are standard material in Western media, these are largely if not entirely absent from Qatar English print media. In these and other ways, the content of Qatar English newspapers is conspicuously more circumscribed than the content of US newspapers. A media research study by NU-Q in 2015 found, however, that Qataris give their news media favorable scores. Most (58 percent) say that the news media in Qatar are credible, and most (65 percent) believe the mass media generally "report the news fully, accurately and fairly."[39] The absence of criticism of local public figures or of reports about criminal proceedings does not appear to leave most Qataris with a sense of being deprived.

The disparity of perception between a Western media consumer and Qataris themselves may lie, at least in part, in a difference in cultural sensibilities. A significant majority of Qataris (75 percent) describe themselves as "culturally conservative."[40] Qataris may have an aversion to public criticism in circumstances in which it might be considered acceptable or even meritorious in US or European societies. An NU-Q journalism student made an illuminating comment in a discussion about a reluctance of Qatar police to arrest drivers for traffic violations, commenting that a roadside arrest would be troublesome in part because it would be embarrassing, not only to the individual and the individual's family but also to the individual's tribe. The comment suggested that some of the disparity between Qatar media and US media may derive from a difference in what the two societies consider acceptable public discourse. The difficulty of defining such sensibilities may explain certain terms of Qatar's 2014 cybercrime law, which imposes criminal penalties for one who, through use of the Internet, "violates social values."[41]

A significant disparity in the degrees of press freedom allowed by Qatar and the United States, however, does not answer the question whether Qataris will have the academic freedom necessary to make significant contributions to science and other advanced scholarship. While Qatar forbids the publication of defamatory information, NU-Q's 2015 media study found that most Qataris (60 percent) say it is acceptable for people to express unpopular ideas on the Internet, and most (57 percent) say they believe in freedom to criticize powerful institutions on the Internet.[42] These statements suggest that Qataris are more receptive to debate and critical thinking than the content of Qatar's English newspapers would suggest. It may be that the ways in which freedom of expression is circumscribed in Qatar will not significantly impair the work of its future scientists and scholars. Whether the challenges posed by conditions in Qatar society will amount to a significant impairment to Qatari scholarship remains to be seen.

The outcome will depend in part on whether Qatar society as a whole is receptive to the government's endeavors to secure the benefits of higher education for Qatar's citizens and whether those efforts prove to be productive. The early results in both respects are promising. Early resistance to female education in Qatar, for example, did not halt this development,[43] and female education now is having profound effects on Qatar society. In a study of informal gatherings (*majalis al-harim*) of Qatari women, NU-Q students discovered that, while Qatari women in times past discussed diet and children, a typical subject today is how to start a business.[44] NU-Q journalism students have reported that the experience of being detained by Qatar police has taught them the value of carrying Northwestern identification and has, on the whole, been confidence building. They report that Qataris appear to be increasingly comfortable with their activities, as NU-Q has acquired a wider reputation for serious and credible work.[45]

Realization of the promises of Qatari higher education will depend in significant part on general acceptance by Qataris of a perspective expressed by Sara Al-Saadi, a Qatari graduate of NU-Q. In a TEDx Talk about the development of a documentary about a Qatar primary school, one that revealed a poor learning environment, Al-Saadi reported that the father of a boy who appeared in the video objected to the documentary, saying it was "very unpatriotic." Al-Saadi said, "We didn't think we were portraying the culture negatively," but rather she and her classmates intended to shed light "on issues that we face in this society but are not discussed publicly." She said, "If we see issues facing our society and we do nothing about them . . . this is what harms our society more than anything else."[46] This perspective, one that sees loyalty to the community in the illumination of issues facing the community, is one that leaves ample room for academic freedom. This perspective may be found not only in the documentary created by Sara and her classmates,[47] but in the work of other NU-Q graduates, such as a documentary on Qatar's limited food supplies[48] and a documentary about the aftermath of a deadly fire at Doha's Villagio shopping mall in 2012.[49]

The willingness to collect and publish facts and analysis, irrespective of concern for reputation, is essential to academic freedom and to the potential for higher education to confer benefits on the society that supports it. This freedom will be essential to the development of scientists and other scholars in the Gulf States who can make notable contributions to the global community of scholars.

Conclusion

In a review of Gulf States education, Gawdat Bahgat, then Director of the Center for Middle Eastern Studies at Indiana University of Pennsylvania, noted that the impressive economic achievements of the Gulf States had not been accompanied by any substantial change in the states' culture and values. He wrote, "The mentality and attitudes of Gulf citizens seem to have changed very little."[50] It is too early to determine whether the predominant culture of the Gulf States will permit the development of a vigorous community of scientists and other scholars, providing a basis for the lasting and independent economic prosperity in the region and contributing significantly to advances in knowledge throughout the world. The early signs, however, provide reason to be optimistic.

The work of students reviewed here reveals a capacity to develop excellent reports of fact and analysis, notwithstanding some constraints, while maintaining a genuine respect for the society's government and culture. If that capacity is manifested in the work of Gulf States scientists and scholars, this work will likely produce the benefits that the Gulf States seek through their investments in higher education and a body of scholarship that, while drawing on local circumstances, will make significant contributions to global development. If any change in the predominant culture is necessary to make way for this development, the early benefits of higher education should facilitate the change.

A final comment made by Sara Al-Saadi in her TEDx talk provides further reason to be optimistic. If the Gulf States succeed in becoming significant participants in the global knowledge economy, it will be because the young people of the region acquire the skills of critical thinking and problem solving necessary to make significant contributions to science and scholarship. As the young people of the region increasingly acquire these skills and apply them to the challenges that are distinctive to the region, they will create and tell stories of their own culture. The work of NU-Q's journalism students provides evidence not only that these young people have the capacity to acquire these skills, but also that they have a great enthusiasm for using them. "We live in a culture that is rich with very interesting stories," Al-Saadi said, "And for us to tell these stories, for us to share these stories . . . we show who we really are. We may break the stereotypes that people have of us, just simply through our stories."[51] That enthusiasm, grounded in Arab perspectives, can be a significant driver in the Gulf States' pursuit of the knowledge-based economy.

Appendix I

Authorities Table

1a) Qatar Government

Qatar Statistics Authority (2 citations)
Qatar Supreme Education Council (2 citations)
Qatar Supreme Council of Health

Qatar National Development Strategy 2011-16
Qatar Annual Health Report
Qatar Ministry of Development Planning and Statistics
Qatar Supreme Judiciary Council
Qatar Advisory Council

1b) Qatar Government representatives

HRH Sheikha Al Mayassa bint Hamad Al Thani, founder and chairperson of Qatar Museums Authority
Supreme Education Council leadership trainer
Supreme Education Council Visual Arts Education director
Ministry of Municipality and Urban Planning head
Supreme Council of Health oral health consultant
Qatar Search and Follow-Up Department official
Qatar Immigration Department official
Qatar Overseas Workers Welfare Administration official
Qatar Ministry of Environment official
Qatar Council for Healthcare Practitioners acting manager
Supreme Education Council department of independent schools official
Qatar Internal Security Force explosives team sergeant

2) Qatar Government-related entities

Kahramaa (Qatar's electricity transmission and distribution company)

2b) Qatar Government-related entity representatives

Kahramaa Conservation and Energy Efficiency Department manager
Kahramaa health, safety and environment department head and senior water quality specialist
Qatar Electricity and Water Company environmental specialist
Qatar Foundation Sustainability & Environmental Management head
Qatar Foundation senior environmental specialist
Hamad Medical Center senior consultant of organ transplantation
Hamad General Hospital transplant coordinator
Hamad General Hospital emergency room doctor
Hamad General Hospital occupational therapist
Domestic Solid Waste Management Center director/plant manager
Primary Health Care Corporation Oral Health Division Manager
Qatar General Cleaning Project public health researcher
Qatar Nanny Training Academy academic manager
Academic Bridge Program assistant director of academic affairs

Mosaab Bin Omair Secondary Independent School for Boys academic vice principal
Al Arqam Secondary School assistant principal

3) Private school representatives

Qatar Academy assistant principal
International School of Choueifat nurse
Newton International School, former deputy head

4a) Private enterprises

Doha News

4b) Private enterprise representatives

Shell in Qatar social investment advisor
Conoco Phillips's Qatar water sustainability center managing director
Jassim Manpower Agency executive director
Doha Plastic executive manager
Qatar Airways duty manager
KLM airlines customer service officer
Fox taxi transport manager
Dr. Sarah's Dental Centres oral surgeon
Veterinary clinic general manager
Construction industry officials
Qatari family therapist

5a) Qatar charitable organizations

Qatar Foundation for Combatting Human Trafficking
Qatar Diabetes Association

5b) Qatar charitable organization representatives

Qatar Dental Society president
Sustainable Qatar president
Education city student-sponsored organ donor public awareness campaign
Fourth-year medical student, Weill Cornell Medicine-Qatar
Third-year medical student, Weill Cornell Medicine-Qatar
Sophomore, Northwestern University in Qatar
First-Year Student, Northwestern University School of Communications
Qatar National Dressage Team founder:
Qatar National Dressage Team coach
Qatar Olympic Committee project developer

6a) Academic institutions in Qatar

Qatar University and its Social and Economic Survey Research Institute (2) Weill Cornell Medical College in Qatar

6b) Representatives of academic institutions in Qatar

Qatar University dean of the College of Business and Economics
Texas A&M University at Qatar chemical engineering professor
Georgetown School of Foreign Service in Qatar professor
Weill Cornell Medicine-Qatar biology professor specializing in ecology and the environment
Weill Cornell Medicine-Qatar professor of surgery
Weill Cornell Medicine-Qatar professor of psychiatry
Carnegie Mellon University in Qatar assistant professor of English and Sociolinguistics
Carnegie Mellon University in Qatar lecturer
Northwestern University in Qatar visiting lecturer
Georgetown University School of Foreign Service in Qatar post-doctoral fellow of Middle Eastern studies and environmental researcher
University College London in Qatar anthropologist
Virginia Commonwealth University in Qatar admissions manager
Qatar University College of Education professional development specialist

7a) International or foreign organizations

World Health Organization (citativar)
World Bank
Columbia University
Amnesty International
The Independent, London
Construction Week Online

7b) International or foreign organization representatives

UN Climate Change Conference, Conference of Parties, Sustainability and Public Engagement Lead
US Occupational Safety and Health Administration certified environmental trainer

8) Religion scholars
Renowned Qatar-based Muslim scholar
Qatar Faculty of Islamic Studies professor
Qatar Islamic Cultural Center preacher and educator
Shiite cleric

9) Individuals relating personal, illustrative anecdotes

      Total: 37

Appendix II

Central Ideas in Student News Reports

1. Maid Abuse. Many housemaids in Qatar are subjected to abuse by their employers, and the Qatar government should do more to protect them
2. Public Transportation. Public transportation services in Doha are inadequate
3. High School. Qatar high schools are insufficiently preparing graduates for college; the Qatar government is working on the problem, but fixing it will take a long time
4. Work Hard. More should be done to alleviate the hardships faced by Qatar's migrant workers
5. Women Students. A predominance of women among university students in Qatar is having both positive and negative effects on Qatari society
6. Going Green. While Qatar has significant environmental issues, there is little public interest in environmental conservation, and the Government is doing little to encourage conservation
7. Water Woes. Although Qatar relies almost entirely on desalinization for drinkable water and has only a two-day water supply, Qataris use water at a high rate, and the Qatar government has taken few steps to encourage water conservation
8. Organ Donation. While Qatar has a substantial need for organ donors and the Government is taking steps to facilitate organ donation, organ donation is not popular and Education City students have undertaken a campaign to increase public awareness and acceptance
9. Health Facilities. Qatar's health care facilities have not kept pace with the growth of Qatar's population, and there is no quick solution available
10. Invisible Community. Qatar has a small Shiite population, and the Qatari Shias keep themselves largely invisible to the general population
11. Tooth Decay. Qatari children have a relatively high incidence of tooth decay as a result of a lack of public awareness of dental health issues, and the Qatar government has launched public awareness campaigns in schools
12. Female Equestrians. Qataris have established a women's national dressage team, and, although some Qataris disapprove of the activity on cultural grounds, the team members see broad support among Qataris for their participation in the sport
13. Waste Management. Qatar residents produce relatively large quantities of waste material; the Qatar government has established a waste processing facility, and it has initiated a public awareness campaign in the schools that emphasizes the society's traditional values

14. <u>Falcon Passports</u>. Qatar issues passports for falcons to celebrate the importance of falcons to traditional Arab culture

15. <u>Alternative Medicine</u>. Conventional and alternative medicine (CAM) is popular among many Qataris, and the Qatar government is considering licensing to ensure safe practice

16. <u>Art Education</u>. The founder and chairperson of the Qatar Museums Authority and other Qataris are seeking to reverse a decision of the Supreme Education Council to eliminate arts education in public schools

17. <u>Nanny Training</u>. In its endeavor to perpetuate Qatari culture, Qatar has established a Qatar Nanny Training Academy

18. <u>High School Absence</u>. Because absenteeism among Qatar high school students is high, with many students poorly motivated and with few adverse consequences for absences, the Supreme Education Council has adopted a system of penalties for absences

Notes

1   Dale F. Eickelman, "The Art of Memory: Islamic Education and Its Social Reproduction," *Comparative Studies in Society and History* 20 (1978), 483-516.

2   Sheikh Tamim bin Hamad al Thani, "Striving for Excellence," Oxford Business Group, *The Report Qatar 2014* (2014) 20, accessed June 29, 2016: http://tinyurl.com/j4yxesh

3   Qatar Supreme Education Council, "Education and Training Sector Strategy, Executive Summary" (2012) 6, 8, 20: http://tinyurl.com/gr24y5s

4   Sheikha Abdulla Al-Misnad, "The Dearth of Qatari Men in Higher Education: Reasons and Implications," Middle East Institute (2012), http://www.mei.edu/content/dearth-qatari-men-higher-education-reasons-and-implications; Lesley Walker, "Qatar University Undergoes Massive Expansion," *DohaNews.com*, May 8, 2014: http://tinyurl.com/p4d54pm

5   Al-Misnad, "The Dearth of Qatari Men in Higher Education."

6   The universities and their course offerings are identified elsewhere in the GCC Higher Education Workshop papers, and they may be reviewed at Qatar Foundation, "Enroll," accessed June 29, 2016: http://www.qf.org.qa/enroll

7   The HBKU colleges include a law school that is associated with Northwestern University. Hamad bin Khalifa University, "About HBKU," accessed June 29, 2016: http://tinyurl.com/zeo4u7z

8   Oxford Business Group, "Interview with Sheikha Moza bint Nasser" *The Report, Qatar 2011* (2011) 26, accessed June 29, 2016: http://tinyurl.com/gl3ctek. The interest in training Arab journalists in western journalism skills is not unique to Qatar. Organizations in the Middle East have sponsored training in western journalism skills for more than ten years, and the interest remains high. See Gordon R. Robinson, "Tasting Western Journalism: Media Training in the Middle East," *Middle East Media Project* (USC Center on Public Diplomacy May, 2005), 1-8, http://tinyurl.com/jzk7m4p; Najiba Kasraee, "BBC Academy's Arabic website is 'number-one training site in Middle East," *BBC Academy*, December 16, 2014: http://tinyurl.com/gtq6zz2

9   In their endeavor to be accurate, journalists must seek to avoid error in several distinct stages of the information reporting process: gathering, processing and dissemination. See discussion at Everette E. Dennis and Melvin L. DeFleur, *Understanding Media in the Digital Age* (Allyn & Bacon, 2010), 203-07.

10   Northwestern University in Qatar, "Doha Stories, NU-Q Journalism Students Report," accessed May 2015, www.dohastories.org. While the 2012 news reports may be examined easily at this website, the 2015 reports are protected by a password. This password may be obtained for academic research

by contacting the author at m-dedinsky@northwestern.edu. The 2015 content is password-protected because there was too little time before posting for final editing.

11 Tim Harrower, *Inside Reporting*, 2d ed. (McGraw-Hill, 2009), 34.

12 Rouda Al-Attiyah, Manar Al-Jamal and Awad Al-Radi, "Artless in Doha," in "Doha Stories, NU-Q Journalism Students Report," posted April 20, 2015.

13 Ghalya Al Thani, Nayla Al-Naim and Nicholas Wong, "Throwing it All Away," in "Doha Stories, NU-Q Journalism Students Report," posted April 21, 2015.

14 Fatima Al-Saai, Noor Jassmi and Mohamed El-Edrisi, "SHEquestrian," in "Doha Stories, NU-Q Journalism Students Report," posted April 22, 2015.

15 According to the World Bank, Qatar in 2013 had a gross domestic product per capita at purchasing power parity of about $136,727 (~ £87,970), more than 2.5 times that of the US, and more than 3.5 times that of the UK. The World Bank, "Data, GDP Per Capita (PPP; Current International $)," accessed June 29, 2016: http://tinyurl.com/lyg5m72

16 In "The Dearth of Qatari Men in Higher Education: Reasons and Implications," Sheikha Abdulla Al-Misnad, the President of Qatar University, noted the availability of attractive options for male Qataris after high school as a reason for the predominance of women among Qatar university students and the impact of this predominance on the initiation and stability of Qatari marriages. Al-Misnad, "The Dearth of Qatari Men in Higher Education."

17 Timothy Eagan, "The End of California?" *The New York Times*, Sunday Review, May 1, 2015: http://tinyurl.com/k3z3m39

18 Daniel Borzellica, "The Male-Female Ratio in College," *Forbes*, February 16, 2012: http://tinyurl.com/8xb5uow; Mark Hugo Lopez & Ana Gonzalez –Barrera, "Women's College Enrollment Gains Leave Men Behind," Pew Research Center FactTank, *News in the Numbers*, March 6, 2014: http://tinyurl.com/m5y9ba8

19 Gawdat Bahgat, "Education in the Gulf Monarchies: Retrospect and Prospect," *International Review of Education* 45 (1999), 130; Daniel Kirk and Diane Napier, "The Transformation of Higher Education in the United Arab Emirates: Issues, Implications, and Intercultural Dimensions," in *Nationbuilding, Identity and Citizenship Education*, ed. Joseph Zajda, Holger Daun, and Lawrence J. Saha (Springer 2009), 134; Christopher Ohan, "An Incompatible Method: the Western Liberal Arts Education Model in Kuwait and the Arab Gulf Region," *Journal of Educational and Social Research*, 2 (2012), 43-52; Sally Findlow, "International Networking in the United Arab Emirates Higher Education System: Global–Local Tensions," *A Journal of Comparative Education*, 35 (2005), 297.

20 Abir Bouguerra, Angel Polacco and Sara Al-Darwish, "Maid Abuse in Qatar: A Growing Problem," in "Doha Stories, NU-Q Journalism Students Report," posted April 24, 2012.

21 Sarah Maslin Nir, "The Price of Nice Nails, Manicurists are routinely underpaid and exploited, and endure ethnic bias and other abuse, the New York Times has found," *The New York Times*, May 7, 2015: http://tinyurl.com/p32doud

22 "Education and Training Sector Strategy, Executive Summary," 13.

23 Oxford Business Group, "Interview with Sheikha Moza bint Nasser."

24 Ibid.

25 "Education and Training Sector Strategy, Executive Summary," 25.

26 "About HBKU;" Sheikh Hamad bin Khalifa Al Thani, "A Solid Core," Oxford Business Group, *The Report, Qatar 2011*, 25; Qatar National Research Fund, "Vision & Mission, accessed June 29, 2016: http://tinyurl.com/zt7jvgr

27 Eric A. Hanushek and Ludger Woessmann, "Universal Basic Skills: What Countries Stand to Gain," OECD Publishing, 36-37: http://tinyurl.com/jfq2xmv; Lesley Walker, "Report: Qatar Ranks in Bottom 10 of Education Index, but shows potential," *DohaNews.com*, May 14, 2015: http://tinyurl.com/gpn4jm6

28 Organization for Educational Cooperation and Development (OECD), "Programme for International Student Assessment (PISA), 2012 Tests, Qatar," *Education GPS*, accessed June 29, 2016: http://tinyurl.com/zvw7nme

29 "PISA 2012 Tests, United Arab Emirates," accessed June 29, 2016: http://tinyurl.com/zylbxs4

30 Liesbet Steer, Hafez Ghanem and Maysa Jalbout, "Arab Youth: Missing Educational Foundations for a Productive Life?" *Brookings Center for Universal Education*, February, 2014, Table 1, 8: http://tinyurl.com/ztys9q4

31 "PISA 2012 Tests, Qatar."

32 Sheikh Tamim bin Hamad Al Thani, "Inaugural Speech" (unofficial translation), *Qatar News Agency*, Local News, Politics, June 26, 2013.

33 Shabina S. Khatri, "Qatar's Education System Grapples with Language Challenges," *DohaNews.com*, October 26, 2013: http://tinyurl.com/glfty3u; Maha Ellili-Cherif and Haitham Alkhateeb, "College Students' Attitude Toward the Medium of Instruction: Arabic versus English Dilemma," *Universal Journal of Educational Research* 3 (2015), 207.

34 Lesley Walker, "Qatar Education Council to tackle rising student absenteeism problem," *DohaNews.com*, September 5, 2014: http://tinyurl.com/jyyd5mm

35 Heba Fahmy, "SEC tries to quell anger among Qatar parents, students over exam scores," *DohaNews.com*, July 5, 2015: http://tinyurl.com/zruqz3p

36 Oxford Business Group, "Interview with Sheikha Moza bint Nasser."

37 Mark Lobell, "Arrested for Reporting on Qatar's World Cup Labourers," *BBC News*, May 18, 2015: http://tinyurl.com/zpo9uw9

38 *Constitution of Qatar* (English translation), Articles 47 and 48, accessed June 29, 2016: http://tinyurl.com/k27pqqa; *Law No. 8 of 1979 on Prints and Publications* (unofficial translation provided by the Doha Centre for Media Freedom for reference only), accessed June 29, 2016: http://tinyurl.com/zgmta2z

39 Everette E. Dennis, Justin D. Martin & Robb Wood, "Media Use in the Middle East 2015: a Six-Nation Survey," Mideastmedia.org (2015), accessed June 29, 2016: http://tinyurl.com/gu7lek7

40 "Media Use in the Middle East 2015," 59.

41 Cybercrime Prevention Law, Law No. 14 of 2014: http://tinyurl.com/hol5nz7

42 "Media Use in the Middle East 2015," 62.

43 Al-Misnad, "The Dearth of Qatari Men in Higher Education."

44 Sama Abduljawad and AlReem Al-Maroei, "Qatari Women: Engagement and Empowerment," *NU-Q in Evanston, the Northwestern Experience in Qatar, Creativity and Innovation, a Student Showcase*, May 13, 2015.

45 Response to audience questions, *NU-Q Student Showcase*, May 13, 2015.

46 Sara Al-Saadi, "Tell the story: Sara Al-Saadi at TEDxEducationCity," TEDx Talks.ted.com, February 1, 2014: https://www.youtube.com/watch?v=EAx2iP4bgmM

47 Sara Al-Saadi, Latifah Al-Darwish & Maaria Assami, "Bader," baderfilm.com, accessed June 29, 2016: https://bader.vhx.tv/watch

48 Maha Al-Ansari and Ardinny Razania, "Food Safety: Qatar is Playing a Risky Game," qatarvironment.org, accessed June 29, 2016: http://tinyurl.com/zl5zywk

49 Rinalda Raviraj and Zena Al Tahnan, "The Villagio Fire Aftermath: What Has Changed?" qatarunderconstruction.org, accessed June 29, 2016, http://tinyurl.com/z4jxfo3

50 Gawdat Bahgat. "Education in the Gulf Monarchies," 129.

51 "Tell the story: Sara Al-Saadi at TEDxEducationCity."

6

Education as Public Diplomacy:
The Soft Power Potential of Qatar Higher Education

Alieu Manjang

This chapter assesses the extent to which Qatar's extensive investment in international students facilitates projecting the country's "soft power." The positive effects of education on the public realm of employment patterns, economic development and the private sphere of marriage and childbearing are unquestionable.[1] Education has also emerged as an effective tool for countries to project their influence globally, promoting their reputation and social, cultural and political values. The result is that education, especially higher education, is not only an avenue for the transmission of knowledge and the development of critical thinking, but also a form of public diplomacy.[2] The recruitment of international students, student exchanges, and academic visits in the field of higher education all have implications for projecting soft power.[3]

Some countries are more explicit than others in using higher education as a form of soft power, shaping the hearts and minds of foreign students. For example, the United States, the United Kingdom and Canada—all prominent in the field of international education—invest foreign aid and private resources to attract and recruit foreign students to enhance their soft power.[4]

Qatar has also joined other developed countries in reaching out internationally through its education institutions. It has heavily invested in the knowledge industry by establishing Education City, with branch campuses of major universities from the United States, Canada, Great Britain, and France. Through Education City, Qatar increased its international educational engagement by inviting prominent academic scholars to its various universities, recruiting and sponsoring foreign students, and engaging in student exchange programs. Similarly, Qatar University, the country's state university, has expanded significantly by admitting and supporting international students to its various programs and colleges.

Despite the mass investment in higher education, however, it is not clear that Qatar is effectively using higher education as a form of public diplomacy. At the official level, Qatar educational officials dismiss categorizing their generous spending on education as a form of soft power. In this regard Sheikha Moza, speaking in Doha at the annual WISE education summit, rejects this connection: "I never thought about it like that. People always think that you should link your foreign aid with your national interests. Does it need to be always like this? I don't see it this way. I see it as a global responsibility towards others."[5]

Not with standing this official denial, most observers accept that Qatar's educational largesse is a form of soft power that seeks to exert international influence through culture and learning.[6]

Soft Power and Education: Public Diplomacy

Joseph Nye coined the term "soft power" in the late 1980s.[7] It is the ability to get a desired outcome through the means of attraction rather than coercion or payment, or getting others to want the outcome that you want. Thus, soft power resides in the ability to frame the preferences of others according to one's own without the means of force; and it is different from hard power, the ability to obtain an outcome through command or coercion.[8]

National sources of soft power are varied, and it includes countries' cultural and political values.[9] The transmission of these values to other countries is known as public diplomacy, the promotion of a country's soft power to win the hearts and minds and hearts of people in other countries. In the nineteenth and twentieth centuries, many countries established special offices to project their culture abroad. In 1883, France created the Alliance Française to promote its language and literature, and the Alliance remains a significant component of French diplomacy to this day. Similarly after World War One, governments established offices to propagate their cause to other countries. The United States, for example, established a Committee on Public Information, tasked with producing propaganda messages that portrayed America in a positive light.

The advent of radio in the 1920s permitted many governments to engage in public diplomacy through foreign broadcasting, promoting favorable images about their countries to foreign publics. This was escalated by the late 1930s with the eruption of World War Two when the Voice of America (VOA) and the British Broadcasting Corporation (BBC) devoted some of their airtimes to carry propaganda for their respective countries by targeting foreign audiences with favorite image of the U.S and the U.K.[10] In the same context, Japan relied upon short wave transmitters to broadcast anti-European propaganda to Southeast Asia even before the war. The Japanese fear of counterpropaganda propelled it to limit receivers to bandwidths used by the Japanese government itself.[11] Similarly, before and during the Word War Two, the Nazis exploited radio to deliver its message to both occupied territories and enemy states.[12]

In the context of Arab World, the 1950s witnessed the pervasive use of radio as a propaganda tool. One of the first and most prominent transmitters was Egypt's Voice of the Arabs, used by former Egyptian President Gamal Abdel Nasser, to spread his messages on Arab unity and revolutions across the Arab world.[13] In addition to radio, films, magazines, and newspapers also contributed to public diplomacy.

International Education as Tool for Public Diplomacy

Education is closely linked to the interests of the nation state.[14] Recent initiatives to engage with the global public in the pursuit of foreign policy interests reveal the interplay between internationalization of education and public diplomacy. The internationalization of education entails attempts of academic intuitions to cope with global academic environment through policies and practices in order to enhance knowledge acquisition and curriculum, and sometimes to enhance revenue flow to the home institution. The policies and practices of internationalization include opening branch campuses abroad, cross-border cooperative arrangements, recruitment of foreign students, student exchange programs and establishing language medium programs.[15]

There are many reasons that universities participate in international projects. One driver is financial gain. Many universities enter into the international market to reap material benefits for establishing new institutions and partnering with universities in other countries. The same quest for revenue drives some countries and universities to recruit international students by charging them tuition fees which contribute to the economic growth of the host institution.[16] Conversely, many other universities and countries enter the field to enhance knowledge and research capability through branch campuses, franchised degree programs, and partnership with local institutions in middle-income countries.[17]

While profit-making and enhancing knowledge and research are significant drivers for the internationalization of higher education, other countries seek to adopt international education as public diplomacy to shape the hearts and minds of international students and to untimely reinforce their soft power. This has become a trend among many countries in the western world, Asia, and the Middle East.

Soft Power as a Motive for Recruiting Foreign Students

Soft power drives many countries in the South and North to recruit foreign students into their universities. It has become a central norm that guides different countries to attract thousands of students to their countries. For instance, the United States annually hosts thousands of foreign students under international education programs. This includes students who come through student visits or academics who come to teach, lecture, do research, and gain work experience in the U.S. There are hundreds of organizations in United States that sponsor or participate in exchange programs of different types. For example, communities, clubs, foundations, corporations, schools, and individuals, as well as the federal government, support foreign student exchange programs. However, the main private agency in the field of international education, the Institute of International Education, is the relevant body that United States relies upon in administering exchange programs between the United States and 74 countries.[18] This organization carries out exchanges under several programs for the Department of State. These include exchanges under the Fulbright and Smith-Mundt Acts, as well as special German-Austrian programs. These programs allow foreign students who come to the United States to attend college; they also permit specialists to come to the United States for advanced training or research; they give university professors opportunities to come to lecture at U.S. universities; as they allow civic and political leaders who come to U.S as individuals or as teams to experience life in the U.S.[19]

While the major objective of these programs may be the transmission of specific skills and techniques to help other countries to alleviate economic conditions at home and elevate the cultural and material levels of life around the world, the Department of State, as the body that regulates the United States' relations with other governments, views the programs as an instrument for increasing understanding, respect, and friendship toward the United States and Americans, as well as a means of supporting democracy abroad, strengthening ties with allies, and securing cooperation for U.S. policy.[20]

Like the U.S., the United Kingdom also maintains longstanding traditions of international education. Annually thousands of foreign students made their way to the U.K. for studying in its universities under various scholarship schemes supported by the government of the U.K. through the Foreign and Commonwealth Office. These scholarships include Commonwealth Scholarships and Chevening Scholarships, which offer awards to outstanding scholars with leadership potential from around the world to study postgraduate courses at U.K. universities. Policymakers have alluded to the importance of these projects as part of the U.K.'s efforts to reinforce its soft power. In 2014, the House of Lord's Committee on U.K. soft power and influence urged the government to double efforts in repositioning education as soft power.[21]

Likewise, Asian countries place significant value on international education. For instance, China offers scholarship programs like the Chinese Government Scholarship-Bilateral Program for International Students to utilize the advantages of the education of international students studying in China to promote it cultural soft power. The Chinese government considers the education of international students in China as a tool to enhance the international influence of China's cultural soft power and Chinese culture. Similarly, Japan, South Korea, and India also use the internationalization of higher education as an instrument to promote their values and cultures to foreign students who come to study in these countries under different types of scholarships and exchange programs.[22]

In the Middle East, countries pursue public diplomacy for soft power purposes through educational institutions. In recent years, Turkey has been expanding educational opportunities to shape Turkish values and extend them beyond Turkey's borders. Turkish educational institutions have engaged in recruiting foreign students through scholarship schemes to tell the story of the new Turkey to a wide-ranging global audience. Thus, Turkey has turned education into a strategic asset for soft power.[23]

International Education in Qatar

The discovery of oil and the subsequent rise in oil revenues facilitated the creation of modern public education systems in the Arabian Gulf and the internationalization of higher education in this region. The Gulf countries have used their economic clout to engage with the world through education. In this regard, several major American and European universities have either opened branch campuses or forged other forms of partnerships and associations with universities in the Gulf States.[24] Qatar is central to this process.

In Qatar as elsewhere in the region, opportunities for formal education were few before the discovery of the oil. In pre-oil Qatari society, the provision of education was confined to *kuttab*, an informal class taught in a mosque or home by a literate man or woman knowledgeable about Islam, where some parents enrolled their children to memorize passages from the Qur'an and learn to read and write. However, with the discovery of oil and the subsequent establishment of Qatar's Ministry of Education in 1956, education was modernized and provided for free to boys and girls alike.[25]

Since then, Qatar expanded its education system with the establishment of its national university in 1973, which started out as a College of Education enrolling both men and women. The establishment of Qatar University set a stage for a revolution in the quality and quantity of higher education offerings in Qatar. The leadership of Sheikh Hamad Bin Khalifa Al-Thani (r. 1995-2013), was a decisive moment in the expansion of higher education in Qatar. Through the efforts of his enthusiastic wife, Sheikha Moza Bint Nasser, Qatar expanded the post-secondary offerings available for Qataris and indeed for the people in Middle East and beyond. This was demonstrated in the establishment of Education City in 1995, a consortium of foreign universities, where the fields of study available include journalism, computer science, business administration, information systems, design, international relations, medicine, and engineering.[26]

The establishment of Education City was followed by an education reform known as Education for a New Era, initiated in 2002 to address issues related to the management and delivery of educational services, the curriculum, the quality of teachers, and the availability of resources. This reform culminated in the establishment of specialized institutes under the Supreme Council of Education (SCE) such as the Higher Education Institute and the Education Institute. Part of this education reform was also the creation of a community college, which is seen as preparatory stage for Qatar's students to move to university. Additionally, in 2003, the emir mandated major reforms at Qatar University (QU). The reform at Qatar University articulated both a new vision and a new mission— and to develop a plan for realizing them.[27]

The creation of the education city and the massive education reform that transformed Qatar University in terms of curriculum and program, represented Qatar's move towards internationalization of its higher education. Over years, this has become an integral part of Qatar's public diplomacy, and it is widely linked to Qatar's efforts to be attractive to international audiences. The internationalization of Qatar education is, therefore, tailored to overall Qatar's foreign policy objective in the last few years. Starting with the Al-Jazeera news network, Qatar is on a mission to gain a stronger profile on the international scene and to increase its public diplomacy.[28] Thus, Qatar is using education, along with Al Jazeera, not only as an influential competitive gain, but also as a way to gain global attention.

For instance, the World Innovation Summit for Education (WISE), considered as equivalent to Davos for the field of education, was first held in December 2010 in Doha as part of Qatar public diplomacy to draw international attention to Qatar.[29]

The concurrent expansion of education in Education City and Qatar University represented the next step in Qatar's internationalization of higher education. The expansion in Qatar University in the past few years resulted in a rapid increase in the number of academics and other university-related staff in Qatar University. It has also helped the University to attract students from the region and has kept the children of expatriates from seeking higher education elsewhere. Thus, Qatar University has become a preferred international destination; and the University is marketing itself as a higher educational hub in the region. This has resulted in the improvement of the university's international student exchange programs.[30] Similarly, the International Student Department supports the growth, progress, and success of international students at Qatar University.[31] These students are recruited in Qatar University, along with the children of expatriates, through relatively inexpensive tuition fees and the wide range of scholarships and financial aid which include: Academic Scholarships for the Undergraduate level, Short-Term Scholarships for the Arabic Program for non-native Speakers, Scholarships for the Islamic world and other countries, Children of Qatar University Employees Scholarships, Inhabitants of Qatar Scholarships, H.H. the Emir of Qatar's Scholarships for Academic Excellence, Scholarships for GCC students and Scholarship for holders of the Qatari High School Certificate.[32]

While Qatar's relative lack of financial constraints and the availability of state revenues facilitated the recruitment of foreign students and the children of expatriates in its university, recruiting foreign students—as part of international education—falls into the overall public diplomacy framework spearheaded by the state.

Theoretical Framework and Research Method

Despite the evidence of growth of Qatar public diplomacy, a significant question remains: To what extent does the recruitment of foreign students contribute to reinforcing Qatar's soft power? There is no research—to the best knowledge of the author—that evaluates whether Qatar's reaching out to world through education is successful.

To this end, this chapter is guided by Nye's[33] perspectives on how a country can increase its soft power potential through recruiting foreign students to its universities. According to Nye, recruiting foreign students allows them to be drawn to the cultures of the host country. Thus, students supposedly return home with a greater appreciation of the host countries' cultural values constitutes a remarkable reservoir for the host country, especially when these students wind up in positions where they can affect policy outcomes.

However, the effectiveness of recruiting foreign students for soft power purposes depends on three contextual conditions which are essential for this positive outcome to occur for hosting foreign students: First, it depends on the depth and extent of social contact and interactions with the host community which allows the students to be drawn to the culture of the host country. Second is the students' sense of belonging to the host community, and the extent to which they have similar identity with the host community. Third, a positive outcome depends on the possibility that students return to their countries and attain influential positions after returning home.

To apply Nye's perspective in the case of Qatar, this study used non-probability sampling to select the study population—international students[34] at Qatar University. The sample included students from the M.A in Gulf Studies Program, the Department of International Affairs, the Department of Islamic Studies, Department of Electrical Engineering, and the Arabic Program for Non-Native Speakers.

The sampling procedure took two forms. The first was to reach the most readily accessible members of the international student sample via e-mail and social networks like WhatsApp, Viber, and Facebook. The second procedure was to use snowball sampling, asking those initially contacted to share the questionnaire with other international students.

The survey instrument was developed through the Survey Monkey website. At the start of the questionnaire, respondents reported demographic information which included gender, nationality, religion, age, college, educational level, and place of residence within Qatar.

In the subsequent section, participants were allowed to indicate their level of social interaction with Qataris, their sense of belonging to Qatari society, and the probability that they will return back to their countries to assume influential positions. For measuring levels of interaction with Qataris, a scale with five possible positions ranging from strongly agree to strongly disagree was used. For example, one statement read: "I always attend Qatari events and functions like weddings and *majlis*." For the measurement of a sense of belonging to the Qatari community, three statements were used. For example, one question was: "Through my interaction with Qataris, I feel that I belong to the society." In the final section of the survey, the possibility of respondents returning back to their countries to attain influential posts was measured with four statements. One statement read: "I will return back to my country once I finish my program at Qatar University."

SPSS data analysis software was used to analyze the collected data. Respondents' nationalities, gender, age, places of residence, education levels and colleges were analyzed. In a subsequent step, each of these demographic variables was cross-tabbed with others.

As for the number of the respondents, a total of 113 international students participated in this survey. Results have been rounded to the nearest tenth of a decimal point. The participants consisted of 69 female students (61.6 percent) and 43 male students (38.4 percent). Among the sample, 101 are Muslims (89.4 percent) while the remaining respondents reported that they are either Christians (2.7 percent) or they are atheists (7.1 percent). The ages of the majority of participants ranged between 18 to 24 years (60.2 percent) while those who reported that they are above 24 constituted 39.7 percent of the respondents. Nationalities of Arab countries dominated the study sample (48.7 percent) followed by nationalities of African countries (excluding Arab countries) 23 percent which is followed by nationalities drawn from Europe, Canada and the US (15 percent). A majority of the respondents either completed or are currently enrolled in B.A programs (48.7 percent), while 23.9 percent are higher school graduates or diplomat holders, and 20.4 percent are either master degree students or holders; the remaining participants consisted of five PhD students or holders, (4.4 percent), and two vocational training students (1.8 percent). Of the respondents 57.1 percent reported that they reside outside the Qatar University hostel with their families, 31.3 percent reported that they are living in the Qatar University hostel, and 11.6 percent are staying outside Qatar University without their families.

The Soft Power Potential of Qatar Higher Education

As per the results of the survey, the responses of the students about their social interactions with the host community suggest that Qatar has minimal opportunity to reap soft power benefits from its recruitment of foreign students. This is because interactions between the international students and Qataris is low, which means that international students do not experience the culture of Qatar and its values. For example, only 14.2 percent of the sample strongly agreed that their social interactions with the host country are high compared to 15 percent who strongly disagreed that they have high social interaction with the host community. Even though 32.7 percent agreed that they interact with Qataris compared to 18.6 percent who rejected that idea, this number is insufficient to suggest that there is a possibility that foreign students are being drawn to Qatar culture when considering the number of respondents who reported that they are neutral or disagreed or strongly disagreed. For example, 20.7 percent of the respondents strongly disagreed that they have Qatari friends compared to 13.5 percent who strongly agreed on this suggestion. A similar result is found when students are asked whether they attend Qatar social functions like weddings and whether they watch local Qatar TV or listen to local radio; in this regards, 28.6 percent and 21.4 percent respectively strongly disagreed or disagreed that they attend these social functions compared to 11.6 percent and 15.2 percent who respectively strongly agreed or agreed that they attend them. Disagreement is also high as to whether students watch local Qatar TV: 49.5 percent either strongly disagreed or disagreed that they watch it compared to 31.9 percent who strongly agreed or merely agreed that they watch Qatar local TV.

The finding that the recruitment of foreign students in Qatar does not contribute to Qatar soft power is also confirmed by the international students' responses to the question of whether they felt like they belonged to Qatari society. This is even more acute when we know that the percentage of the respondents who strongly agreed or agreed that they have similar identities (language, religion) with the host country (46.4 percent compared to 25 percent who strongly disagreed or disagreed) is lower than the number of respondents who reported that these identities do not make them feel that they belong to the society (43.4 percent compared to 34.4 percent who agreed or strongly agreed that they belong to the host community). The importance of having similar identities with the host country becomes less relevant when we consider the number of international students who are neutral to admit that their identities encourage them to interact with the host community. For instance, 31.9 percent of the respondents are neutral to agree that their identities support them to have social interactions with Qataris compared to 28.3 percent who strongly agreed that their identities drive them to mingle with the host community socially.

Additionally, the possibility that Qatar's investment in hosting foreign students in its university will be a goodwill gesture for Qatar soft power becomes lower when we take into account the percentage of foreign students willing to return back to their countries, and who are optimistic that they will attain influential political positions when they return. For example, only 13.4 percent and 10.7 percent strongly agreed or agreed that they will return back to their countries after their studies in Qatar, while 27.7 percent and 15.2 percent strongly disagreed or disagreed about that idea. Likewise, the number of international students who have not made up their minds about going home after their studies is significant. For example, 33.1 percent of the respondents are hesitant to agree with this proposition. This percentage is higher than those who strongly agree that they will not go back (15.2 percent) and it is higher than those who indicated that they will return 13.4 percent.

Among the respondents, only 19 percent (3.5 percent strongly agreed and 15.9 percent agreed) are optimistic that they will hold influential positions when they return back to their countries; this percentage is lower than those who are pessimistic about this idea (23 percent strongly disagreed and 18.6 percent agreed). The remaining percentage, 38.9 percent, could not decide whether opportunities await them to attain influential posts in their respective countries.

Most of the respondents to this survey share a common religion and language with Qataris. In this regard, 96.4 percent of the respondents reported that they are Muslims, while 48.7 percent come from Arab countries. The importance of this in the context of soft power is that similarity between in culture attracts people to interact.[35] Despite the low level of interaction between foreign students and the Qatar community, those who reported that they are Arabs and Muslim tend to have higher level of social interaction with Qataris. For example, 14.9 percent and 33.7 percent of Muslim respondents agreed strongly or agreed that they have social interactions with the host community. This result is even higher among Arabs, as 18.2 percent and 38.2 percent strongly agreed and agreed that they have high social interactions with the host community compared to 9.1 percent and 14.6 percent of those strongly disagreed or disagreed that they have social contacts with the host community.

This opportunity for Qatar to optimize soft power by recruiting foreign students falls flat by this lack of contact with the host community. For example, the overall responses to the questionnaire suggest that students have minimal exposure to Qatari culture and society.

For instance, a high proportion of those who reported that they were Arabs and Muslims disagreed that they interact with Qataris through attending social functions and gatherings or by having a Qatari friend, or by watching local Qatari TV or listening to local radio. In this regard, among the Arab respondents, 40 percent strongly disagreed or disagreed that they attend functions like weddings and a *majlis*, compared to 27.3 percent who strongly agreed or agreed to this statement. Of the Arabs, 45.1 percent either disagreed strongly or disagreed that they watch local Qatar TV or listen to Qatar Radio, compared to 27.3 percent who strongly agreed or agreed.

Likewise, respondents who identified as Muslim strongly disagreed or disagreed that they attend weddings or *majlis* (48 percent compared to 29 percent who strongly agreed or agreed); most of the Muslim students also disagreed or disagreed that they have Qatari friends (51.5 percent compared to 33.3 percent who agreed strongly or just agreed); or that they watch local Qatar TV or listen to Qatar Radio (48.5 percent compared to 34.7 percent who agreed strongly or agreed that they watch Qatar local TV or listen to Qatar Radio).

Despite some shared identities between the local community and most international students, these similarities do not make international students feel that they can ever belong to the local community. In this aspect 39 percent of Muslim students denied that they feel a sense of belonging to the local community when they interact with Qataris; while 37.6 percent reported that they did.

Another challenge that undermines Qatar's effort to reap soft power benefits from its investment in foreign students is the fact that most of the respondents who interact with the local community do not see themselves as returning to their countries of origin after finishing their studies. Strikingly, 33 percent of them could not make up their minds about leaving Qatar after their programs. In the same context, only 18.8 percent of the respondents are optimistic about the suggestion that they have a chance to hold an influential position once they return back to their countries. The remaining portion of the Muslim respondents (39.6 percent) could not foresee whether they would be employed in an influential position.

A similar trend is found among Arabs as only 11 percent reported that they will return to their countries after their studies in Qatar University compared to 61.8 percent who reported that they would not return back to their countries. Like Muslim respondents, Arab respondents are also negative about the possibility of assuming influential posts in their countries. For example, 43.6 percent are pessimistic compared to 18.8 percent who are optimistic.

Conclusion

The results of this survey indicate that foreign students have a low level of social interaction with the local population. This could be ascribed to the closeness of Qatari society. Despite the advanced relative development of infrastructure and education, Qatar society resists the social acceptance of most expatriates and foreign students. The development achieved by Qatar is not a response to a gradual process of social change which also goes along with changes in attitudes and beliefs; rather, it is strongly connected to oil revenues which Qatar accumulated from the oil boom in the mid-1970s.[36] Thus, the imbalance between material development and social change explains why Qatar is still a traditional society with patriarchal ethos and conservative religious social and cultural norms that inhibit wider interaction between Qataris and foreigners in general. The material advancement only compounded the isolation of Qataris from the expatriates. Oil wealth made Qataris distinguishable from others in the society. Their lifestyle and attire made them even more prevented distinctive. This others who could not afford this lifestyle or to embrace Qatari attire as regular dress from interacting with them socially. This is confirmed by why many respondents disagreed that they have Qatari friends or that they attend social functions like wedding and *majlis*, and this could be the reason why even international students with Arab and Islamic backgrounds disagreed that they have sense of belonging to the society despite the fact that share a similar language and religion with the host society. This distancing is compounded by the favorable and exceptional treatment rendered to Qataris in the university, hospitals, immigration department, and other institutions that render service to Qataris and expatriate communities alike.

In other countries both the local and international students share school buses and other services within the university. For example, at Al-Azhar University in Egypt, local and foreign students share the same buses to and from the university. This sharing contributed to increasing the level of foreign students' interaction with local communities and the students in particular. Even though local and international students do not share dormitories in Al-Azhar, the high level of interaction that occurs among local and foreign students sustains long-term social relations beyond the university campus. This is manifested in international students being invited by local students to visit their villages in countryside, and to attend their social functions like weddings and festivals. In contrast to Al-Azhar, no Qatari uses university student buses; neither are they accommodated in Qatar University's hostels. Most Qatari male university students have their own cars or are dropped off by family drivers at universities, while family drivers deliver most female students to universities. Thus, opportunities to interact with Qataris are minimal.

This lack of opportunity of interaction is compounded by other factors:

Many Qatari students are full-time students while they are also full-time employees elsewhere; consequently these students spend little time on campus, and they rarely engage in extracurricular activities. They make little use of campus resources. These types of students primarily come to campus to attend lectures; thus, they miss the benefit of being part of the overall educational environment. Therefore, their chance of making friends is minimum due to the shortness of time they spend on campus. Such a phenomenon is not distinctive to Qatar University; the Qatar Faculty of Islamic Studies is populated by Qataris who only turn up for lectures and have little interaction beyond the classroom with foreign students in the same program.

Social pressure emanating from family obligations is another factor that constrains Qatari students' length of stay in campus, minimizing their chance to make friendships with foreign students that could be extended outside the campus. In most cases, Qatari students live in extended family settings and everyone is expected to take part in family life. Within this culture, men are expected to assist in the family business, especially in the case of the eldest son. In some cases, they are required to assist in family-related duties. Women are expected to socialize daily with other female household members and visitors, as well as accompany the family when visiting relatives. These obligations force them to spend less time on campus.

The policy of gender separation that limits mixed classes and the movement of students between the male and female campuses is yet another factor. This policy limits opportunities for building friendships through group works and other student activities.

The low number of Qatari male students at Qatar University, especially at the graduate level, represents another reason for minimal interaction between Qatari students and international students. University enrollment among male Qataris is generally low compared to that of females, and this is especially evident at Qatar University. This could be ascribed to the fact that Qatari males attend universities abroad on Qatari government scholarships. It could also be due to the fact western universities in Education City attract Qatari students who meet exigent entry requirements or those who pursue their degrees in specializations unavailable at Qatar University. For instance, in the QU M.A. Gulf Studies Program, only one male Qatari has graduated since its inception in 2012.

In addition to this, expatriate faculty members, administrators, and staff, and not Qatari nationals, occupy most positions that have daily interaction with students. For example, in the Gulf Studies program none of the lecturers is Qatari, while only one Qatari female administrator exists out of three. This is another factor that restricts the opportunity for foreign students to build relations with Qatari students, staff, and lecturers.

This project also indicates that a large portion of foreign students are either unwilling to return back to their countries or hesitant to agree that they will consider going back home once they finish their studies. This could be due to the following factors:

Employment opportunities are available in Qatar labor market for university graduates with the attractive salaries and packages offered to those who remain in Qatar. Despite the Qatarization policy that prefers Qataris over non-Qataris in employment, the mega-development plans prompted by the state necessitates that Qatar absorb graduates among foreign students to supplement the small labor pool of skilled nationals. Immigration law allows international students to change their student visa to a work visa provided that they have a Qatari sponsor.

Family ties are another factor that drives foreign students to admit that they will stay in Qatar after their graduation. This is even acute when we consider the number of expatriate children in Qatar University, whose residency status in Qatar is determined by that of their fathers

Summary Recommendations: The recruitment of international students has little potential for propagating Qatari soft power. International students have minimal interactions with Qataris, do not feel that they belong to the society, and are unwilling to return back to their countries because of perceived lack of opportunities. Despite the Qatari concern with public diplomacy and soft power, Qatar's heavy investment in international students does not go beyond absorbing them into the local labor market.

Securing a positive public diplomacy outcome for higher education in Qatar necessitates the participation of non-government sectors and community-wide participation. In this regard, government and educational institutions should encourage communication through social media, traditional media, and informal communication between local and international students to project Qatar's image and values.

Qatar University should also encourage both local and international students to build social and intellectual ties that could expand beyond educational environments. This would pave the way for international students to experience Qatar cultures and ideas; it will also increase the possibility of positive outcomes.

Class work and extracurricular activities should be designed to involve both local and international students; and there should be a policy to encourage foreign students to get exposed to Qatari society and culture, both popular and "high."

Alumni engagement should be encouraged by the government as part of its public diplomacy. This could become the largest global network through which Qatar could advance its public diplomacy interests.

Notes

1   John Brennan, "Higher Education and Social Change," *Higher Education* 56, no.3 (March 2008): 381–93. doi:10.1007/s10734-008-9126-4.

2   William Jones, "European Union Soft Power: Cultural Diplomacy and Higher Education in Southeast Asia," *Silpakorn University International Journal* 9-10 (October 2009): 44.

3   Caitlin Byrne and Hall Rebecca Hall. "International Education as Public Diplomacy," *International Education Association of Australia* (June 2004): 2-3: http://www.ieaa.org.au/documents/item/258 (accessed 29 June 2016).

4   Carol Atkinson, "Does Soft Power Matter? A Comparative Analysis of Student Exchange Programs, 1980-2006," *Foreign Policy Analysis* 6 (January 2010): 14. doi:10.1111/j.1743-8594.2009.00099.x.

5   "Sheikha Moza: The power behind Qatar's global lessons", *BBC World Service*: http://www.bbc.com/news/business-29997174 (accessed on 29 June 2016).

6   Osman Antwi-Boateng, "The Rise of Qatar as a Soft Power and the Challenges," *European Scientific Journal* 9, no. 31 (December 2013): 300.

7   Joseph Nye, *Soft Power: The Means to Success in World Politics* (New York: Public Affairs Press, 2004), 2.

8   Joseph Nye "Soft Power and Higher Education," Internet and the University Forum (2003): 33–60: http://tinyurl.com/gppc7cz (accessed 29 June 2016).

9   Nye identified three sources upon which the soft power of a country primarily rests: Culture, political values, and foreign policies (see Nye, "Soft Power," 33).

10 Ibid.

11 Anthony Rhodes, *Propaganda: The art of persuasion: World War II* (New York: Chelsea House Publishers, 1976), 255.

12   Sean Murphy, *Letting the Side Down: British Traitors of the Second World War* (Sutton Publishing Ltd, 2006): 85-87. Kamel Labidi, "The Voice of the Arabs is speechless at 50," *The Daily Star*: http://tinyurl.com/zbfsppp (accessed 29 June 2016).

13   Caitlin Byrne et al., "International Education as Public Diplomacy," 2.

14   Ibid.

15   Elmo Wilson and Bonilla Frank, "Evaluating Exchange of Persons Programs," *Public Opinion Quarterly* 19 (January 1955), 22. doi:10.1086/266539.

16   Ibid., 24.

17   Ibid., 21.

18   Ibid.

19   Ibid.

20   Caitlin Byrne and Hall Rebecca Hall, "International Education as Public Diplomacy." 3.

21   Yiwei Wang, "Public Diplomacy and the Rise of Chinese Soft Power," *Annals of the American Academy of Political and Social Science,* 616, March 2008), 257-73.

22   Kalin Ibrahim, "Soft Power and Public Diplomacy in Turkey," *Center for Strategic Studies* 16, no. 3 (Autumn 2011), 5-23: http://tinyurl.com/hme64pr (accessed 29 June 2016).

23   Sheikha Abdulla Al-Misnad, "The Dearth of Qatari Men in Higher Education: Reasons and Implications," *Middle East Institute*: http://tinyurl.com/jj3ofs7 (accessed 29 June 2016).

24   Cathleen Stasz, Eide Eric and Francisco Martorell, "Post-Secondary Education in Qatar: Employer Demand, Student Choice and Policy Option," *Rand Cooporation* (2007): 11-13: http://tinyurl.com/gr4ydca (accessed 29 June 2016).

25   Hiba Khodr, "The Dynamics of International Education in Qatar: Exploring the Policy Drivers behind the Development of Education City," *Journal of Emerging Trends in Educational Research and Policy Studies* 2, no. 6: 514-25: http://tinyurl.com/zcgxvpd (accessed 29 June 2016).

26   Ibid.

27   "Qatar Knowledge Diplomacy," November 15, 2014: http://tinyurl.com/jh7knzb (accessed 29 June 2016).

28   Ibid.

29   "Student exchange Programs," *Qatar University*: http://tinyurl.com/jgl5q6m (accessed 29 June 2016).

30   "International Students," *Qatar University*: http://tinyurl.com/he4a6q6 (accessed 29 June 2016).

31   "Academic Scholarships - Scholarship Types and Condition," *Qatar University*: http://tinyurl.com/z3tslhv (accessed 29 June 2016).

32   Joseph Nye, "Soft Power and Higher Education," 41-49.

33   "International students" in this study refers to students with student visas and to the children of expatriates. Although the children of expatriates are not considered as international students, they share many characteristics with international student. Although the State of Qatar does not technically place foreign residents in the same category, they are included in this study. First; both categories of student benefit from the cheap tuition fees and scholarships offered by the University; second, they are both considered as non-nationals vis-à-vis Qataris; third, none of them are entitled to Qatari citizenship regardless of the period they stay in the country. Significantly, some of the children of expatriates acquire international student status once their parents leave the country. For more information about Qatar residency law and student visas, see: http://tinyurl.com/jxrv8ka

34   Joseph Nye, "Soft Power and Higher Education," 42.

7

The Health of Nations: The Evolution and Structure of Public Health Higher Education in the GCC

Muhammad H. Zaman and Katie Clifford

This chapter focuses on understanding the need and challenges to build and sustain public health capacity within GCC countries in order to meet the new demands for a rapidly changing regional health landscape. In the last four decades, the GCC states have seen rapid development along with increase in life expectancy, decrease in maternal and infant mortality, and overall improvements in the quality of life of their citizens.[1] This has been done, in part by rapid urbanization, creation of new and state-of-the-art hospitals and substantial improvement in water sanitation.

The creation of medical "cities" that feature state-of-the art equipment in hospitals as well as medical staff, some trained at leading world institutions, has raised the level of quality in hospital care within the region. That said, with changes in lifestyle and urbanization, new challenges associated with high impact chronic diseases, in particular diabetes, obesity, cancer, cardiovascular ailments, and mental health issues have posed new and complex problems for the GCC states that require rethinking the existing public health systems in place.[2]

The incidence of some of these diseases in the GCC, particularly diabetes and cancer, is among the highest in the world.[3] Consequently, addressing public health challenges requires not only change in policies but also the creation of new educational models to train the workforce and create domestic research and technical capacity to meet these new challenges.

Many GCC states have taken creative approaches to educate their local workforce. These include university-industry collaboration in biotech, international initiatives focused on applying innovation to health, and accelerating the growth of local public health education programs through partnerships with western universities. The countries that comprise the GCC each face their unique public health hurdles but also share common challenges in improving health outcomes for their citizens and non-citizens alike. These recent challenges have been the catalyst for many GCC nations to begin investing in the future of public health, particularly through local higher education institutions.

Health and Healthcare Financing: Meeting the Needs for A Growing Population

It is important to understand the landscape of public health in the region. Over the last fifty years, there has been exponential regional economic growth. This growth has drawn people from all over the world to this region, in search for work opportunities at every employment level. For example, in 2011, expatriates constituted 87 per cent of the population in Qatar and 84 per cent of the population in the UAE.[4] In 2010, it was estimated that 8.3 million expatriate workers emigrated to the UAE alone.[5] In addition to a surge in expatriates, there are large populations of documented and undocumented migrant workers working on the expansive construction projects found in many GCC states. Unlike the expatriate community, the migrant worker population often has a much lower income, lower education levels, and face greater occupational health risks tied to construction jobs. With a high influx of foreigners comes the financial issue of extending public services to this population, specifically health care services. The majority of GCC countries provide publicly-funded health care to their populations.[6] Natural resource wealth has allowed these countries to provide health services to their relatively small populations. However, with the large number of expatriates now making up the majority of the population, GCC countries are concerned that they will not be able to cover this new population's health costs. While public health care is offered at no cost to citizens, expatriates often pay a heavily subsidized rate that does not come close to covering the costs incurred by the government to run highly specialized hospitals with expensive equipment and highly skilled workforce employed in these hospitals.[7]

In some countries, the burden placed on the healthcare systems by non-citizens has already become a contentious issue, and government response has been controversial. In 2013, the Kuwaiti government restricted foreigner access to public hospitals to the afternoons, after complaints by Kuwaiti nationals who were having to wait for treatment. Some view the new system as "racist", while others see it as the only means of timely healthcare delivery for Kuwaiti nationals.[8] Similar barriers to healthcare have been faced by the Bidun population, a group of "stateless" peoples who have resided in Kuwait for generations, yet are considered by the government to be illegal immigrants. While the Kuwaiti government has extended free healthcare to the Bidun, lack of documentation required by public hospitals and the inability to afford services at private facilities have kept this poverty-stricken population from accessing needed care.[9]

The Burden of Chronic Non-Communicable Disease on the Health Care System

The economic growth the GCC states have led to a socioeconomic change among its population, resulting in a lifestyle change for many of its citizens. Along with increased wealth has come a more sedentary, less active lifestyle[10] and a high-fat, unhealthy diet.[11] These changes have led to a drastic increase in obesity among the population, with an average 40 per cent of GCC nationals classified as obese.[12] In turn, these unhealthy lifestyle choices related to increased obesity have resulted in numerous chronic health problems for these countries.

Cardiovascular disease is a leading cause of death in the GCC nations, acting as the cause of 45 per cent of early deaths in the region[13] In 2010, it was estimated that 29 per cent of all deaths in the emirate of Abu Dhabi were due to cardiovascular disease.[14] This trend is expected to continue into the future, with a projected increase of 419 per cent in cardiovascular treatment demand in the GCC.[15] The increased future need for cardiovascular treatment is not only a public health crisis, but also a fiscal emergency. Projections estimate that between 2006 and 2025, cardiovascular treatment as part of the GCC total health care spending will increase from 12 per cent (US$1,428,000) to 24 per cent ($13,752,000).[16]

Similarly, cases of cancer are on the rise, and are affecting younger populations in the GCC than compared with other countries.[17] In 2010, it was estimated that 16 per cent of all deaths in Abu Dhabi were due to cancer, with that rate doubling in the UAE by 2020.[18]

Correspondingly, poor health habits have led the GCC to have some of the highest diabetes rates in the world, with its prevalence in the population at 25 per cent in the UAE,[19] 17 per cent in Saudi Arabia, 15 per cent in Bahrain and 14 per cent in Kuwait.[20] In the UAE, this staggeringly high rate rises to 40 per cent of Emiratis over the age of 60.[21] In response to its own public health battle against diabetes, Qatar created the online National Diabetes Registry in 2013 in order to compile data on patients, monitor trends, and share information with other countries and institutions. Also recognizing the severity of all chronic non-communicable disease in its country, Qatar crafted the National Health Strategy 2011-2016, with the goal to promote a healthier lifestyle change to prevent these diseases, and strategies that allow for earlier detection.[22]

Exacerbating these chronic non-communicable diseases is the population demographics in GCC countries. GCC nationals aged 65 and older is estimated to swell to 14.2 million in 2050, up from 1.2 million in 2015.[23] In general, elderly populations require more frequent and intensive health care, and often are afflicted with the costly conditions described above. While the GCC countries have made great strides in reducing infant mortality rates and lengthening life expectancy, they will now be responsible for the health care of a much larger elderly populations than they have had in past years.

These "lifestyle" diseases have put both a financial and logistical strain on the health systems of GCC countries, contributing to rising medical costs as well as creating demand for more and increasingly specialized physicians.

Dependence on a Foreign Workforce

Aside from the growing financial costs of health care, states in the GCC are also confronted with a lack of qualified clinicians and a dependence on an expatriate workforce. In GCC states, the average number of physicians is 20 per 10,000 people, about half of 40 physicians per 10,000 people found in Europe.[24] In addition, the majority of clinicians in the region are foreign, with an average of 75 per cent of physicians in GCC states being non-nationals.[25] The problem of local staff shortages in public health is also felt acutely, with very few medical students opting into a career in public health. According to a 2013 survey of King Saud University medical students, only 6.6 per cent planned to enter community medicine, the second lowest discipline apart from anesthesia.[26] Many universities in the GCC have recently recognized the lack of public health practitioners graduating from local medical schools, and are beginning to offer public health degree programs to non-physicians.

Figure 1: Percentage of Expatriate Clinicians in the GCC Health Care Sector, 2001-2002

	Expatriate physicians (%)	Expatriate nurses (%)
Bahrain	30	48
Kuwait	63	90
Oman	78	55
Qatar	89	91
Saudi Arabia	78	79
UAE	82	96
GCC average	75	79

Source: Mona Mourshed, Viktor Hediger and Toby Lambert, "Gulf Cooperation Council Health Care: Challenges and Opportunities" *Global Competitiveness Reports 2006*, World Economic Forum, http://tinyurl.com/n9vy5me (accessed 29 June 2016).

This dependence on a foreign workforce is a major cause of instability in the health system, as the turnover rate is high for non-GCC nationals in health fields. This also affects the quality of care as patients are unable to develop a relationship with primary care physicians, and can also lead to instability of a particular department with the departure of experts in a given area. The dependence on non-nationals is also a major reason for poor development of certain highly specialized, but desperately needed areas, such as mental health and pediatric psychiatry.

There are a number of reasons that GCC states must rely on an expatriate workforce to act as clinicians in their health care systems. The rapid rise in chronic non-communicable diseases will require more physicians and nurses than can be currently provided by GCC state nationals. As these diseases become more of a burden on the health care system in the future, lack of local clinicians will continue to be an issue as there are not enough GCC nationals enrolling in medical school to adequately serve the population. This may be in part due to the unwillingness of GCC nationals to take lower-paying positions, such as jobs as nurses or physicians' assistants, as well as the limited number of institutions that are able to train students in public health professions.[27]

Oman is an exception in the region for improving local capacity. The Omani government recognized this as a crisis of health worker capacity and took steps to strengthen their own health workforce and, in 1991, set out a five-year health development strategy. A main aspect of this strategy was the policy of "Omanization," or local capacity building, of the workforce in all sectors, including health care. The government of Oman saw the value in increasing the number of nationals in the health workforce, resulting in an increase of Omanis employed by the Ministry of Health from 52 per cent in 1990 to 68 per cent in 2007.[28] Overall, in 2007 the 58 per cent of the Omani health workforce were nationals. The first step taken was to improve the health infrastructure of the country, building hospitals, clinics, and other much needed health facilities. Next, and arguably most important, Oman invested heavily in their national medical education infrastructure by establishing regional nurse training institutes, helping to ensure that nursing staff would be distributed across the country. These Ministry of Health institutes expanded, training nurses in more specialized fields, such as midwifery. The expansion also established new institutes, educating the Omani population in public health and pharmacy professions. Once graduates finished the nursing program, the Ministry of Health prioritized their hiring over expatriates and foreign health workers. Furthermore, when Oman was eventually in need of nurses with advanced degrees, instead of sending Omani staff abroad to acquire MSN degrees, they partnered with foreign universities to bring the education opportunities to the country. The expansion of educational opportunities continued, with programs for the continued professional development of health care staff.

Once the health facilities were constructed and the local health workforce were being trained, the Ministry of Health brought together a workforce planning team in order to outline the operational and managerial aspects of their expanding health care system. With government support, an advanced health information system and constant re-evaluation of their methods, the workforce planning team was able to supervise operations and plan for projected future health care worker need. By 2012, these efforts have resulted in Oman having 24.3 physicians per 10,000 people and 58.3 nurses per 10,000 people.[29]

Oman's successes were due to a number of laborious, yet necessary, decisions they made throughout the process of "Omanizing" the healthcare sector workforce. Omani leadership, particularly Sultan Qaboos bin Said, recognized the importance of a quality workforce for health development and prioritized the creation of an Omani medical education system.[30] In 1986, the publically-funded Sultan Qaboos University and the College of Medicine and Health Sciences was established, providing Omani citizens a free medical education and all but guaranteed jobs in the health sector after graduation.[31] Still, the medical education system in the country is relatively young, and Oman is still working to increase local training opportunities in specialized medicine. In 1975, Oman had only 52 medical specialists in the country, but that number rose to 2,162 in 2008 and is expected to grow to 2,228 by the end of 2020.[32]

Oman has also made efforts to improve professional development and promote lifelong learning for local physicians with the creation of the central steering committee for continuing professional education (CPE) by the MOH. While the MOH provides leadership and guidance in CPE initiatives, as well as an accreditation system, CPE opportunities are implemented at the hospital level. The Oman Medical Specialty Board, the regulatory body heading continuing education initiatives, has even created an online forum where clinicians can submit CPE activities for review, and the healthcare community can find out about upcoming conferences and seminars.[33] Lastly, throughout each step of the process, the MOH and WHO consultants worked to gain the support and trust of health officials who would be critical in the successful roll-out of the workforce development plan. On the advice of the WHO, the MOH included policy-makers and regulators at the beginning of strategy development, and took their suggestions and considerations seriously. In 1992, the WHO advisor helped organize a workshop for high-level MOH officials, held as a retreat outside of Muscat. The goal of the retreat was to explain the health workforce development strategy, its importance to the improvement of the Omani healthcare system, and to field any concerns from MOH executives. These initiatives gave rise to similar workshops for high- and mid-level administrators in the MOH, in which the Minister of Health attended, showing his support of the plan.[34]

Public Health in the GCC: Investments

The extraordinary economic growth experienced by the GCC states has also been felt in the health care sectors of those nations. The need for having local capacity, through education and training, is reflected in the recent investments in the health sector. Estimates have projected the healthcare and pharmaceutical markets of the GCC will increase from US$46 billion to $133 billion in the next five years.[35] The potential impact of these investments and the challenges faced by the GCC nations in restructuring the local public health system within their respective nations are highly significant.

Medical Cities

"Medical cities" modeled after innovation hubs are being created in the GCC to foster innovation, decrease the cost of travel between facilities, and bring various stakeholders in the health sector in close proximity. These medical cities are often all-inclusive, consisting of hospitals with specialized treatment facilities, research and diagnostic labs, medical training centers, rehabilitation therapy, and housing. The medical cities model is limited in its ability to be scaled in all locations, requires GCC governments to budget substantial funds to these projects, and often provide land to develop. The large, urban populations found in GCC countries are also mobile enough to access these health facilities, making them a lucrative endeavor.[36] However, the ability to staff these medical cities with local physicians and public health professionals is a challenge. Until GCC countries are able to educate a strong local workforce, medical cities will be forced to rely on the foreign doctors and health workers.

Saudi Arabia, the largest healthcare market in the Middle East, is building some of the biggest of these medical cities. The King Fahad Medical City contains four hospitals that hold over 1,000 beds, and is estimated to serve 2 million outpatients and 50,000 inpatients each year.[37] The Saudi Ministry of the Interior is also funding the King Abdullah Medical City at a cost of US$6.7 billion, which will consist of two cities with 1000 beds each.[38] Despite rapid expansion of health care facilities in Saudi Arabia estimates expect that at least 115,544 beds will be needed in 2018, up from 11,241 beds in 2013.[39]

Similar ventures in other regions are also ongoing. The construction of the Sheikh Khalifa Medical City in Abu Dhabi will provide 838 beds among three hospitals.[40] Oman is in the process of constructing two medical cities at a cost of US$1 billion each, as well as planning the development of additional hospitals and medical centers.[41] The Sultanate drafted its strategy for the future in its Health's Vision-2050, which focused on the best ways to provide health care in an urban setting and to a growing population.[42]

Qatar has also allocated a substantial amount of money to invest in its health care system. As the fastest growing health care market in the GCC with a compound annual growth rate of 23 per cent,[43] Qatar has budgeted US$7.8 billion to improve health services.[44] A number of these improvements will come in the construction of medical cities, which will receive investments of US$ 1.1 billion between 2014 and 2019.[45]

Public Health in the GCC: Innovative Partnerships

The strength of any public health system lies not only in what technologies it can acquire, but also in its ability to integrate various disparate components of the system, to innovate and to respond to crisis. In this section, we will analyze the role innovation plays within the public health system in the GCC, the role of higher education institutions and the ability of the system to respond to external perturbations, such as MERS and Ebola.

In 2011, the World Bank reported that the research and develop expenditure, as percent of GDP, for Kuwait, Oman and the UAE was 0.09 per cent, 0.13 per cent and 0.49 per cent, respectively.[46] Compared to the U.S. 2011 expenditure of 2.76 per cent of GDP, funding of innovation and research development in these GCC countries are strikingly low. In addition to a lack of funding, major players in GCC innovation are not sufficiently connected to each other, with governments, agencies, business and academia building bilateral partnerships but failing to align all stakeholders together.[47] Additionally, while there have been some efforts in creating a culture of innovation, the efforts have focused largely in engineering and technology, with few applications in health, which remains outside the domain of technological innovation. However, recent efforts are aimed at bridging this gap and to encourage innovation in science and technology through local, regional and international partnerships.

Qatar has been at the forefront of health care innovation and partnership, hosting the annual World Innovation Health Summit (WISH) organized by the Qatar Foundation.[48] WISH is an initiative to foster innovation in healthcare and share those findings with global collaborators from every part of the health care sector. International corporations like Aetna and Philips sponsor the event, connecting the private sector with government officials and local researchers of the fastest growing health care market in the Middle East. Aside from acting as a forum for health care collaboration, WISH has taken part in affecting policy change. WISH officials acted as part of the Qatar delegation at the 2014 World Health Assembly, the policy-making committee of the World Health Organization.

In addition to the WISH initiative, Inconet – GCC2 is an international science, technology and innovation network established in 2014 between the European Commission Directorate General for Research and Innovation and GCC countries.[49] This three-year funded project is closely tied to the EU Horizon 2020 program, which is focused on finding innovative solutions for societal changes, including those in the public health arena. Inconet – GCC2 focuses on bilateral research, connecting innovators interested in finding solutions to specific societal issues, including public health challenges. The initiative encourages capacity building in countries without strong support through researcher mobility programs and the open sharing of knowledge and findings. This exchange of knowledge and sharing of research facilities will accelerate health research that will eventually inform health policy decisions in the GCC.

Ministries of Health and multilateral global health agencies have been working together over the past decade on projects that inform and change health policy in the GCC. In 2001, the UAE Ministry of Health and the World Health Organization undertook a joint research project and discovered that 25 per cent of Emiratis were diabetic, compared with the global average of 5-7 per cent.[50] This startling statistic has focused the attention of the Emirate government to the epidemic of obesity-related disease in their country, helping to formulate policy.

There are also regional collaborations within the GCC that are created to foster regional cooperation among countries. Established in 1976, the Executive Board for Health Ministers Council for GCC states is comprised of the six GCC member states, plus the Republic of Yemen, and works to encourage cooperation between ministries of health in each country.[51] However, the ability of the organization to foster innovation has largely been limited and interactions with educational institutions are non-existent.

Another regional organization created to bring together the leaders of GCC health care to facilitate innovative solutions to local health issues is the GCC Healthcare Innovation Congress.[52] The Congress holds an annual meeting attended by members of the healthcare industry, health ministries, physicians, health IT technicians, and pharmaceuticals companies, in order to explore the latest biotech innovations and share successful strategies for public health programming. This organization, while leaner than the Health Ministers Council, also focuses on pharmaceutical companies and health policies, such as "e" and "m-health," and less on creating a culture of innovation in health.

The Role of Universities in Health Innovation

Historically, the role of universities in the GCC states in fostering innovation, in particular in the health sector, has been limited. This has been a function of the university structure, limited understanding of the need for innovation, poor integration of health and technology and a fragmented public health policy. However, over the past decade, certain countries in the GCC have encouraged collaboration between universities and industry, resulting in increased partnership between these two sectors. According to a 2011 World Economic Forum report, Qatar has risen in the ranks of countries with local university-industry research collaboration with a score of 5.3, indicating "intensive and ongoing" R&D collaboration,[53] when compared to their score of 4.2 in 2008.[54] Saudi Arabia has also increased the number of collaborations in its own country, with a rising score of 4.3 in 2011,[55] compared to 3.8 in 2008.[56] These scores are quite an impressive when compared to those of Switzerland (5.8) and the U.S. (5.7), top leaders in university-industry partnerships. Still, other GCC states have room for improvement in regards to the extent of collaboration between their universities and private sector businesses. Kuwait, Bahrain and Oman rank as countries with limited collaborations, scoring 3.2, 3.3 and 3.8, respectively,[57] only a slight improvement over their 2008 scores of 3.1, 2.8 and 3.7.[58]

The United Arab Emirates

In 2008, the Ministry of Higher Education and Scientific Research in the United Arab Emirates (UAE) established the National Research Foundation (NRF) in order to make the nation a globally competitive innovator through supporting local research and constructing a knowledge-based economy.[59] The NRF is focused on the promotion of innovation in higher educational institutions in the UAE, and advises the Ministry on the funding and implementation of national research programs in local universities. In encouraging local innovation in higher education, the NRF also helps build partnerships between universities, government agencies and the private sector. One of the top priorities of the Foundation is to support "linkage" between publically-funded research and industry, as well as encourage an entrepreneurial spirit throughout its research initiatives.

Abu Dhabi University, and its leadership has made innovation and entrepreneurship one of its key priorities. In addition to graduate programs in engineering and innovation, ADU also offers undergraduate degrees in Public Health, with a particular focus on the health challenges and healthcare issues of the UAE.[60] This curriculum includes courses on a range of topics with three main concentration focuses: health policy management, health promotion and environmental health. Yet unlike the College of Engineering, there is no noted collaboration between the Innovation Center and ongoing biotechnology research, and the public health degree program. The opportunity for ADU to integrate their current innovation initiatives into the public health sphere is one that should be seriously considered as the public health program grows.

United Arab Emirates University (UAEU) also offers one of the few public health programs in the GCC region, offering MPH and PhD graduate degrees, and integrating public health training into the undergraduate education of UAEU medical students. Housed in the College of Medicine and Health Sciences (CMHS), the Institute of Public Health's Zayed Bin Sultan Center for Health Sciences has created a MPH program targeted towards public health professionals working in government, non-profit organizations and in the healthcare service setting.[61] The Center recognizes the need for flexible class scheduling for current public health practitioners, and has crafted a part-time program that lists development of "lifelong learning skills necessary for professional development" as one of its primary learning outcomes.

Offering a wide array of academic concentrations, including occupational and environmental health, refugee mental health, clinical epidemiology, and social and behavioral health, a running theme throughout each focus is to understand the context in which public health issues emerge. The program objectives state that students should understand the socio-economic, behavioral and cultural factors that lead to disparities and differing health outcomes, as well as how our current world is shaping population health.

The UAEU aims to foster innovation, and has an Intellectual Property and Patents Unit in the Graduate Studies and Research Department to help students and faculty in the technology transfer process.[62] In May 2015, the Unit held a workshop to help inventors in the UAEU community learn how to best commercialize and protect their innovations. They've also held events on campus, such as the International Conference on Innovations in Information Technology, and have integrated project-based learning into their engineering department curriculum. However, the spheres of innovation and public health have not yet intersected at UAEU, and the population health department remains isolated and solely focused on research. Current UAEU industry research partners are primarily from the material and petroleum sciences, such as the Semiconductor Research Corporation, Intel and Takreer. While the University supports innovation in other departments, it has yet to link entrepreneurial and innovative thinking to public health research.

Saudi Arabia

The King Saud bin Abdulaziz University for Health Sciences has been a pioneer in public health education, establishing one of the first graduate-level public health programs offered in the gulf region.[63] The mission of the College of Public Health and Health Informatics is to create the public health leaders of tomorrow through providing students with a premier education focusing on high-quality research, evidence-based decision-making, and sound ethics. Masters students can concentrate in health informatics, epidemiology, biostatistics, public health, and health systems and quality management, and the program is not limited to physicians, like many MPH programs in the region.

Qatar

The Qatari branch of the Weill Cornell Medical College is deeply invested in collaborative public health research, education and community outreach. As the only medical school in Qatar, the Weill Cornell Medical College has worked incessantly to establish a translational public health research program that include a sustainable and collaborative research community investigating both nationally-relevant and global public health issues.[64] The College has outlined and is taking the following steps for employing research to enact public health changes: using the "bench to bedside" concept to guide locally-relevant initiatives; creating a strong public health educational program to build Qatar research capacity; and establishing the Division of Global and Public Health for the formation of public health policy, education and research.

The Division of Global and Public Health (GPH) at Weill Cornell Qatar, collaborative by institutional design, values cooperation in public health efforts. Created with the belief that "health is a shared responsibility,"[65] the Division of GPH is focused on partnering with other universities and institutions, both locally and globally, to prepare their medical school graduates take on the public health challenges of today. The Division addresses pressing public health issues through a model of medical school training that focuses on three main components: education, research, and community engagement.

A desire for global collaboration is especially evident in the educational efforts at the Division of GPH, which offers Weill medical students the opportunity to investigate global health off-campus as well as encouraging international students to attend on-campus global health courses. The Global Health Internship Program invites international undergraduates to study at the College, taking courses on global public health and visiting health facilities in the Doha area. Conversely, the Global Health Education and Research Program offers enrolled students the opportunity to spend two months working at a Tanzanian hospital after their first year of medical school, discovering challenges faced in the field through experiential learning. Senior medical students preparing to complete their degree are also given an optional introduction to global health, with a four-week Population Health and Primary Care Perspectives elective course that examines both regional and global health care delivery systems. In keeping with the importance of collaboration, the College brought university faculty, students and healthcare professionals from across Qatar held the Global and Public Health and Academic Health System Symposium in March 2015. The conference delved into traditional and non-traditional therapies in integrative medicine, and assessed the future (the "fifth wave") of public health.

In 2007, as an effort to provide medical students with the most comprehensive global public health education, the Division of GPH created the Center for Cultural Competence in Health Care. The mission of the Center is to encourage healthcare equity and reduce disparities among local and global underserved populations. The Division of GPH believes that the solution to this issue partly lies in cultivating healthcare providers who take a "culturally competent and patient-centered approach" to their practice. The Center provides workshops for students, residents and other healthcare professionals on how cultural competency, or lack thereof, can affect how they make medical decisions and the way that patients access healthcare services. These workshop trainings not only focus on competency in Qatari culture, but train participants in how best to administer healthcare services in any cultural setting different from their own.

Similar to their educational initiatives, the Division of GPH encourages both local and global research collaborations, but prioritizes research initiatives that focus on the public health issues facing Qatar. Current ongoing projects at the College in Qatar include research on diabetes, obesity, injury due to motor vehicle accidents, and use non-traditional medicine. The Qatar branch also regularly collaborates with the Weill Cornell Medical Hospital in the U.S. on nationally-relevant research, such as exploring the genetic basis of type II diabetes in Qataris and the link between metabolic syndrome and osteoarthritis.[66] Through partnering with a well-renowned institution, Qatar has accelerated their public health and medical research capacity, taking advantage of the support and resources provided by the Weill Cornell Medical School.

In addition, the Division of GPH does some community outreach work. In order to provide quality trainings, the Center for Cultural Competence works closely with cultural leaders and community associations in developing their curriculum. The Division of GPH also releases reports in both English and Arabic on relevant public health topics such as diabetes, obesity, heart disease, H1N1 flu and alternative medicine. These reports, written by faculty at the College, discuss in non-scientific language the current state of these public health issues, and prevention and treatment measures.

In addition to Weill Cornell Medical College – Qatar, Qatar University (QU) has recently emerged as a leader in public health education, offering both a Bachelor of Science and a Master's degree in Public Health. The University aligned themselves with the Qatar National Development Strategy (2011-2016), which identified the need for both infectious and non-communicable disease prevention, improved maternal and child health services, improvement in occupational health and healthy lifestyle promotion.[67] QU is working to educate the future, and many argue, first, generation of Qatari public health practitioners, in order to create an "informed and empowered public health workforce" able to address current and future local health challenges. The Department of Health Sciences does this through an educational model that relies heavily on experiential learning and public health research. QU requires students to complete internships, where they connect students with public health organizations and health care facilities.[68]

Well-defined learning outcomes, focused on public health in the local context, guide undergraduates through their course of study and help administrators measure the overall success of the program. QU has an inspiring vision for how their program can enhance the currently lacking public health environment in Qatar. The University sees their graduates as future public health leaders in government and as policymakers, on both the national and regional levels. The program also prepares graduates to manage public and private health services, and public health research and governmental and non-governmental institutions.

Both the BSc and MPH programs are fairly new, and neither have had a graduating class yet. Still, enrollment has been promising. On average, each year 40 students are accepted into the BSc public health program, with all of those students being female.[69] Undergraduates in the program choose to concentrate in health education or health management. The graduate program, currently in its inaugural year, is the first and only MPH program in Qatar. The graduate program is half the size of the undergraduate, with 20 students enrolled and 2/3 of those students female. The undergraduate and graduate programs are comprised of both Qatari and non-Qatari students, with foreign students coming primarily from Bahrain, Pakistan, India, Syria, Palestine, Jordan, Egypt, Lebanon and Sudan. MPH students will choose to concentrate in either epidemiology or health system improvement, and can take classes either full- or part-time. While the program attracts many recent graduates, the flexible scheduling offered targets working health care professionals in fields such as medicine, nursing, nutrition and public health. At present, only nine faculty members, all expatriates, are dedicated to teaching public health courses, but the University aims to hire more in the near future.

Response to Events Outside the Region

The strength of the public health system, its resilience and its innovative capacity depends greatly on its ability to respond to external perturbations. The complex and often tragic stories emerging from West African states of Sierra Leone, Guinea and Liberia, in response to the Ebola outbreak of 2014 demonstrate the high toll of poorly functioning health systems. The question in the context of GCC states therefore becomes, how prepared are these countries for an outbreak of Ebola or MERS and what is being done at the institutional level to increase innovative capacity within the region. While there have been substantial discussions at the government and the ministry level to address the growing challenge from MERS (Middle East Respiratory Syndrome) and more recent challenge of Ebola, the role of university-based academic researchers or innovators in coming up with new technologies have been minimal. There have been few, if any, policy papers from public health practitioners and no involvement from the engineering or technological sectors. This is in contrast to strong participation from universities outside the GCC (particularly in the US and Europe) that have played a major role in debating policy, creating new technological solutions and developing new control and management programs with the help of the local governments.[70]

Conclusion

The public health system of the GCC countries, like all other nations, is complex. In our study, interviews, and analysis, we note that in addition to the inherent complexity of disease management and public awareness, there are three additional challenges that the GCC nations face. The first one is high dependence on non-local staff, at all levels in the health system. The second is emphasis on individual health versus public health, and lack of awareness in the public about health practices. This is also leading to new financing models that are aimed towards encouraging integrated public/private healthcare partnerships. The third aspect of complexity arises from public health still being outside the folds of innovation policy. Innovation policy in the region has focused historically on oil and gas, and more recently in attracting IT firms to the region. Because of emphasis on high-end healthcare for individuals and less emphasis on population health, historically there has been little incentive to develop new and innovative solutions for local problems. While there has been a strong tradition of partnership with international organizations in the domain of health, they have focused largely on hospital equipment and hospital staffing and less so on innovation. Patent policies that have been fragmented and lack of local capacity has also contributed to this challenge. That said, recent efforts at Abu Dhabi University and in Qatar through the Qatar Biomedical Research Institute are planning to foster innovation and research in public health. The rapid growth of international institutions, particularly research-focused institutions of higher education, has allowed GCC to attract attention and reputable human resources in research and scholarship. However, the engagement of these institutions in addressing local problems of public health has been limited. Lack of innovation also makes the region vulnerable to public health challenges that may or may not originate within the GCC (such as Ebola and MERS) and for which there is limited local capacity, and marginal emphasis on innovation.

The public health system within the GCC needs to restructure for the changing regional and global climate. From a policy perspective, it needs to develop innovative capacity that is able to handle public health emergencies and on the other needs to engage a broad set of local, regional and international institutions that focus on effective, efficient and scalable solutions that are focused on awareness, research and solution implementation. In this regard, the role of local universities, curriculum development, university-hospital partnership, university-industry linkages and international research collaborations, that in the field of public health have historically has been ignored, needs to made a corner stone of public health policy.

Notes

1   William L. Cleveland, *A History of the Modern Middle East*. (Boulder, USA: Westview Press, 2004).
2   "Global Status Report on Noncommunicable Diseases 2010," WHO: http://tinyurl.com/6zbhq9j (accessed 29 June 2016).

3   Rory Jones, "Diabetes Epidemic Hits Persian Gulf Region," Wall Street Journal, February 10, 2014: http://tinyurl.com/ofbszmj (accessed 29 June 2016).

4   "UAE, Qatar have highest expat ratio in GCC," Emirates 24/7, September 11, 2013: http://tinyurl.com/p9x7hoz (accessed 29 June 2016).

5   "National Population by Emirate and Sex 2010 Mid-Year Estimates," United Arab Emirates National Bureau of Statistics: http://tinyurl.com/42aufp6 (accessed 29 June 2016).

6   Soeren Mattke *et al.*, "Population Health Management and the Second Golden Age and Diversifying Economies," Rand Health: http://tinyurl.com/nawkpbg (accessed 29 June 2016).

7   Mona Mourshed, Viktor Hediger and Toby Lambert, "Gulf Cooperation Council Health Care: Challenges and Opportunities" *Global Competitiveness Reports 2006*, World Economic Forum: http://tinyurl.com/n9vy5me (accessed 29 June 2016).

8   Courtney Trenwith, "First Kuwaiti Hospital Starts Morning Ban for Expats," Arabian Business, June 3: 2013, http://tinyurl.com/pz9ybre (accessed 29 June 2016).

9   "Kuwait: Stateless 'Bidun' Denied Rights," Human Rights Watch, June 13, 2011: http://tinyurl.com/ntbgxh9 (accessed 29 June 2016).

10   RM Mabry *et al.*, "Evidence of physical activity participation among men and women in the countries of the gulf cooperation council: A review," *Obesity Reviews* 11 (2010): 457-64.

11   Musaiger NA Abdulrahman, "Food consumption patterns of adults in the United Arab Emirates," *J R Soc Promot Health* 118 (1998): 146-50.

12   Mourshed, "Challenges and opportunities," 56.

13   Sophia Antipolis, "CVD time bomb set to explode in Gulf region in 10 - 15 years," *European Society of Cardiology*, February 13, 2013: http://tinyurl.com/o7anp4c (accessed 29 June 2016).

14   "Health Statistics 2010," Abu Dhabi Statistics Centre: http://tinyurl.com/o9lamqp (accessed 29 June 2016).

15   Mourshed, "Challenges and opportunities," 56.

16   Mourshed, "Challenges and opportunities," 59.

17   Saleh Al-Othman *et al.*, "Tackling cancer control in the Gulf Cooperation Council Countries," *Lancet Oncology* 16 (2015): e246 – e257.

18   Thomas Loney *et al.*, "An analysis of the health status of the United Arab Emirates: the 'Big 4' public health issues," *Global Health Action* 1 (2013): 1-8.

19   Padmakumar Ram, "Management of Healthcare in the Gulf Cooperation Council (GCC) countries with special reference to Saudi Arabia," *International Journal of Academic Research in Business and Social Science* 4 (2014): 24-41.

20   "GCC Healthcare Industry Report 2014," Alpen Capital: http://www.alpencapital.com/industry-reports.html (accessed 29 June 2016).

21   Ram, "Management of Healthcare," 27.

22   GCC Healthcare Industry Report, 55.

23   Ram, "Management of Healthcare," 37.

24   Marc Bornstein, "Medical cities: A new approach to healthcare in the Middle East," *Arab Health Magazine*, Show issue 2015: http://tinyurl.com/ppbfy4o (accessed 29 June 2016).

25   Mourshed, "Challenges and opportunities."

26   HM Abdulghani *et al.*, "What determines the selection of undergraduate medical students to the specialty of their future careers?" *Medical Teach* 35 (2013): S25-S30.

27   Ram, "Management of Healthcare," 62.

28   Basu Ghosh, "Health workforce development planning in the Sultanate of Oman: a case study," *Human Resources Health* 7 (2009).

29   "Global Health Observatory Data Repository: Density per 1000 Health Workforce, 2012," WHO: http://tinyurl.com/jxxjzha (accessed 29 June 2016).

30   Ghosh, "Health workforce development."

31   Gillian White, "Transforming education to strengthen health systems in the sultanate of Oman," *Sultan Qaboos University Medical Journal* 12 (2012):429-34.

32   Moeness Alshishtawy, "Medical Specialties in Oman: Scaling Up through National Action," *Oman Med Journal* 24, no. 4 (2009):279-87.

33   "Continuing Professional Development," *Oman Medical Speciality Board*: http://www.cpdoman.com/home.aspx. (accessed 29 June 2016).

34   Ghosh, "Health workforce development," 12.

35   "GCC pharma, healthcare markets to cross $133 billion in 5 years," Emirates 247, January 27, 2014: http://tinyurl.com/nsfux9w (accessed 29 June 2016).

36   Bornstein, "Medical cities."

37   Ram, "Management of Healthcare," 26.

38   Bornstein, "Medical cities."

39   Ram, "Management of Healthcare," 32.

40   Ram, "Management of Healthcare," 26.

41   Moeness Alshishtawy, "Four Decades of Progress: Evolution of the health system in Oman," *Sultan Qaboos University Medical Journal* 10, no. 1 (2010):12-22.

42   GCC Healthcare Industry Report, 53.

43   "Qatar and UAE are fastest growing healthcare markets in the GCC," *Nuviun Digital Health*, April 24: 2014, http://tinyurl.com/nsmovsd (accessed 29 June 2016).

44   GCC Healthcare Industry Report, 55.

45   "Qatar and UAE fastest growing."

46   "Research and development expenditure (% of GDP), 2011," The World Bank: http://tinyurl.com/2wsb92k (accessed 29 June 2016).

47   Barry Jaruzelski *et al.*, "The Role of Coherent Linkages in Fostering Innovation-Based Economies in the Gulf Cooperation Council Countries," *The Global Innovation Index* (2012): 109-120.

48   World Innovation Summit for Health 2015: http://www.wish.org.qa/home (accessed 29 June 2016).

49   Inconet – GCC2: http://www.inconet-gcc.eu/ (accessed 29 June 2016).

50   Ram, "Management of Healthcare," 27.

51   The Executive Board of Health Ministers' Council for GCC States: http://tinyurl.com/pkhsll5 (accessed 29 June 2016).

52   GCC Healthcare Innovation Congress: http://tinyurl.com/ppjs2pu (accessed 29 June 2016).

53   Klaus Schwab, "The Global Competitiveness Report 2010–2011," World Economic Forum: http://tinyurl.com/2crw9ws (accessed 29 June 2016).

54   Michael E Porter, "The Global Competitiveness Report 2008 – 2009," *World Economic Forum*: http://tinyurl.com/p5z3l8p (accessed 29 June 2016).

55   Schwab, "Global Competitiveness 2010," 491.

56   Porter, "Global Competitiveness 2008," 489.

57   Schwab, "Global Competitiveness 2010," 491.

58   Porter, "Global Competitiveness 2008," 489.

59   "About," *Ministry of Higher Education and Scientific Research at the National Research Foundation*: http://www.nrf.ae/aboutus.aspx (accessed 29 June 2016).

60   "Bachelor of Science in Public Health", *Abu Dhabi University*: http://tinyurl.com/prm7h6y, (accessed 29 June 2016).

61   "Institute of Public Health," *United Arab Emirates University College of Medicine and Health Sciences*: http://tinyurl.com/h4sao7p (accessed 29 June 2016).

62   "UAEU organizes a technology commercialization workshop to support innovation," *United Arab Emirates University*: http://tinyurl.com/pjjd34m (accessed 29 June 2016).

63   "College of Public Health and Health Informatics", King Saud bin Abdulaziz University for Health Sciences: http://tinyurl.com/nz8ufpz (accessed 29 June 2016).

64   Lotfi Chouchane *et al.*, "Medical education and research environment in Qatar: a new epoch for translational research in the Middle East," *Journal of Translational Medicine* 9, no.1 (2011):16.

65   "Division of Global and Public Health," Weill Cornell Medical College in Qatar: http://qatar-weill. cornell.edu/gph/ (accessed 29 June 2016).
     "Health Care Policy and Research Department," Weill Cornell Medical College: http://tinyurl. com/gr277ea (accessed 29 June 2016).

66   "About the program," Qatar University College of Arts and Sciences: http://tinyurl.com/orpwyk8 (accessed 29 June 2016).

67   Anayat Durrani, "Public Health Degrees Equip Arab Students for Regional Concerns," US News & World Report, September 2, 2015: http://tinyurl.com/nlto3w5 (accessed 29 June 2016).

68   Abdellaif Al Husaini, interview by Muhammad Zaman and Katie Clifford, telephone call, September 1, 2015.

69   "Fighting Ebola: A Grand Challenge for Development," USAID: http://tinyurl.com/jvyc7sh (accessed 29 June 2016).

8

Science and Engineering Education in the GCC: Challenges and Transformations

Afreen Siddiqi, Laura Diaz Anadon, and Venkatesh Narayanamurti

The GCC states have enacted policies and programs for reducing economic reliance on oil and gas export revenues and have expanded other industrial sectors and services. The multi-decadal plans, motivated in part by prevailing theories of economic growth[1] from technological innovation,[2] envision future knowledge-based economies in the region.[3]

The GCC states in general, and especially Saudi Arabia, Qatar, and the UAE, have made substantial investments over the last decade in developing domestic institutions of higher education and research. These countries have expanded state-funded scholarships for higher education of their citizens in foreign countries, established new universities, broadened the mission of existing universities to include research, and established technology parks to foster university-industry linkages and stimulate entrepreneurship. For example, Saudi Arabia allocated 210 billion Saudi Riyals (approximately 56 billion USD) in 2014 for education and training that accounted for 24 per cent of the total national budget excluding defense spending. Of this allocation, 10 per cent (22 billion SR, equivalent to 5.8 billion USD) were for foreign scholarships in higher education for Saudi students.[4] Qatar reportedly allocated 2.8 per cent of its GDP for scientific research and development projects,[5] and UAE ranked third among all Arab states (where Qatar topped the list) with a gross expenditure on R&D at 0.49 per cent in 2011.[6]

With economic diversification agendas, there has been particular focus on technical education institutions. The extensive efforts are bearing some fruit, and several indicators reflect positive trends. In a knowledge-based economy, it is not only sufficient to import and impart knowledge, but to also consistently *generate* new knowledge. In that measure, some of the traditional metrics of scientific output (peer-reviewed publications and patents)[7] show large increases in the past decade.

An analysis of the global share of journal article publications from GCC countries in science and engineering disciplines shows that while GCC states periodically gained and lost share during 1981-2005 (Fig. 1), since 2006 there has been consistent advancement for Saudi Arabia, UAE and Qatar.[8] The total share for GCC countries changed from 0.1 per cent in 1981 to 0.7 per cent in 2013. In 1981, Saudi Arabia had 0.07 per cent, Kuwait 0.03 per cent, while

UAE, Qatar, Oman and Bahrain each had around one thousandth of a per cent share. This changed to 0.54 per cent for Saudi Arabia, 0.07 per cent for the UAE, 0.049 per cent for Qatar, 0.039 per cent for Kuwait, 0.029 per cent for Oman, and 0.0092 per cent for Bahrain in 2013.

Saudi Arabia and Qatar have made the most gains compared to the other GCC countries;[9] however, this rapid increase has attracted discussion and debate. The experts point to a combination of policies that incentivize research activities from faculty (for instance, all principal investigators of research projects receive additional monthly payments of at least $1500 for the duration of the project),[10] as well as programs of extensive international collaboration and engagement of foreign researchers.

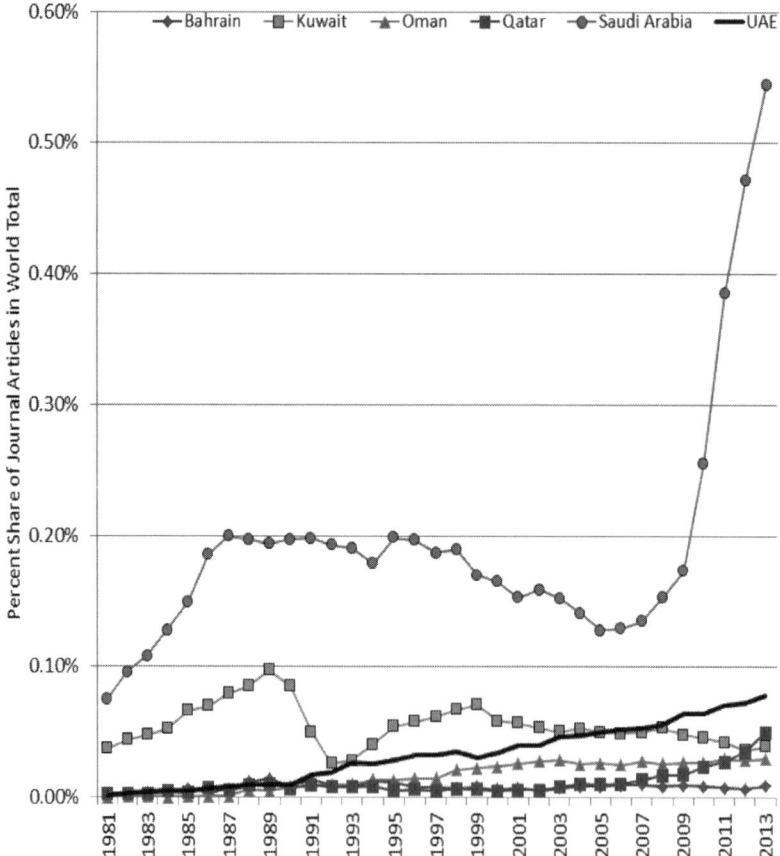

Figure 1: Share of journal publications of GCC countries from 1981-2013 has fluctuated, however Saudi Arabia, UAE, and Qatar have consistently increased their share since 2006.

While on one hand the trends look positive for Saudi Arabia, UAE, and Qatar, the trend for Kuwait, Oman, and Bahrain are either stagnant or decreasing. Furthermore, even for Saudi Arabia, the level of catch up that is needed is evident in its small footprint in the global scientific research arena. For comparison, the US had a global share of 19.2 per cent, China 12.5 per cent, and South Korea ~3 per cent in 2013.[9]

Annual publications are only a partial measure of the state of scientific enterprise, and when other indicators are considered there is continued concern about the level of development in local capacity,[11] and focused science and technology policies.[12] Other metrics such as that of enrollment in technical degree programs,[13] quality of teaching and research, and employment of graduates in private-sector technical positions show a mixed picture. The impact of recent efforts — in particular for Qatar, UAE, and Saudi Arabia — in expanding local science and technology capabilities remains an important open question.

There is an extensive literature on the ailing systems of education in the Arab world, and experts (ranging from private consultants to academic researchers) have examined the problems and prescribed solutions for the Middle East and North Africa at large as well as for specific countries.[14] Overall, MENA countries — of which the GCC states are a part — have made large gains since the 1960s in primary education. The quality and access of higher technical education, however, remains deficient.

There have been extensive state-led efforts to address this issue in the last decade, but with mixed results and persistent questions of long-term development. We examine the challenges in science and engineering (S&E) as perceived by local faculty and researchers. Here, we report on our findings from semi-structured interviews with senior university administrators, faculty, and industry executives in Saudi Arabia, Kuwait, the UAE, and Qatar, and synthesize and discuss the emergent themes.

Data Collection and Analysis

In this study, which is part of a larger project on investigating the state and challenges in science, technology, and innovation in the Middle East, we explored the perspectives of key stakeholders. In the results and analysis presented here, we draw from over 80 semi-structured interviews in more than 20 different institutions with faculty, senior administrators (including university presidents, VPs of research, and college deans), and senior executives of technology companies conducted during 2013-2015 (Table 1). The interviews, lasting 30-90 minutes, were semi-structured with common questions about challenges and follow up questions that differed based on the answers of the experts.

The interviews with university administrators (with variations for other institutions and interviewees) included questions about the vision and mission of the university, their perception of the big challenges in strengthening science and engineering in their institution and more broadly in the country, strategies for increasing enrollment for local citizens in technical education, nature of existing collaborations and partnerships with other universities and industry, and impact of international collaborations (if any) on their institution.

Table 1: List of Institutions Where Interviews Were Conducted

Saudi Arabia	King Abdullah University for Science and Technology (KAUST); King Abdullah Economic City (KAEC); King Fahd University of Petroleum and Minerals (KFUPM); Dhahran Techno Valley (DTV); Saudi Oil Company (Saudi Aramco)
Qatar	Qatar University; Texas A&M – Doha; Weill-Cornell Medical College – Doha; RAND Corporation – Doha; Qatar Foundation
UAE	Masdar Institute of Science and Technology; Khalifa University; UAE University – Al Ain; Masdar – Energy; Abu Dhabi Technology Investment Company; Abu Dhabi Technology Development Committee;
Kuwait	Kuwait University; Gulf University of Science and Technology; Ministry of Higher Education; Sabah Al Ahmed Center for Giftedness and Creativity; Kuwait Society for Advancement of Arab Children; Kuwait Foundation for Advancement of Science; Kuwait Institute for Scientific Research; Advanced Technology Company

The responses in some cases were specific to the country; however, there were some consistent and often-repeated themes that touched upon both the problems as well as solutions on what would be needed to make some of the emerging positive trends as not symbols of transient growth but indicators of lasting education reform.

In the following sections we first provide a brief overview of some key projects and education initiatives that have been taken in the countries of study over the last decade, and then present and elaborate on the continuing challenges that were discussed in the interviews.

A Decade of New Ambitions, Investments, and Institutions

Policy makers in the GCC have viewed higher education in science and engineering as a necessary element for building local technical expertise needed to run the engine of industrial development and economic diversification. Starting from mid to late 1990s, the issue of education was brought in sharp focus with ambitious policies rolled out in Qatar. Saudi Arabia, under new leadership in 2006, followed with its own agenda of revamping and revitalizing education in the country. The leadership in the United Arab Emirates also pursued goals of a highly educated citizenry and a vision of a future knowledge-based economy. Kuwait, with a longer history of education and local research as compared to other GCC states, has struggled but sought to further build its scientific enterprise.

In Saudi Arabia, some key developments included the establishment of King Abdullah University of Science and Technology (KAUST) that was inaugurated in 2009, Princess Nourah Bint Abdul Rahman University established in 2008, and a number of new programs and initiatives at King Fahd University of Petroleum and Minerals in Dhahran.[13] In 2001-2004 period, the fraction of graduates in science and technology programs was only 12.5 per cent (as compared to 66.6 per cent in business administration, accounting, and psychology) in the country. In efforts to increase enrollment and access, 35 new technical colleges were opened to provide technical education and vocational training by 2008.[16]

In the UAE, Masdar Institute of Science and Technology was established in 2007 in Abu Dhabi, and new and expanded facilities for Khalifa University of Science and Technology (formerly Etisalat college) have been built. A number of additional developments such as Masdar City with a Free Zone to attract foreign technology companies, location of International Renewable Energy Agency (IRENA) headquarters *etc.* are all part of many recent steps in creating a base of locally resident educators and researchers in critical technology areas.[17]

Qatar embarked on its ambitious agenda of higher education with strong state support. The Qatar Foundation (QF), established in 1995, spearheaded many initiatives, including the Education City in Doha, that hosts several campuses of foreign universities connected to science and engineering, such as Texas A&M, Weill-Cornell Medical College, and Carnegie Mellon University.[18] QF has also launched World Innovation Summit for Education (WISE) to annually convene practitioners and scholars in Doha from around the globe to share best practices and approaches for promoting education. In addition, Qatar Science and Technology Park and Qatar National Research Fund have been created with the aim of steering national development in strategic areas.[3]

Kuwait announced a $150 billion economic diversification plan in 2009.[19] The Kuwait Foundation for Advancement of Science and Kuwait Institute for Scientific Research developed new strategic plans for growth and reform, and Kuwait University established international research collaborations with foreign universities in technical areas of national relevance (such as a large collaborative program with MIT on research in energy and water technologies). In addition, several programs were funded in international policy schools (including London School of Economics in the UK) to foster research on regionally critical issues such as economic growth and diversification.

Continuing Challenges in Science and Engineering Education and Research

The enthusiasm in the regional science communities, due to the government investments and support, is marked with caution. A sense of uncertainty pervades given the past history of the region and continuing questions about its geo-political and socio-economic spheres. Furthermore, experts recognize that new infrastructure and new hires alone will not be sufficient for bridging the significant gaps in science and technology that have continued to widen with time, address systemic issues of poor education quality, and affect how science is valued in the larger society. These broader issues had some bearing on the factors that emerged from the semi-structured interviews, that included i) questions on continuation of education policies with sustained state-support for S&E (even during economic downturns), ii) calibration of expectations (that are often not matched with constraints and risks in the development of nascent programs), iii) incentives for attracting, retaining, and integrating talent, iv) creation of culture of excellence and self-reliance, and (v) building networks for engagement of local industry, researchers, and decision makers.

Sustained Policy and State Support for Lasting Reform

The GCC states have had a checkered past in S&E, with repeated patterns of some progress followed by regression over the last thirty years (At least as measured by publications output shown in Fig. 1). This history has left lingering uncertainties among senior faculty and administrators who remain concerned for sustained long-term policy emphasis on education and research. In our interviews, this issue was often mentioned as the key factor that will determine the long-term outcomes. A high-ranking administrator expressed concern that "The resources that are needed to create permanency [in knowledge capital] are up for question…They need to provide continued and assured support to build a knowledge economy".[20] The senior administrators called for "continuation of forward-looking" policies in S&E, and emphasized the need for sustained high-level state support — pointing out that for nascent programs and new establishments it is a matter of survival. While established institutions have some capacity to withstand cyclical funding, the new programs need a sufficient period of nurturing such that they develop internal strength and capabilities for future independent functioning and growth.

A few senior officials pointed to the need for stable funding that assure steady availability of resources and continuation of the universities missions, with one of them noting that, "Relying on public support makes universities vulnerable. Endowments can help stabilize the finances and give flexibility and independence to universities to pursue what they see as their objectives."[21]

Setting Expectations for Long-Term Impacts

The expectations for some of the newly established technical institutions have been narrowly cast for producing near to-medium term (5-7 years) results. The returns on "investment" (made through state funding) are being sought in the form of patents, start-ups, and other measurable outcomes directly or closely linked to economic indicators. These expectations stem in part from the goals and visions of a knowledge economy, along with attitudes prevalent in corporate management cultures to which some of the decision-makers are closely linked or engaged.

A number of interviewees discussed the difficulties of conforming to short-term output expectations, and emphasized the need to recognize the long time scales that are involved in realizing desired benefits from universities and education programs. One senior administrator described this issue as, "There is some impatience from the government to show immediate results, and there is a focus on the short-term report cards. However, one cannot leap frog everything. There are some things that cannot be leap- frogged, and one of those things is a solid foundation of an educated population".[22]

A more suitable approach for calibrating expectations is one in which the focus is shifted from short-term, direct impacts, to long-term indirect impacts that result from institutions of higher learning. Lester *et al*, in a wide-ranging study on universities, innovation, and impacts on local economies, discussed this issue:[23]

> A university can also play an important role as a public space for ongoing conversations, involving local industry practitioners, about the future direction of technologies, markets and local industrial development. This public space can take many forms, including meetings, conferences, industrial liaison programs, standards forums, entrepreneur/investor forums, visiting committee discussions of departmental curricula, and so on. The conversations between university and industry people that occur in these spaces are rarely about solving specific technical or commercial problems. But they often generate ideas that later become the focus of problem solving both in industry and in universities. The importance of the public space role of the university and its contribution to local innovation performance is frequently underestimated.

The highly regarded technical universities of US and Europe — whose successes the regional policy makers seek to emulate — have followed long paths of development (on the order of decades and centuries) fashioned partly by circumstance and partly by strategy. Thus, while global recognition and high standing is a worthy upfront goal, it is necessary to provide time and continued support to achieve such goals. Our interviewees pointed out the need for devising strategies that take into account not only the distinctive challenges confronting new institutions in a globalizing world, but also the unique local realities of the region. As Brinkely *et al*. aptly note:[19]

> High-profile examples of successful national and regional economies, based on blockbuster licenses on university-patented research and technology transfer to small and medium enterprises (SMEs) and start-ups, have become a gold standard and universal blueprint for policymakers but have limited relevance in many settings.

Attracting Local and Global Talent for Building Enduring Capacity

Saudi Arabia, Qatar, and UAE have actively sought to attract and relocate top talent to gain international visibility and a jump-start in research.[24] A common issue that was repeatedly mentioned in our interviews, from university presidents to college deans, was of the "chronic shortage of human capital."[25] Some of the regional universities have created significant incentives for attracting highly qualified faculty and researchers through generous financial resources, the construction of world-class infrastructure, and provision of state-of-the art lab facilities and equipment. These are important steps for seeding and establishing institutions, however, they are insufficient in themselves. The retention and *further* recruitment of good talent for long-term institutional growth requires a system that provides professional fulfillment and ample opportunities for career-advancement.

For GCC nationals, the difficulty of their integration into scientific research once they return from foreign training and education is a critical issue. The significant scientific asymmetry between the countries in which they train and their countries to which they return has been a major barrier in their retention and local integration for scientific work. While some new universities have created world-class research laboratories in the region, the quality of facilities for scientific research remains inadequate and under-staffed in most public universities in the GCC. A senior administrator, commenting on the need for establishing world-class local institutions for graduate-level research, noted that

> Currently, the students go abroad for PhDs, and come back as "strangers". They do their research on very high end problems, stem cells, or other advanced topics and come back to find that they cannot do any work back home since there is no support system, labs, and other colleagues. They then either "die" as researchers, or wait for a long time to get their labs set up etc. and simply tag up with colleagues abroad to publish and do work.[26]

For the expatriates in S&E in the region, the interviews highlighted issues of the high turnover of faculty and researchers. It was pointed out that short-term visa policies and contractual jobs lead to a constant churn of people that arrests quality improvement and institutional development. This dynamic undermines productivity and impedes the cumulative processes of learning and scholarship. These issues have been discussed and documented but remain unaddressed as they connect with complex and sensitive issues of immigration policy and ultimately national identity. The policies of importing labor on short-term contracts have enabled successful construction projects and large-scale physical development of the region, but experts question the efficacy of such policies for developing local intellectual capital and knowledge-based economies.

Preparing Future Scientists and Engineers

Students in S&E programs, needed for a healthy pipeline of future scientists and engineers, are at the core of efforts in nations seeking to build capabilities in science and technology. However, in the GCC states, the enrollment in S&E programs of local students is not resulting in positive national trends. The experts in our interviews pointed to inadequate student preparation and insufficient incentives for local careers in research and engineering as key factors behind this issue.

The faculty noted that on national scales, the entering university students in GCC countries are not adequately prepared in math, science, and English (the language of engineering education in the region). The poor quality of teaching in schools leaves students with analytical, quantitative, and communication skills that are not at par with requirements of university-level S&E degree programs. Furthermore, while enrollment is low to begin with (as compared to enrollment in humanities and management programs), there is also high attrition as inadequately prepared students struggle in S&E and then switch to other programs. Some also noted that the quality of teaching in many state universities is also deficient, feeding into a vicious cycle of reinforcing student perceptions of S&E being difficult. In some cases, the universities have a higher fraction of students enrolled in the humanities due to lack of sufficient number of facilities for S&E programs. Science and engineering education requires more funds, expensive facilities, and resources — often a challenge for universities to secure.[11]

Additionally, the low enrollment in S&E is partly due to lack of awareness and exposure to careers in science. One research dean observed: "It comes down to exposure. If they are not exposed to careers in medicine and research, not aware of what these fields entail, the type of work, the quality of life style etc., the students will not know and will not choose these fields. They need exposure to consider this as a career path."[27]

In terms of career choices that impact students' selection of training and degree programs, the well-paying public sectors jobs and generous social security stipends for GCC nationals create secure and lucrative career paths. Therefore, many young graduates are unwilling to take up demanding careers in research or undertake risks with untested technology start-ups. While some graduates from technical universities prefer private sector technical jobs and are pursuing dynamic careers, they are a small fraction. Additionally, government-mandated hiring quotas for nationals[28] in private sector businesses are leading to adverse dynamics of eroding competence required for securing jobs and lack of incentives for students to pursue demanding degree programs.

Creating Culture of Excellence and Building Domestic Expertise

Several faculty members and senior administrators pointed to a dire need for bringing about a cultural transformation that seeks excellence and one in which challenging work is embraced, critical thinking is promoted, and a self-reliant attitude of original problem solving is expected.

One high-ranking administrator (who was formerly active in research as a faculty member) explained: There is a culture of sub-contracting the research out to others, and there are no incentives to change. Even [the national research agency] does research by sub-contracting it to outside consultants who will do the actual work, write a report, and that's it. If one wants to go back to revise, or refine the work, then the consultants ask for more money and a new contract for that revision. A contractual type of research enterprise does not help solve the national problems.[29]

Some called for fostering an environment where "ambition" and "drive" is kindled and rewarded, and pointed out that the low enrollment in science and engineering is also partly due to student hesitation in taking on challenges.

Connecting Nodes to Build Networks: Engaging Science, Society, and Policy

An eco-system where researchers and entrepreneurs can convene with shared professional interests is needed for education and research to thrive. The importance of clusters, wherein specialized institutions and actors are located in close proximity, synergistically interact to impact innovation and industrial competitiveness has been extensively documented.[30] The universities need to be strongly linked with their host societies – that is part of the success of the higher education system in Europe, US and other countries, and one that is conspicuously deficient in most Arab countries.[13] Many universities in the region are isolated nodes where they may be islands of potential future excellence, but are far removed from local society and disconnected from the local economies. In the GCC, there are weak (and in some cases missing) linkages within and across local universities, between universities and local industries, and between universities and decision-making bodies in national governments.

Some of the faculty in our interviews pointed out that institutional isolation (rather than constructive competition) is prevalent in many cases, stifling collaboration and limiting the potential for creating larger clusters of academic and research excellence in the region. One professor observed that the "hardest collaborations are between universities in the same country in the GCC. There is competition [among] the universities [as they want] to be seen as better than the rest so that they can attract more government funding. The universities have deep rivalries and do not collaborate."[31]

Visiting faculty fellowships among local universities, multi-university local collaborative research projects, and provisions for faculty to immerse and engage with domestic industry on short leaves of absences are rare or not present altogether. Furthermore, there is little to no opportunity for paid consulting by faculty — experts in engineering and scientific disciplines — in local industries. In fact, in most state universities in the region, faculty members are not permitted to consult for private firms.[32] There are few to no councils of technical experts from academia connected to active research and teaching that advise decision-makers or serve in decision-making capacities in government.

Conclusions: Towards the Road to Transformation

The challenges and developments in higher education, research, and industrial development have been studied and reported since the GCC states laid out visions for future economic diversification.[33] There are, however, comparatively few studies that have sought to examine persistent and broader societal issues that are reining back the potential for local development despite the efforts for change.[34]

Our study finds that while the goal of building local capacity in science and engineering has been taken up by national governments, the scale and scope of efforts is not commensurate with the needs. Additional investments in people and places will be required. Furthermore, recognizing that impacts of institutions of higher learning are more than directly measurable impacts on national GDP is critical. In a knowledge economy, some of the most important assets are highly qualified people and new ideas.[23] Aligning expectations in consort with the unique local context and aiming for long-term societal benefits will better serve and support the mission of regional transformation and societal advancement.

A healthy ecosystem of research and collaboration has yet to take root in the GCC, and at the system level — from elementary education to employment — there are many weak links and in some places missing elements. The challenge of education culture, rather than curriculum, looms large and daunting yet is necessary to address if real and positive change is to be realized.

The areas for improvement are greatly interlinked. A culture of embracing challenges is unlikely to emerge if there are no incentive structures to reward taking on such challenges. In one sense, the most important takeaway is that for technical capabilities and enterprises to emerge, incentives need to be fashioned to attract and retain a willing workforce that would seek to tackle local socio-economic, and environmental challenges. Financial drivers will be key factors for incentivizing participation in technical careers. However, the societal benefits and welfare that can come about from scientific teaching and research — including public health, safety, and environmental improvements — also need to be emphasized and highlighted to attract a new and motivated generation of students, researchers, and entrepreneurs. Lastly, but perhaps most importantly, societal appreciation of the benefits of higher education and local research in S&E is crucial (and currently a missing link) that can help sustain long-term policies and state support for strengthening local institutions.

Notes

This research was supported by a grant from The Kuwait Program at Harvard Kennedy School.

1   J. A. Schumpeter, _The Theory of Economic Development_ (Oxford University Press, 1934).
2   C. Freeman, Technology Policy and Economic Performance: Lessons from Japan (London, Pinter, 1987).
3   "Qatar National Development Strategy 2011~ 2016: Towards Qatar National Vision 2030," Qatar General Secretariat for Development Planning, Doha, 2011. "Educating the Next Generation of Emiratis: A Master Plan for UAE Higher Education," United Arab Emirates Ministry of Higher Education and Scientific Research, Office of Higher Education Policy and Planning, 2007.
4   http://tinyurl.com/zpwjxsp
5   "Qatar Tops Gulf and Developed Nations in Research Spending," _Arab News Express_, July 2, 2012: http://tinyurl.com/nbhaod7.
6   L. Veale, "What is Being Done About the State of Science in the Arab world?" _MIT Technology Review_ – Arabic Edition, February 10, 2015: http://tinyurl.com/jq4pxgp
7   R. M. May, "The Scientific Wealth of Nations," _Science_ 275 (5301) (1997), 793-96.
8   We used publications data (of full journal articles and excluding such items as conference proceedings and review articles) from the Science Citation Index-Expanded from the Web of ScienceTM Core Collection. A paper was attributed to a country publication count if _any_ author of the paper had an address located in the given country of search. The world total count was adjusted accordingly to determine the fractional share of each country in world total publications for each year.
9   A. Siddiqi, J. Stoppani, L. D. Anadon, V. Narayanamurti, "Scientific Wealth of Middle East and North Africa: Productivity, Indigeneity, and Speciality in 1981-2013" (under review).
10 M. Al-Ohali, and J. C Shin., "Knowledge-Based Innovation and Research Productivity in Saudi Arabia," in _Higher Education in Saudi Arabia_, ed. Smith and Abouammoh, 95-102.
11 A. B. Zahlan, _Science, Development, and Sovereignty in the Arab World_ (New York: Palgrave Macmillan, 2012).

12   M. Sioufi, "It's Not Just About Oil: Kuwait Needs a Science and Technology Policy to Harmonize the Country's Efforts of Advancing Sciences," *MIT Technology Review – Arab Edition*, May 12, 2015.

13   L. Smith and A. Abouammoh, Eds., *Higher Education in Saudi Arabia; Achievements, Challenges and Opportunities* (New York, Springer Link, 2013).

14   "The Road Not Traveled: Education Reform in the Middle East and North Africa," *MENA Development Report* (The World Bank, Washington, D C, 2007); M. Barber, M. Mourshed, F. Whelan, "Improving Education in the Gulf," special edition: Reappraising the Gulf States, *McKinsey Quarterly 2007*, 39-47; Z. Bunglawala, "Nurturing A Knowledge Economy in Qatar," *Policy Briefing*, Brookings Doha Center, 2011.

15   Ibid.

16   M. A. Ramady, *The Saudi Arabian Economy: Policies, Achievements, and Challenges*, Second Edition, (New York: Springer, 2010).

17   http://tinyurl.com/hlwvzee.

18   D. P. Hajjar, et al. "Prospects for Policy Advances in Science and Technology in the Gulf Arab States: The Role for International Partnerships," *International Journal on Higher Education* 3, no. 3 (2014), 45-57.

19   I. Brinkley, W. Hutton, P. Schneider, K. C. Ulrichsen, "Kuwait and the Knowledge Economy," London School of Economics and Political Science, Report No. 22 (April 2012).

20   Senior university administrator, name withheld by request, February, 2015.

21   Senior university administrator, name withheld by request, February, 2015.

22   Senior university administrator, name withheld by request, March, 2013.

23   R. Lester, "Universities, Innovation, and the Competitiveness of Local Economies: A Summary Report from the Local Innovation Systems Project – Phase I," MIT Industrial Performance Center Working Paper 05-010 (2005).

24   Q. Schiermeier, "Middle Eastern Promise," *Nature*, 500 (2013), 111-12.

25   Academic dean, name withheld, December, 2013.

26   Senior university research administrator, name withheld, April, 2014.

27   Research dean, name withheld, December, 2013.

28   H. Mustafa, "Saudization Program Not Helping Saudi Arabia's Economic 'Competitiveness,'", *Al Arabiya*, September 5, 2013: http://tinyurl.com/pau62am.

29   Senior university research administrator, name withheld, April 2014.

30   M. Delgado, M. E. Porter, and S. Stern, "Clusters, Convergence, and Economic Performance," NBER Working Paper Series, National Bureau of Economic Research, 2012.
     O. Sorenson, J. W. Rivkin, L. Fleming, "Complexity, networks and knowledge flow," *Research Policy* 35 (2006), 994–1017.

31   Senior university research administrator, name withheld, April 2014.

32   Academic dean, name withheld, February 2015.

33   A. Zewail, "Dire need for a Middle Eastern science spring," *Nature Materials* 13 (2014), 38-320.

34   A. Siddiqi and Laura D. Anadon, eds., Science and Technology Development in the Gulf States: Economic Diversification through Regional Collaboration (Berlin: Gerlach Press, 2016).

9

Afterword: State-Society Dialogues in the GCC Knowledge Economy

Rogaia Mustafa Abusharaf

In the foreword to the Qatar National Vision 2030, the "knowledge economy" is depicted as an "authentic" key to human, economic, environmental and social development that has "emerged from intensive consultation across Qatari society. It is based on the guiding principles of Qatar's Permanent Constitution. It reflects the aspirations of the Qatari people and the resolve of their political leadership" to transforming themselves.[1] This claim to authenticity informs the title of this chapter. It raises questions of meaning for the state-society dynamic, as the former aspires to diversification and gender inclusivity. In the Qatar National Vision's articulation of its goals of "charting economic and social progress in modern societies," and by invoking the language of nationalization, Qatar, like other Gulf monarchies, strives to shift perceptions *vis-à-vis* expatriate labor, sustainability, security, and self-fashioning through "nation branding in late modernity."[2] As a vehicle for constructing new citizen identities in a world ridden with competitiveness over resources, higher education and citizenship are inseparable from concerns over reliance on expatriates. It is reductive to conclude that Gulf nationals merely resent foreigners sharing in the "wealth of their nations;" such reliance on foreigners is often met with mixed responses. Pursuing modernity and progress through the knowledge economy as a major objective of nationalization begs the question as to what strategies or adaptive preferences should be adopted by Gulf societies to mediate between authenticity and modernity. This is particularly important in a section of the Qatar document addressing what being an educated population means overall:

> A world-class educational system that equips citizens to achieve their aspirations and to meet the needs of Qatar's society their aspirations and to meet the needs of Qatar's society, including: educational curricula and training programs responding to the current and future needs of the labor market; high quality educational and training opportunities appropriate to each individual's aspirations and abilities; accessible educational programs for life-long learning. A national network of formal and non-formal educational program that equip Qatari children and youth

with the skills and motivation to contribute to society, fostering a solid grounding in Qatari moral and ethical values, traditions and cultural heritage; a strong sense of belonging and citizenship; innovation and creativity…(among others).[3]

The document proceeds by listing several key 'human development outcomes' expected to accrue from higher education and preparedness of citizens in the labor markets through increased diversification cognizant of the important role of women's participation at the highest levels of economic and political leadership.

An in-depth reading of what it means to be an educated citizen as inscribed in the Vision's enumerations of the above attributes, provides potential opportunities for dialogues about citizenship, modernity, cultural heritage and the paradoxes they present. Given the weight placed on preservation of culture and morality while discussing higher education as a modernizing force leads us to ask the following questions: What modernity? From whose perspective is the quest for it being advanced as an objective necessitated by the demands of a globalized 21st century universe? Can we consider a context-specific Gulf-vernacularized alternative modernity as a conceptual frame within which the overall projects of capacity-building, and reconciliation of competing visions within the region is comprehended? What are the cultural, political, and economic dimensions of knowledge economy in the global discourse on preparedness and competition? These questions are important for GCC societies to which this volume addresses itself.

Invariably, the leadership in all Gulf societies deploys the language of a knowledge-based economy (defined by the OECD as "the driver of productivity and economic growth, leading to a new focus on the role of information, technology, and learning in economic performance")[4] as their states continue to witness a meteoric rise in the numbers of universities and colleges, both national and "offshore" college campuses, public and private (see Stoll in this volume). As Dale Eickelman argues "the reason for the rapid growth in higher education in particular, is not unique to the region." Higher education, as Karoly argues, "is propelled by the rapid pace of technological change, as well as the interdependent, global economy, forces that together demand a workforce with the capacity for leadership, problem solving, and collaboration and communication in a wide range of economic sectors. Within this context, the education and workforce development systems are critical for supporting human capital development throughout the life course."[5] As Eickelman demonstrates, "the global growth in higher education—extending beyond the original capacity of existing institutions—has produced a variety of responses, including the creation of new kinds of institutions and adaptation of the old."

The subject of reorienting education through expanding public and western institutions is one of the theoretical and practical concerns of this volume. The knowledge economy as a transformative discourse is not as clear-cut as the extant literature leads us to conclude. There are important rifts in Gulf societies to be considered as far as the debates on higher education as a modernizing force. The use of English as a medium of higher education instruction is emblematic of the sahism between the forces of Arabization and those of advocating western-style curriculum. In an instructive ethnography of these palpable tensions, Sally Findlow sheds light on the relationship between higher education, language shift, and cultural (re)production through such post-colonial educational bilingualism.[6] Her work documents the recalibration of collective identities through mass higher education in one Arab Gulf country within the context of "recurrent pan-Arab and Islamist-tinged nationalism." Her conclusion, that "language and higher education (can act) as tools or fields for cultural transformation and for resistance identity construction,"[7] is telling of the anxieties about language as a tool of cultural imperialism as evidenced in the debates about offshore campuses.[8] As Eickelman shows (this volume), these competing narratives are evident in the rubrics entailed in liberal arts education which is equivocated with secularism. As this volume illustrates, both the traditional and the modern are in constant tension given the marked shifts in demography, labor markets, urbanisms, and cosmopolitan ambitions as in the case of Dubai when upon entry into its extravagant airport, one is greeted with "Dubai: The Center of Now," whereas in another portal the greeting reads "Our Heritage, Our Responsibility." By focusing on these paradoxes with regards to different types of higher education in Iran and Saudi Arabia, Keiko Sakurai (this volume) explores why and how these countries resist compromising their religion-cultural norms despite accepting major institutional characteristics of Western universities. Her conclusions about the interaction between Islam and the "Western model," which produces the unique type of universities in Iran and Saudi Arabia, is an illustrative example of these tensions. A different response, however, is clear in Abdulrahman Al-Salimi, who identifies the patterns of transformation of religious learning in Oman: tradition and modernity. He writes:

The last fifty years make a period of great change in the role of religious leadership and education in the Sultanate of Oman. The country moved from bifurcated leadership between an Imam and a Sultan to a single political authority. These decades also witnessed the modernization of the state. These factors combined to reshape the place of religion and religious education in society. Whereas previously religious leaders have relative autonomy and more direct political influence, now they were brought under the auspices of the government with their focus circumscribed to religious matters. The structures and foci of religious education were then reshaped so that tradition provided a platform for progress and the more zealous ideologies emerging in the region could be held at bay. This has permitted Oman to modernize and engage with a global society in an amicable, non-sectarian, manner.[9]

Sheikha Al-Misnad, the former President of Qatar University, elucidated both patterns of accommodation and protest as far as the conflicting responses to education in her work on the development of modern education in the Gulf, engaging with issues as complex as family constraints, social structures, the transition from *kuttab* to Arabian mission western-style led education[10]. If Grant McCracken is right when he posited "When modern routines emerge, the pattern holds. For a moment, these new routines appear to win the day, but eventually they prove merely to be an addition to the standing set,[11] then the shifting boundaries of the traditional and the modern must be incorporated as a paradox that the states must confront head-on. Read in this context, the knowledge economy as vehicle for nationalization can be understood as a facet of social change, with great expectations pinned on self-reinvention.

According to Kapiszewski, for this transformation to occur "states plan to upgrade their educational systems, subsidize work by nationals, force companies to hire more nationals, and try to modernize the work ethic and attitudes of natives of these countries."[12]

This project is not without its critics. Both Sheikha Al-Misnad and Gawdat Bahgat expressed concerns regarding the seeming lack of alignment between degrees pursued by students and labor market needs.[13] Although efforts at aligning educational attainment with labor market priorities are clear as evident in Zaman and Clifford's (this volume) examination of the trajectories of public health education in the GCC, we cannot assume that it will eliminate the reliance on foreign labor. Within the quest for nationalization as we see in our chapter on science and engineering education in the GCC (Siddiqi *et al.*, this volume), in-depth analysis of the challenges surrounding science and education are numerous in light of the poor education quality that mitigates the opportunities of latent attainment without continued reliance on global talent dealing with the soft power potential of higher education in Qatar (see Manjang, this volume) with respect to the continued support of foreign students. Stoll's contribution to the conversation on a "branch" campus in Qatar dovetails with the work of Laila Kadiwal and Irfan Rind, who argue in the context of Dubai that students and teachers are both transformed as "selective cosmopolitans who negotiate cross-cultural influences pragmatically and ambivalently" (2008:689).[14] Namie Tsujigami's work on shifting aspirations in Saudi Arabia (this volume) is a relevant example of the ways in which the Kingdom is negotiating a powerful cultural current with respect to diversity and inclusion of women in the public realm.

Knowledge-Economy Beyond the Obvious

In concept and practice, a knowledge-based economy in the GCC States must be located both within the changing landscape of the realities of state rentierism and the economic safety net accrued from it by Gulf nationals. In his work on late rentierism in the GCC, Matthew Gray was critical of rentierism's inability to adjust to globalization, new technologies, and social change and development priorities. He explains rentierism's main tenet as follows: "since the state receives external income and distributes it to society, it is relieved of having to impose taxation, which in turn means that it does not have to offer concessions to society such as democratic bargain or development strategy." Whether this social contract stays put or becomes part of a bigger renegotiation of "an evolving ruling bargain" is a broad question that lies beyond the scope of this project.[15] Suffice it to say that investment in higher education built on solid economy may be considered here as one of the adaptive strategies that concerns Gray as conspicuously absent from the state's calculations. Read in this context, the knowledge economy can be understood as a dialogue between state and society with the expectation that the latter should spare no effort at pushing their citizens to reinvent themselves. As a vehicle for constructing new identities in a world ridden with competition over scarce resources, higher education becomes an urgent socioeconomic, cultural, and political project. In light of the vast demographic, economic, and social considerations punctuating the drive for higher education, the astonishing rate of urbanization as a factor in the states' modernizing projects is worthy of note. When the knowledge economy as a transformative discourse is seen as an element in the structural shifts afoot, we can begin to address how urbanism as a way of life has enabled Gulf citizens to make choices about their future aspirations. Zaman and Clifford's study (this volume) provides a powerful evidence of urbanization and the new demands it dictated for a rapidly changing regional health landscape.

This volume is an effort to navigate some of the opportunities and challenges in "building universities that lead" (see Eickelman, this volume). The subject of higher education in the neoliberal age lends itself to the interdiciplinarity reflected in it. Tackled from the perspectives of journalism (Dedinsky, this volume) to international relations (Manjang, this volume), anthropology (Eickelman, this volume), history, science and medicine (Zaman, Siddiqi *et al.*) the discourse and practice of higher education in this volume tried to illuminate the dialectics of state and society as seen through the lens of institutions of higher learning. The efforts are timely and laudable, but ironies remain as GCC societies venture forth with ensuring that sustainability, diversification, and competition in the global marketplace of ideas can come to fruition. The Gulf region has historically played an important role in providing opportunities for foreign workers and afforded many valuable opportunities throughout the histories of its cities from Muscat and Mutrah, Dubai, Abu Dhabi, Al Aïn, Dammam, and the old cities of Hofuf, Doha, Manama, and Muharraq, Kuwait City, Basrah, Bandar Abbas, and Bandar Lengeh. All have forged an early learning environment regardless of the traditional nature bestowed at the time. Therefore, adapting to global challenges and fluctuating market forces is a process and not merely a by-product. What remains significant in the knowledge economy discourse is in the end what is considered by state and society to be relevant and negotiable.

Notes

1. State of Qatar General Secretariat for Developing and Planning, "Qatar National Vision 2030" (Doha, Qatar, 2008), Foreword.
2. Christopher S. Browning, "Nation Branding, National Self-Esteem, and the Constitution of Subjectivity in Late Modernity," *Foreign Policy Analysis* 11, no. 2 (2015): 195–214.
3. General Secretariat for Developing and Planning, "Qatar National Vision 2030," 16.
4. It is important to note here that in the context of knowledge economy, performance can defined as active national labor force engagement in all aspects of socioeconomic development.
5. Lynn a. Karoly, "The Role of Education in Preparing Graduates for the Labor Market in the GCC Countries," *SSRN Electronic Journal*, 2010, http://papers.ssrn.com/abstract=1554716.
6. Sally Findlow, "Higher Education and Linguistic Dualism in the Arab Gulf," *British Journal of Sociology of Education* 27, no. 1 (2006): 19–36: http://www.jstor.org/stable/30036113
7. See also Sally Findlow, "International Networking in the United Arab Emirates Higher Education System: Global–local Tensions," *Compare: A Journal of Comparative and International Education* 35, no. 3 (2005): 285–302: http://tinyurl.com/zd575y2

8   Paul Lefrere, "Competing Higher Education Futures in a Globalising World," *European Journal of Education* 42, no. 2 (2007): 201–212.

9   Abdulrahman Al-SalimiI, "The Transformation of Religious Learning in Oman: Tradition and Modernity," *Journal of the Royal Asiatic Society* 21, no. 02 (May 18, 2011): 147–157: http://tinyurl.com/gmdvc8d

10   Sheikha Al-Misnad, *The Development of Modern Education in the Gulf* (London: Ithaca Press, 1985).

11   Grant McCracken, "Transformations : Identity Construction in Contemporary Culture," in *Transformations: Identity Construction in Contemporary Culture*, 2008, xxiii.

12   A Kapiszewski, "Population, Labour and Education Dilemmas Facing GCC States at the Turn of the Century.," in *Cross-Roads of the New Millennium. Proceedings of the Technological Education and National Development (TEND) Conference* (Abu Dhabi, 2000): http://eric.ed.gov/?id=ED447278

13   Gawdat Bahgat, "Education in the Gulf Monarchies: Retrospect and Prospect," *International Review of Education* 45, no. 2 (1999): 127–36.

14   See Matthew Gray, "A Theory of ' Late Rentierism ' in the Arab States of the Gulf," *Center for International and Regional Studies*, no. 7 (2011): 1–50.

15   For in-depth analysis Mehran Kamrava, *Beyond the Arab Spring: The Evolving Ruling Bargain in the Middle East* (London: Oxford University Press, 2013).

About the Contributors

Rogaia Mustafa Abusharaf is Associate Professor of Anthropology at Georgetown University-Qatar Campus. Her books include *Wanderings* (2002), *Transforming Displaced Women* (2009), and several edited volumes, most recently *Africa and the Gulf Region* (co-edited with Dale F. Eickelman, 2015).

Laura Diaz Anadon is Assistant Professor at the Kennedy School of Government at Harvard University and Visiting Senior Lecturer in the Department of Science, Technology, Engineering, and Public Policy at the University College London. Professor Anadon's research focuses on innovation institutions, energy and technology policy, managing uncertainty, and the policy implications of the interdependencies of resources. She has advised policy makers internationally and worked as a consultant for various international organizations. She was a co-editor of *Transforming U.S. Energy Innovation* (2014).

Katie Clifford is the program coordinator for the Global Health Initiative in the biomedical engineering department at Boston University. She holds a B.S. in biology, and an M.P.H. degree with a concentration in epidemiology and international health. In 2007, she completed her Peace Corps service in Zambia, where she focused on sustainable agriculture, nutrition, and women's health. Her area of interest lies at the intersection of global public health and technological innovation, with an emphasis on reproductive and maternal health.

Mary L. Dedinsky is Director of the Journalism Program at Northwestern University in Qatar. She is an Associate Professor in Residence at NU-Q, a former Associate Dean of Northwestern's Medill School of Journalism, and a former Managing Editor of the *Chicago Sun-Times*.

Dale F. Eickelman is Ralph and Richard Lazarus Professor of Anthropology and Human Relations at Dartmouth College (USA). His books include *Knowledge and Power in Morocco* (1985), *The Middle East and Central Asia: An Anthropological* Approach (4th edition, 2002), *Muslim Politics* (co-authored with James Piscatori, new edition, 2003), and *Africa and the Gulf Region* (co-edited with Rogaia Mustafa Abusharaf, 2015). He is a former President of the Middle East Studies Association of North America and since 2003 has been Relationship Coordinator for the Dartmouth College-American University of Kuwait Program.

Alieu Manjang is a Ph.D. candidate in Gulf studies at Qatar University. He also works at the university as a graduate teaching and research assistant. He also holds two M.A. Degrees. One is in Gulf Studies (Qatar University, 2015). His thesis was on "The Arab Spring and Gulf Foreign Aid: The Case of Qatar Foreign Aid to Africa. He also holds an M.A. in Public Policy in Islam from the Faculty of Islamic Studies, Hamad Bin Khalifa University, Qatar, 2012). His thesis was entitled "*Waqf* an an Instrument for Human Development: The *Maqasid* Perspective." In 2009 he received a B.A. in Journalism and Mass Communication from Egypt's Al-Azhar University. His areas of interest include the foreign policy and international politics of the Arab Gulf States, with a specific focus on Gulf-African relations, and education and migration in the Gulf.

Venkatesh Narayanamurti is the Benjamin Peirce Research Professor of Technology and Public and Policy at Harvard University. He was formerly the John L. Armstrong Professor and Dean of the School of Engineering and Applied Sciences and Dean of Physical Sciences at Harvard. He is an elected member of the American Academy of Arts and Sciences and the National Academy of Engineering, and has served on numerous advisory boards of the U.S. government, research universities, and industry. He is the author of more than 240 scientific papers and lectures widely on condensed matter and applied physics, solid state, computer, and communication technologies, and on the management of science, technology and public policy.

Keiko Sakurai is Professor at the School of International Liberal Studies, Waseda University, Japan. Her publications in English include *Shaping Global Islamic Discourses The Role of Al-Azhar, Al-Medina and Al-Mustafa*, co-edited with Masooda Bano (2015); *The Moral Economy of the Madrasa: Islam and Education today*, co-edited with Fariba Adelkhah (2011); "Iran: Three Dimensional Conflicts," in *Education in West Central Asia*, ed. Mah-E-Rukh Ahmed (2013); "Shi'ite Women's Seminaries (*howzeh-ye 'elmiyyeh-ye khahran*) in Iran," *Iranian Studies* 45, no. 6 (2012); "Muslims in Contemporary Japan," *Asian Policy* 5 (2008); and "University Entrance Examination and the Making of an Islamic Society in Iran," *Iranian Studies* 37, no. 3 (2004).

Afreen Siddiqi is a Visiting Scholar in the Science, Technology, and Public Policy Program at Harvard Kennedy School and is a Research Scientist at the Massachusetts Institute of Technology. Her expertise is in complex socio-technical systems analysis, including water, energy, and food security in developing regions, and science and technology policy. She has worked with major companies in energy, instrumentation, and aerospace sectors, and with international academic research institutions. She is currently leading a research study on university and industry linkages in the GCC.

Daniel C. Stoll is Senior Adviser to the Dean and Associate Dean at Georgetown University's School of Foreign Service in Doha, Qatar. His books include: *International Conflict Over Water Resources in Himalayan Asia* (2013, co-authored with Robert Wirsing and Christopher Jasparro); and *The Politics of Scarcity: Water in the Middle East* (1988, co-editor and contributing author with Joyce Starr).

Namie Tsujigami is Project Associate Professor at the Centre for Middle Eastern Studies, the University of Tokyo (UTCMES) and Sultan Qaboos Chair in Middle Eastern Studies. As Visiting Researcher at the King Faisal Centre for Research and Islamic Studies since 2005, she conducted fieldwork ron women's movements, networks, agency, and transnational migration in Saudi Arabia. Among her publications is *Gender and Power in Contemporary Saudi Arabia: A Discourse Analysis from the Perspective of Foucauldian Theory of Power* (2011, in Japanese), completed with a Grant-in-Aid for Scientific Research (KAKENHI), an award provided to creative and pioneering research. Her most recent publication is *Gender Order in the Muslim World: Women's Struggle after the 'Arab Spring'* (2014, in Japanese).

Muhammad H. Zaman is Howard Hughes Medical Institute Professor of Biomedical Engineering and International Health, Boston University. His research focuses on global health, innovation and innovation policy and the role of higher education in improving local capacity to address high impact global public health challenges.

Index

Al Misnad, Sheikha 'Abdulla: 1, 137-38
Al Misnad, Sheikha Moza bint Nasser: 73, 79, 81, 93, 96
Al Sa'ud, King 'Abdullah bin 'Abd al-'Aziz (r. 2005-2015): 30, 33-34
See also: King Abdullah University of Science and Technology
Al Sa'ud, King Faisal bin 'Abd al-'Aziz (r. 1964 – 1975): 26, 43-44
Abu Dhabi: 10-11, 23, 58, 64, 108, 112, 114, 119, 126-27, 139
Abu Dhabi University: 114, 118
Abusharaf, Rogaia Mustafa: 6, 141
admission standards: 4, 16, 58
American University of Kuwait: 12, 15-17, 20, 141
Anadon, Laura Diaz: 6, 141
"Arab Spring": 3, 45, 141-2
AUK: *See* American University of Kuwait
Khamenei, Sayyed Ali Hossein (1939-): 31, 36-37
Khomeini, Sayyid Ruhollah Musavi (1902-1989): 24-25, 27-28, 31, 35
Al-Azhar University: 102, 141

Bahrain: 1, 43, 45, 80, 108-9, 114, 118, 124
    education in: 1, 80
    health: 108-9, 114, 118
    universities in: 114, 118, 124
    women in: 43, 45
BBC (British Broadcasting Corporation): 82, 93

Carnegie Mellon University: 15, 87
China: 2, 12-13, 95, 125
    education in: 12-13, 95, 125
    government: 95
    universities in: 13, 95, 125
Clifford, Katie: 5, 138-39, 141
co-education: 27, 30-31, 34
Committee for the Promotion of Virtue and the Prevention of Vice (*al-Hai'a*). *See* Saudi Arabia, *al-Hai'a*

continuing education (CPE) : 5, 111
Council of Higher Education: *See* Council of Higher Education, Saudi Arabia
curricula, educational: 3, 10, 16-19, 20, 24-25, 28, 31-32, 34, 36, 38, 44, 57, 59-60, 67, 94, 96, 114-15, 117, 119, 129, 133, 135-36
    agriculture: 2, 25
    architecture: 2, 17, 30
    arts: 17, 25, 30, 33, 59, 76, 85, 89
    business administration: 32, 39, 96, 127
    computer science: 15, 38, 96
    economics: 17, 32-33, 35
    engineering: 2, 6-7, 15, 17, 25-27, 29-34, 38, 57, 59, 87, 98, 112, 114-15, 118, 123-34, 138
    evolution: 14, 31
    health and medical: 5, 106, 110, 115-18, 138
    history: 14, 16, 32, 35, 139
    journalism: 4, 15, 72-91, 96, 139
    language: 6, 9, 12, 14-18, 34, 36, 39, 64-65, 80, 93-94, 99-100, 102, 117, 130, 135-37
    law: 25, 33, 35, 39
    mathematics: 6, 16, 80, 130
    physical education: 30, 44, 53
    political science: 35
    psychiatry: 109
    religious studies: 2, 35, 44
    science: 6, 7, 11, 23, 26, 28, 30-31, 33-34, 51, 57, 73, 79-80, 83-84, 113, 123-34, 138-39
    theology: 25, 30
    technology: 6, 11-12, 17, 23, 26, 28, 30-33, 35-36, 57, 59 113-15, 123, 125-27, 129-31, 136

Dedinsky, Mary L.: 4, 139, 141
degree programs: 16, 58, 67, 94, 109, 130-31
development projects: 29, 42, 107, 112-13, 130, 136, 139. *See also*: economic development
diversification, economic: 123, 126-27, 136, 139
Doumato, Eleanor: 44, 49, 53
dress codes: 2, 29, 33, 102

economic development: 58, 64, 92. *See also* development projects
economic hardship: 48
economies: 12, 15, 58, 73, 123, 129-30, 132
    global: 15, 18, 136
    local: 129, 132
    petroleum-based: 43, 72
    regional: 129
education
    advanced: 16, 34, 74, 78, 80, 83, 101, 130
    modern: 34, 48, 137
    primary (elementary): 16, 20, 28-29, 79-80, 83, 125
    public: 4, 43, 49, 76, 81, 95
    religious: 24, 35, 137
    secondary: 9, 13, 29, 79-80
    tertiary: 11, 27-28, 57
    undergraduate: 27, 115
    women's: 43, 83
Education City: *See* Qatar, Education City
education policy: 28, 30, 37
education reform: 96, 126
Effat University: 27, 30
Egypt: 38, 102, 118
Eickelman, Dale F.: 136-37, 139, 141
English language: 2, 6, 9, 12, 14-18, 23, 26, 33-34, 38, 64-65, 80, 82-83, 117, 130, 136
enrollment: 25-27, 30, 33, 77, 103, 118, 125, 127, 130-31
    female: 30, 77
entrepreneurship: 10, 114, 123
environmental issues: 30, 76-77, 88, 115, 133, 135
Europe: 2, 23, 55, 72, 99, 129, 132
    France: 92-93
    United Kingdom (U.K.): 3, 92, 95
exchange programs: 16-17, 59, 92, 94

family: 3, 45-52, 61, 64, 77, 79, 82, 102-103, 137. *See also* kinship, social networks
fatwas: 46
feminism, global: 43, 53
feminization: 43, 45, 51-52
Ferdowsi University: 32
financial aid: 27, 48-50, 60, 64, 97
Findlow, Sally: 136
foreign aid: 92-93, 141
foreign education providers: 56
foreign institutions: 8
foreign students: 5, 27, 32-33, 36-38, 92, 94-95, 97-104, 118, 138
freedom of speech: 31, 73, 81
free-trade zone: 32-33

GCC: *See* Gulf Cooperation Council
gender
    gender equality: 43
    gender segregation: 18, 20, 29-31, 38
George Mason University: 19, 69
Georgetown University: 15, 55-71, 87, 141-42
Gray, Matthew: 138
growth
    economic: 19, 57, 94, 107, 111, 127, 136
    educational: 2, 9, 13-15, 25-26, 44, 119, 126-28
    population: 42, 51, 88
Gulf Cooperation Council: 2, 5-6, 9-11, 14-15, 18-20, 43, 72, 97, 106-15, 118-19, 123-33, 135-36, 138-39

Hamad bin Khalifa University (HBKU): 4, 73, 80, 89, 141
health
    diseases: 106, 108-9
    ebola: 112, 118-19
    epidemiology: 115-16, 118, 141
    global: 113, 116
    healthcare: 5-7, 13, 88, 107-19
    mental: 106, 109, 115
    MERS (Middle East Respiratory Syndrome): 112, 118-19
    public: 5, 6, 74, 76, 106-22, 133, 138, 141-42
Hertog, Steffen: 45
higher education
    American: 19-20, 62
    globalization of: 56, 68-69
    modern: 24, 38
    private: 1, 8-9
    Western: 72
human capital: 6, 57, 129, 136
    development: 136
human rights: 31, 44, 51

IAU: *See* Islamic Azad University
ICIS (International Center for Islamic Studies): 36
Imam Muhammad ibn Saud Islamic University: 26, 35
Imam Sadiq University: 35
infrastructure: 5-7, 11, 59, 66, 101, 110, 127, 129
    information systems and technology: 17, 66, 96
international education: 92, 94-97
internationalization: 19, 33, 94-97
international relations: 15, 96, 139
International Renewable Energy Agency (IRENA): 127
Internet: 82-83

Iran: 2, 8, 23-41, 137
    1979 Revolution: 24-31, 36-40
    education in: 2, 23-41, 137
Iraq: 25-26, 32, 36
Islam
    gender norms: 29-31
    Islamic education: 20, 23, 34, 36-38
    Islamic law: 24, 27, 29, 38
    Islamic seminaries: 23, 38
Islamic Azad University (IAU): 25-26
Islamic University of Medina (IUM): 3, 26, 34, 37-38
Islamization: 28, 31-32
IUM: *See* Islamic University of Medina

job market: 18, 79

K-12 education: 10
kafala (labor sponsorship system): 61-62, 66
KAUST: *See* King Abdullah University of Science and Technology
King Fahd University of Petroleum and Minerals (KFUPM): 8, 126-27
kinship: 3, 48, 51, 53. *See also* family, social networks
King Abd al-Aziz University: 32
King Abdullah University of Science and Technology (KAUST): 2, 11, 27, 30-34, 126
King Faisal University: 26
King Saud University: 2, 30, 109

labor market: 43, 45, 50-52, 103-04, 135, 138-39
Lebanon: 14, 118
liberal arts: 2, 11, 15-16, 31, 60, 73, 137

Manjang, Alieu: 4-5, 138-39, 141
marriage: 45, 47, 50, 52-53, 77, 92
media
    censorship: 14, 16, 61
    mass: 82
    news: 4, 31, 74-82, 88-89, 96
    social: 98, 104
medicine: 25, 50, 57, 59, 89, 96, 109-11, 115-18, 131, 139
MIU: *See* Mustafa International University
modernization: 43, 45, 137
Mustafa International University: 36-38

Narayanamurti, Venkatesh: 6, 142
Nasser, Gamal Abdel (President of Egypt, 1956-1970): 93
National Research Foundation (NRF): 114

natural resource wealth: 107
New York University system: 10-11, 58, 64, 69
Northwestern University: 15, 70, 72-73, 83, 86-89, 141
NYU: *See* New York University system

OECD: *See* Organization for Educational Cooperation and Development
oil: 2-3, 25, 34, 37-38, 42-46, 51, 95-96, 102, 119, 123, 126
Oman, Sultanate of: 1, 5, 8-9, 12, 15-19, 68, 80, 109-14, 124, 137
    education in: 1, 8-9, 12, 15, 17, 68, 80, 137
    government: 5, 110-14
Organization for Educational Cooperation and Development: 80, 136
organizations
    foreign: 87
    non-profit: 25, 70, 86

patriarchal system: 52, 102
politics: 24, 35, 44, 82, 102, 139
population: 5-6, 26-27, 42, 44, 46, 51, 58, 64, 76, 88, 98, 101, 107-10, 115-16, 119, 129, 135, 139
Princess Nourah bint Abdul Rahman University: 126
private sector: 30, 113-114, 131

Qatar: 1, 4-10, 15-16, 20-23, 39, 43, 55-105, 107-109, 112-14, 116-19, 123-29, 135-38
    Education City: 8, 15-16, 20, 56, 59, 64, 70, 73, 80, 86, 88, 92, 96-97, 103, 127
    education in: 4-5, 8, 16, 20, 55-105, 117, 126
    government: 55, 73-85, 88-89, 103
    society: 75, 77, 88, 96, 98-101, 104, 135
    Supreme Council of Education (SCE): 96
Qatar Foundation (QF): 15, 59, 63-65, 70, 73, 80-81, 86, 89, 126-27
Qatar National Research Fund: 127
Qatar National Vision: 6, 64, 133, 135
Qur'an: 34, 37

religious establishments: 23, 38
Ridge, Natasha: 42-45

Sakurai, Keiko: 2, 137, 142
Saudi Arabia: 2, 3, 8-9, 23-54, 63, 68, 80, 108-9, 112, 114-15, 123-26, 129, 137-38, 142
    Council of Higher Education: 28
    education in: 2, 30-33, 44, 52

government: 30, 42, 44-45, 49, 53
al-Hai'a (Committee for the Promotion of Virtue and the Prevention of Vice): 44
women in: 3, 42-54
School of Foreign Service (SFS): 15, 55-56, 59-60, 62-66, 70, 87, 142
Sharif University of Technology: 32-33
Shi'ism: 28, 36-39, 142
Siddiqi, Afreen: 6, 142
social networks: 3-4, 48, 98. *See also* family, kinship
social sciences: 16, 25, 28, 31-32, 57
"soft power": 4-5, 57, 92-105, 138
Stoll, Daniel C.: 3-4, 138, 142
student exchange programs: *See* exchange programs
Sultan Qaboos University: 8, 12, 15, 110
Syria: 32, 118

Texas A&M University: 15, 59, 87, 126-27
textbooks: 1, 16, 25, 44, 53
Tsujigami, Namie: 3, 138, 142
tuition: 14, 18-19, 25-26, 34, 49-50, 64, 94, 97, 105

United Arab Emirates (UAE): 8, 10-11, 15, 19-20, 23, 58, 63, 80, 107-09, 112-15, 123-29. *See also* Abu Dhabi
higher education in: 8, 10-11, 15, 19-20, 23, 58, 63, 80, 114-15, 123, 125-27, 129
United Arab Emirates University (UAEU): 115
United Nations (U.N.): 57, 77, 87
United States (U.S.): 4, 10, 13-14, 18-19, 21, 23, 46, 59, 61-62, 64-66, 72, 77-78, 81-82, 92, 94-95, 112, 114, 117, 141, 142

universities
academic freedom: 14, 16, 61
accreditation: 1, 8, 9, 19, 39, 111
dormitories/housing in: 3, 5, 17, 47, 66, 102, 111
extracurricular activities: 15, 102, 104
Ivy League: 15-17, 59, 86-87, 116-17, 126-27
private: 2, 5, 8-9, 13, 17, 19-20, 25-27, 33, 37
public: 3, 49-51, 5, 130
women's: 30
University College of London: 15
University of Nizwa: 12, 17, 20, 22
University of Tehran: 25, 32-33
University of Tokyo: 47
urbanization: 5, 106, 139

vilāyat-i faqīh (guardianship of the *faqīh*): 24, 27-28, 35, 37

Wahhabism: 24, 35, 37
waqf (religious endowment): 37, 141
water conservation: 7
water sanitation: 5, 106
Weill Cornell Medical College in Qatar: 15, 59, 86-87, 116-17, 126-27
Wilkins, Stephen: 56
Willoughby, John: 43, 51
workers, foreign: 23, 76, 139
World Bank: 11, 58, 87, 90, 112
World Economic Forum: 114

Zaman, Muhammad H.: 5, 138-39, 142